# THE GUARDIAN YEAR 2006

# THE GUARDIAN YEAR 2006

### EDITED BY KATHARINE VINER

*To Saira*
*with lots of love*
*from*
*Kath*
*xxx*

**theguardian**

Atlantic Books
London

First published in hardback in Great Britain in 2006 by Atlantic Books on behalf of Guardian Newspapers Ltd. Atlantic Books is an imprint of Grove Atlantic Ltd.

Copyright © Guardian Newspapers Ltd 2006. The following pieces are all 2006 copyright ©:

Inside Iraq's hidden war © Ghaith Abdul-Ahad
Inside the Asbo capital of Britain © Eric Allison
The British in Basra © Jasem al-Aqrab
A face transplanted © Julian Baggini
Explosion in the suburbs © Naima Bouteldja
*The Da Vinci Code* and the next pope; *United 93*: I needed to lie down in a darkened room afterwards. So will you © Peter Bradshaw
*The X-Factor*; I'm too old for MySpace © Charlie Brooker
The day the sky fell in © Matthew Engel
Why resurgent religion has done away with the country vicar © Giles Fraser
Iran: the next big test of the west © Timothy Garton Ash
Bad science: Brain Gym © Ben Goldacre
Revolution in the Andes © Richard Gott
On Lebanon © David Grossman
The return of snobbery © John Harris
Tony Blair should sack Gordon Brown © Robert Harris

On smoking being banned © David Hockney
A tale of two BBCs; What on earth are British soldiers doing in Afghanistan? © Simon Jenkins
Live blog from the Brit awards © Dorian Lynskey
Down with decaf © Lucy Mangan
India and China need a new way of becoming modern © Pankaj Mishra
Omega 3s and a great cognitive leap backwards © George Monbiot
Arctic Monkeys: *Whatever People Say I Am, That's What I'm Not*. The real deal – for now; The death of *Smash Hits* © Alexis Petridis
Off-peak © Jenni Russell
Out of the ordinary © Jon Ronson
The right to self-defence in the Middle East © Ahmed Samih Khalidi
Sorry Mr President, Katrina is not 9/11 © Simon Schama
It is an amputation – on widowhood © Katharine Whitehorn

The moral right of Katharine Viner to be identified as the editor of this work has been asserted in accordance with the Copyright, Designs and Patents Act of 1988.

The Guardian is a registered trademark of the Guardian Media Group Plc. Guardian Books is an imprint of Guardian Newspapers Ltd.

Every effort has been made to contact copyright holders. The publishers will be pleased to make good any omissions or rectify any mistakes brought to their attention at the earliest opportunity.

9 8 7 6 5 4 3 2 1

A CIP catalogue record for this book is available from the British Library.

ISBN 10: 1 84354 529 2
ISBN 13: 978 1 84354 529 3

Printed and bound in Great Britain by William Clowes Ltd, Beccles, Suffolk

Atlantic Books
An imprint of Grove Atlantic Ltd
Ormond House
26–27 Boswell Street
London WC1N 3JZ

# CONTENTS

# INTRODUCTION

You could be forgiven for thinking that public and political life in Britain had got stuck in the last couple of years. So much seems familiar: the perennial Blair/Brown tussles, the continuing fallout from the government's alliance with the Bush administration and joint excursions in the Middle East, a would-be Tony Blair leading the Conservative party, cultural and political conflict between Muslims and the west, MPs resigning because of alcoholism and gay affairs, royals dressing up as commoners, England performing disappointingly in the World Cup.

But as I looked back over the range of a year's *Guardian* coverage, it became clear how much had been shifting beneath the surface. Those familiar tales have been given new twists: an overheard conversation – in which George Bush addressed the prime minister 'Yo, Blair' – laid bare the humiliating reality of the US-UK special relationship; videos of soldiers beating and abusing Iraqi prisoners exposed the myth of the British army as a benign occupying force in Basra; and Afghanistan, where the conflict was presumed to be over, turned into a killing field for British squaddies, prompting Simon Jenkins to wonder what on earth they're doing there.

The Muslim world might still be the crucible for world relations, but the war in Lebanon ushered in a new balance of forces in the Middle East, and the latest round of 'culture wars', over the publication of anti-Muhammad cartoons in a Danish newspaper, triggered some riveting debates about racism, freedom of speech and respect, reflected here in Gary Younge v Philip Hensher.

At home, the never ending Blair/Brown saga and the 'cult of the centre' across the political parties left many voters alienated from Westminster politics, wrote Seumas Milne, while New Labour's one-time cheerleaders were either falling for David Cameron, as detailed by Jonathan Freedland, or turning on Tony Blair's heir apparent – the prime minister should sack his chancellor, wrote Robert Harris. And Prince William dressing up as a working-class 'chav' for a party? John Harris showed how that was a reflection of a wider, newly acceptable form of snobbery. (The only twist to England's World Cup disappointment, mind you, was just how disappointing they were: they got what they deserved, wrote Richard Williams – absolutely nichts.)

In other ways, too, the year as seen through the prism of *Guardian* reporting and commentary is both exciting and alarming: full of conflicts, moral bafflement and confusion. So while it is widely acknowledged that the overriding crisis of our time is global warming and the environmental threat to the planet – a chilling example of the dramatic shift is outlined here by Ian Sample – governments still largely leave it to individuals to change their gas-guzzling behaviour, as with *Guardian* editor Alan Rusbridger and his decision to convert to an electric car. When it comes to producing the children who will inherit that legacy, says Madeleine Bunting, there is a culture of contempt for parenthood that means it takes a 'spectacular act of rebellion' to have a baby at all; but from Libby Brooks' perspective, that might not be due to lack of desire, as it is harder than ever to find someone to start a family with. Joseph Harker is concerned about whether the St George's flag, which fluttered everywhere this summer, has really shed its racial connotations – but there has been less debate about how to tackle the growing racism and discrimination faced by British Muslims, as highlighted in Urmee Khan's light-hearted and insightful piece. We flock to read the book and see the film of *The Da Vinci Code*, about a religious conspiracy theory – while we witness, shows Giles Fraser, the slow break-up of the Church of England.

There are other interesting juxtapositions. The government votes to ban smoking in public places, much to David Hockney's disgust, while children are pumped full of fish oils, the manufacture of which, says George Monbiot, will wipe out the world's fish stocks for good. There's little discussion about how new technology may be changing our brains, writes Jackie Ashley – and yet, as revealed by Ben Goldacre, schools send children on the scientifically questionable Brain Gym courses. We delight in an MP's appearance on *Celebrity Big Brother*, while the deputy prime minister shows that allegations of sexual harassment are no barrier to his keeping his job. And a British woman gives birth, after egg donation, at 62 – perhaps for the wrong reasons, argues Catherine Bennett – while the leading fashion trend is what Jess Cartner-Morley calls the 'dead socialite look', and a young woman undergoes the first-ever face transplant.

(If you find these changes unnerving, turn to Polly Toynbee's article 'Let's celebrate the utter bloody goodness of the world today' for a bracing corrective.)

Actually, there are plenty of reasons for straightforward delight this part year: from Arctic Monkeys' debut album, to the staggering change in social attitudes reflected by the first gay civil partnership ceremonies, to the England cricket team's elegant and dramatic winning of the Ashes – even the news that, because of the rise in the price of copper, a 2p piece was now worth 3p, as discovered by Richard Adams and Patrick Collinson. Even a comedian swimming the Channel for charity becomes a source of great joy in the hands of Nancy Banks-Smith.

As well as reflecting the kind of year we had, the breadth and diversity of this collection also highlights some of the things that the *Guardian* does particularly well. In my view that includes giving a voice to non-British writers to write about events in their home country, such as Ghaith Abdul-Ahad spending time with insurgents in Iraq; Naima Bouteldja explaining the riots that rocked the Paris banlieues in November; Jasem al-Aqrab, who is from Basra, responding to what British troops are doing in his home town; David Grossman, who is Israeli and Ahmad Samih Khalidi, who is Lebanese, discussing the war in Lebanon; and Pankaj Mishra demystifying the growth of India and China. They provide from-the-ground insights and analysis rare in the British press.

It also includes Rory Carroll's article about his kidnapping in Baghdad and the terrifying 36 hours he spent as a hostage – demonstrating the great risks foreign correspondents in Iraq take for their work; the revealing investigation by Sarah Boseley into the selling of Herceptin as the latest wonder drug for breast cancer; Sandra Laville's moving interview with a survivor of the July 7 2005 London tube bombings; and some superb writing, from Katharine Whitehorn's devastating description of life as a widow to Simon Schama's challenge to George Bush over his government's response to Hurricane Katrina. There's a lot of funny writing too, from Tim Dowling and Matthew Norman to Jon Ronson and Marina Hyde.

And from the year that the *Guardian*, by converting to a full-colour Berliner (midsize) format, underwent massive changes of its own, there are articles from the Guardian Unlimited website that herald a far greater revolution in the way people consume news – such as Georgina Henry's piece looking at how web users engage with the new Comment Is Free blog site, which launched in March; Dorian Lynskey's live blog from the Brit awards; and Rob Smyth's minute-by-minute commentary of England's defeat by Portugal.

The article that stands out, however, and was nominated most often when I was preparing this collection, is Matthew Engel's piece on the death from cancer of his 13-year-old son Laurie. 'The day the sky fell in' is both brilliantly written and startling in the emotional truths it conveys, and, in a year marked by political infighting and disappointment, cultural confusion and disillusionment, is beautiful for the clarity of the love at the heart of it. It's hard to imagine a reader who would not be moved by the article, or indeed who would not find something to intrigue, entertain or inform in this collection.

Katharine Viner, London, September 2006

# AUTUMN

# OUR MOST RADICAL CHANGE IN 50 YEARS

## Tania Branigan

One summer morning in 2003, far below the busy London streets, a carriageful of tube passengers were wrestling with their papers. 'It's like origami,' muttered one woman as she folded and refolded a broadsheet. 'I do feel uncomfortable,' complained another, as pages flapped against her neighbour.

It was a common enough scene, with a curious twist. Aldwych station closed in 1994; the train was going nowhere. *Guardian* researchers were trying to determine whether readers shared the editor's enthusiasm for the continent's shapelier newspapers in place of Britain's stout, unwieldy broadsheets.

The experiment – and its conclusion: yes – heralded the paper's biggest change for well over 50 years.

'We are going to remake the paper from the bottom up,' promised the editor, Alan Rusbridger. The broadsheet would become a mid-sized 'Berliner': 12 cm shorter and 6 cm narrower. But changing the format changed every aspect of the paper.

The *Guardian* is not just about chasing scoops or laying out elegant features. It is also a factory, which must manufacture and distribute a complex product all over Britain, in just a few hours, six days a week.

'This project is simultaneously about a building programme, machinery, steel, components, advertising grids, retail display and distribution, as well as font sizes, colour palettes and the tone and quality of journalism,' said Carolyn McCall, chief executive officer of GNL. The bill would run to £80m. The process, warned experts, would take three years. The *Guardian* has done it in one and a half.

'We simply refused to believe that it would take three years and that we couldn't do it faster than we were led to believe,' said executive editor

Sheila Fitzsimons. 'We approached this project with an obsession about detail and a healthy degree of ignorance.'

The switch to a smaller paper was accelerated when the *Independent* and then *The Times* relaunched as tabloids in late 2003. The *Guardian* had considered such a change, but staff feared it would damage the paper's character. The limited space of a tabloid front page lends itself to a single story, often projected by strong, even strident, writing and headlines.

The Berliner format was different. 'It was raw, but it was very clear that something was going on in terms of setting yourself apart; looking like an intelligent newspaper; story counts ... Something about the shape makes it feel authoritative and intelligent,' said Mark Porter, the creative director, who designed the sample copy.

There was one huge drawback. Switching to a tabloid would have taken weeks. The same presses could be used because it would be half the size of a broadsheet. Becoming a Berliner would take years.

'Every single way you look at it, we are changing everything we do and how we do it,' explained McCall at the start of the project. 'My peers in the newspaper industry think I'm absolutely bonkers.' The board of the Guardian Media Group disagreed. In spring 2004, it gave the go-ahead. 'The business case was so well made and the arguments so overwhelming, the trust was absolutely all on side,' said Liz Forgan, chair of the Scott Trust.

Most newspapers answer to shareholders seeking to maximise their returns. But all shares in the Guardian Media Group are owned by the Scott Trust, whose remit is to safeguard commercial success while upholding the values laid down by the paper's longest-serving editor, CP Scott: 'Honesty, cleanness [integrity], courage, fairness, a sense of duty to the reader and the community'.

But, added Scott in the same essay, these could only prosper where the editor and business manager marched hand in hand. The Berliner would depend on such a partnership.

By late summer, the project team had ordered the most advanced presses in the UK. The three machines can each print up to 90,000 copies an hour. The new technology also makes the *Guardian* the first full-colour newspaper, and allows us to print across the 'gutter' or inside margin, permitting stunning photographic spreads across two pages.

Porter was charged with making the most of this opportunity.

'To redesign completely any newspaper of this stature is unbelievable and once in a lifetime,' he said. 'But Hillman's design [the current version] is acknowledged as the most important piece of newspaper design in 30 years. To be doing what supplants that is quite scary.'

He admitted he was trying to square a circle, producing a paper that was 'modern but classic; authoritative but distinctive'.

'If everyone else is shouting louder and louder, the only way you can be heard is by talking in a normal tone of voice – or even whispering,' said Porter.

The challenges facing the *Guardian* go way beyond competition among newspapers. By the end of 2004, less than half the population was reading a national newspaper each day. In a time-compressed world, where people are bombarded with information, the press can easily be overlooked. If it fails to reflect the complexities of real life, readers will soon dismiss it as irrelevant.

'It's not only about reinterpreting the paper for a particular age, but making the case for what we do and saying it has validity,' said Rusbridger.

So five wide columns have replaced the broadsheet's eight. There are smaller headlines, more analysis and background and a specially commissioned typeface uniting disparate elements. Both the journalism and design are calm and restrained. But the high-quality colour printing allows each page and each picture to sing.

Hundreds of miles away from *Guardian* headquarters, sparks arced out into the cavernous MAN Roland foundry as a worker poured liquid steel from a huge vat. The sideframes for the third press were being cast here while, not far away, colleagues ran tests on the two completed machines.

Bavarian-based MAN Roland has built printing presses for more than 150 years, selling them to 164 countries. But this, said its managing director, Gerd Finkbeiner, was a first: 'It's the shortest timetable we've ever done for a build of that magnitude; a tremendous logistical process.'

The weight of the presses – each 44 metres long, 13 metres high and 8 metres wide – required the floors at the print plants in Manchester and the capital to be reinforced with steel and concrete. The new site in Stratford, east London, was rebuilt to incorporate all the equipment needed. By early 2005, when workers began to construct the machines, huge sheets of polythene still stood in for walls and pigeons flapped around the ceiling.

Meanwhile, the IT and commercial departments were operating at full stretch. New designs meant new electronic templates for pages. The size meant a different system for selling advertising space. To readers, the *Guardian* is best known for its journalism. But within the industry, the other departments are as well-known and respected.

'The ad department, which takes more advertising than any national newspaper, has consulted on the changes widely, from creative directors to clients, from planners to buyers,' said McCall. Commitment and sheer will kept the Berliner on course while the same staff produced the existing paper. 'You're trying to keep the business on track and hold your nerve. Yet you're planning a massive project delivery – it's quite stressful to say the least,' she admitted.

The reassuring news was that research groups were embracing the Berliner with an enthusiasm that surprised even its creators. When the current design by David Hillman was introduced in 1988, it prompted over 1,000 letters in 5 days, the vast majority negative. Now it is regarded as a seminal piece of 20th-century newspaper design.

Matching its impact was a daunting task. Then, in mid July, came the 'lightbulb moment', said Paul Johnson, deputy news editor, who led the editorial side of the redesign. Porter dropped Hillman's iconic masthead, with its instantly recognisable combination of Garamond Italics and Helvetica Bold. In its place was a lower-case masthead in the new Guardian Egyptian font. The last-minute decision meant extra work for everyone. It would also be a shock to readers. But it was fresh, simple, stylish – and, the team believe, right.

With weeks to go before launch, the layout staff practised designing pages, advertising teams went to the market to present the new paper and journalists hit the phones in search of interviews and exclusives.

Several miles across London, test pages were whirring from the presses: blocks and bars of yellow, cyan, magenta and black, as if Bridget Riley had commandeered the relaunch. One wall was stacked with reels of paper, each containing 19,700m sheets. Close by, the 10,000 litre tanks had been filled with thick, treacly, concentrated ink.

Images, sent from the *Guardian* headquarters, are drawn on to flat aluminium plates with a laser. Each page requires four plates – one for each colour ink – attached to cylinders rotating around a 'blanket' cylinder that picks up the ink and transfers it to paper. Next, the long ribbon of paper is sliced in half, folded and chopped again. Extra sections are inserted before the papers are wrapped, dropped onto pallets and loaded on to lorries to make their way to newsagents and readers' doorsteps. 'It has got to be like clockwork,' said Derek Gannon, the operations director. 'I think of it like *The Italian Job* – all those Minis have to be going round in exactly the right place at the right time.'

If imitation is truly flattery, the new paper has already succeeded. Trinity Mirror, News International and the Daily Mail and General Trust have all announced they are buying new presses and moving to full colour by 2008. The Berliner has arrived three years ahead of its rivals.

But that is only half of the equation. 'You can never know as much about a paper as the people who read it,' said Joe Clark, the printing, distribution and circulation director, who has worked for the paper for almost 20 years. 'I read it every day, but I still know less than my dad or my brother: they phone me up and say "I can't believe you've done this."'

Next week, it's your verdict that truly counts. We hope you will approve. The Berliner has the same big ideas, but in a small – and, dare we say it, perfectly formed – package.

'It's an anxious moment when you produce your little baby and wait for people to respond to it,' reflected Rusbridger. 'If they say it is beautiful and intelligent – that will do me.'

September 12 2005

# SORRY MR PRESIDENT, KATRINA IS NOT 9/11

## Simon Schama

Slipstreaming behind the annual rituals of sorrow and reverence for 9/11, George Bush has decreed that, five days later, on the 16th, there is to be a further day of solemnities on which the nation will pray for the unnumbered victims of Hurricane Katrina. Prayers (like vacations) are the default mode for this president who knows how to chuckle and bow the head in the midst of disaster but not, when it counts, how to govern or to command. If you feel the prickly heat of politics, summon a hymn to make it go away. Make accountability seem a blasphemy.

Thus has George Bush become the Archbishop of Washington even as his aura as lord protector slides into the putrid black lagoon, bobbing with cadavers and slick with oil, that has swallowed New Orleans. No doubt the born-again president is himself sincere about invoking the Almighty. But you can hear the muttered advice ... in the White House: Mr President, we were in trouble after 9/11, the unfortunate episode of the schoolroom, *My Little Goat* and all that. But do what you did then, set yourself once more at the centre of the nation. Go to the epicentre of the horror and embrace its heroes. Make yourself the country's patriotic invigorator and all may yet be well.

So this weekend it was predictable that the president would shamelessly invoke the spirit of 9/11 to cover his shamefully exposed rear end – 'resolve of nation ... defend freedom ... rebuild wounded city... care for our neighbours'. But comparisons with 9/11 – the fourth anniversary of which was marked in New York yesterday – will only serve now to reinforce the differences between what the two calamities said about America, and especially about those entrusted with its government. The carnage of 9/11 generated an intense surge of patriotic solidarity, even with America's Babylon, a city scandalously and notoriously indifferent to heartland values. This was because the mass murders had been committed by people who defined foreignness: theocratic nihilists who equated pluralist democracy with depravity A hard-ass city supposedly abandoned to the most brutal forms of aggressive individualism (a fiction it liked to cultivate) showed instead the face of American mutualism, as volunteers poured into the smouldering toxic crater. Blood and food donations piled up and a mayor disregarded his personal safety to be where he had to be, in the thick of the inferno, his daily press conferences astoundingly bullshit-free, unafraid of bearing bad news, treating his fellow citizens, *mirabile dictu*, like grown-ups.

The rest of the country looked at Zoo York and, astoundingly, saw images and heard stories that made themselves feel good about being American: the flag of defiance flown by firemen amid the Gothic ruins, the countless tales of bravery and sacrifice among those trapped inside the towers. For all the horror, this could be made into a good epic of the American character. It was this redeeming sense of national community that protected the president from any kind of serious political scrutiny whenever he invoked 9/11 as the overwhelming reason for launching the invasion of Iraq. As John Kerry found to his cost, unexamined passion triumphed over reasoned argument. Bush won re-election simply by making debate a kind of treason, an offence against the entombed.

Out of the genuinely noble response to 9/11, then, came an unconscionable deceit. Out of the ignoble response to Katrina will come a salutary truth. For along with much of New Orleans, the hurricane has swept away, at last, the shameful American era of the fearfully buttoned lip. Television networks that have self-censored themselves into abject deference have not flinched from their responsibility to show corpses drifting in the water, lines of the forlorn and the abandoned sitting amid piles of garbage outside the Convention Centre, patients from Charity hospital waiting in the broiling sun in vain for water and medical supplies, helicopters too frightened of armed looters to actually land, but throwing bottles of water down from their 20-foot hover. Embarrassed by their ignorance of the cesspool that was the Convention Centre, members of the government protested that it was hard to know what was really going on 'on the ground'. All they had to do was to turn on the TV to find out.

Millions of ordinary Americans did. And what they saw, as so many of them have said, was the brutality, destitution, desperation and chaos of the Third World. Instead of instinctive solidarity and compassion, they have witnessed a descent into a Hobbesian state of nature, with Leviathan offering fly-by compassion from 30,000 feet up, and then, once returned to the White House, broadcasting a defensive laundry list of deliveries, few of which showed up when and where they were needed. Instead of acts of mutual succour, there was the police force of Gretna, south of New Orleans, sealing off a bridge against incoming evacuees, and turning them back under threats of gunfire. Instead of a ubiquitous mayor with his finger on the pulse, and the guts to tell the truth, enter Michael Brown, a pathetically inadequate director of the Federal Emergency Management Agency, Fema, hounded from his 11-year tenure as supervisor of commissioners and stewards of the International Arabian Horse Association by legal proceedings. Instead of summarily firing 'Brownie', the president ostentatiously congratulated him on camera for doing 'a heck of a job'.

Only on Friday, in an attempt at damage control, was the hapless Brown 'recalled' to Washington, his position as Fema director intact.

And instead of an urban community of every conceivable race, religion and even class brought together by trauma, another kind of city, startlingly divided by race and fortune, has symbolised everything about America that makes its people uneasy, ashamed and, finally, perhaps lethally for the conservative ascendancy and its myths, angry. A faint but detectable whiff of mortality is steaming up, not just from the Louisiana mire, but from this Republican administration. Call me a cynic but is it entirely a coincidence that suddenly the great black hope of moderate Republicanism, Colin Powell, is everywhere, publicly repenting of his speech to the UN (and by implication damning those who supplied him with unreliable intelligence), and offering, unbidden, his own lament for the institutional meltdown that followed the breach of the levee? The administration is already thought of as a turkey and the turkey vultures are starting to wheel.

Historians ought not to be in the prophecy business but I'll venture this one: Katrina will be seen as a watershed in the public and political life of the US, because it has put back into play the profound question of American government. Ever since Ronald Reagan proclaimed that government was not the answer but the problem, conservatism has stigmatised public service as parasitically unpatriotic, an anomaly in the robust self-sufficiency of American life. For the most part, Democrats have been too supine, too embarrassed and too inarticulate to fight back with a coherent defence of the legitimacy of democratic government. Now, if ever, is their moment not to revive the New Deal or the Great Society (though unapologetically preserving social security might be a start) but to stake a claim to being the party that delivers competent, humane, responsive government, the party of public trust.

For the most shocking difference between 9/11 and Katrina was in what might have been expected in the aftermath of disaster. For all the intelligence soundings, it was impossible to predict the ferocity, much less the timing, of the 9/11 attacks. But Katrina was the most anticipated catastrophe in modern American history. Perhaps the lowest point in Bush's abject performance last week was when he claimed that no one could have predicted the breach in the New Orleans levees, when report after report commissioned by him, not to mention a simulation just last year, had done precisely that. But he had cut the budget appropriation for maintaining flood defences by nearly 50%, so that for the first time in 37 years Louisiana was unable to supply the protection it knew it would need in the event of catastrophe. Likewise Fema, which under Bill Clinton had been a cabinet-level agency reporting directly to the president, had under his successor been turned into a hiring opportunity for political hacks and cronies and had disappeared into the lumbering behemoth of Homeland Security. It was Fema that failed the Gulf, Fema that failed to secure the delivery of food, water, ice and medical supplies desperately asked for by the Mayor of New Orleans, and it was the president and his government-averse administration that made Fema a bad joke.

In the last election campaign, George Bush asked Americans to vote for him as the man who would best fulfil the most essential obligation of government: the impartial and vigilant protection of its citizens. Now the fraudulence of the claim has come back to haunt him, not in Baghdad but in the drowned counties of Louisiana. In the recoil, disgust and fury felt by millions of Americans at this abdication of responsibility, the president – notwithstanding his comically self-serving promise to lead an inquiry into the fiasco – will assuredly reap the whirlwind.

# BONDAGE AT 36,000 FEET

## Peter Preston

Cry victory for Tampere, Rzeszow, Kaunas and, indeed, Bydgoszcz! They – along with 85 other faraway places with strange-sounding names – have just made Ryanair your carrier of supreme choice: more bums (3.26 million of them) on more seats in August even than BA. It's another triumph for Michael O'Leary, for rampant expansion – and for sheer, unadulterated, un-Irish nastiness. Welcome to MasochismAir.

Here we are again, waiting to check in with 102 people in front of us because the bus from the big city – 60 miles away – arrived five seconds before we did. Nothing's moving. A Croatian girl at the front has left her passport in the hotel (60 miles away). A Spanish boy thought that identity cards would get him on a plane to Stansted.

And the familiar business of the baggage rebalancing is already far advanced. Right down those two stretching, desultory queues, lads in trainers have their suitcases open on the floor, shuffling stuff back and forth. 'Is it under 15 kilos now?' 'No, still bloody 17- and a half.' Piles of jeans and T-shirts are slyly decanted into a black garbage bag to be carried through below check-in sightlines – then stuffed into hand luggage. The floor itself is strewn with mounds of crumpled cotton debris, as though Mandelson's China boycott has gone flops in a trice.

Occasionally, after glum altercations, company weight watchers dispatch cursing transgressors to queue at an overflow office and pay for their sins. When does a £40 ticket cost you double the money? When you're 10 kilos over a load. Expletives seldom deleted. So back to the crawl through security and the sharp-elbowed rush when the boys with the black bags disregard any hope of an orderly boarding routine (as explained via a defective loudspeaker system). So to seats so closely packed you can hear the first squeaks of incipient pulmonary embolism starting four rows away.

Nasty? Of course. But insanely cheap some of the time (unless you're old, young, disabled or want to change your booking) and relatively efficient most of the time. MasochismAir takes you to places you never knew existed, destinations without reasonable alternatives. That's not the whole of its branding success, though.

For O'Leary doesn't play emerald super-yob by accident. He's just a 'jumped-up Paddy' who 'doesn't give a shite', because he says so. Worried about the environment? Then 'sell your car and walk'. Worried about Europe's commissioners? They're 'morons'. Fill in the blanks after B and A 'and you get bastards'. His most unctuous ballad is called 'Screw the share price, this is a fares war'. He's honed Mr O'Nasty, the guy who liked to charge extra for wheelchairs.

One lurking strand of Ryanair's subliminal pitch, in short, seems to translate BO down that stretching queue into Bloody Ordeal. This isn't supposed to be a pleasant experience circa 1986, with welcome smiles and blond stewardesses handing out cocktails. This is a carefully constructed obstacle race. O'Leary's increasing operational shift from Stansted to Luton puts the airport of reality-TV choice back at screen centre. I'm a nonentity, get me out of here.

And, of course, it works brilliantly, 3.26 million times over. Decades of airline marketing tried to make flying a wondrous experience, full of cosseted comfort and luxurious treats. The truth, though, was always grimly different. The ordeal was constant, it just wasn't made into a selling point.

Michael O'Leary has put that straight for ever. Bondage and humiliation still function at 36,000 feet. Ryanair prospers because indignity sells. There's the same retrospective glow from the standing and scrabbling as you get from kneeling in front of a pile of jeans in Primark, Peckham, and finding a £5 pair that fit. I went, I fought, I endured – and now I have a bargain tale to tell. Call it victim consumerism: classless examination by indignity.

How does BA strike back? The good news, maybe, is that they've finally got the message, courtesy of Gate Gourmet, days of inaction and buckets of bile. On my last long-haul test a few days ago, check-in pushed a scrap of paper back over the desk along with my boarding pass.

What's this? It was a voucher to spend $20 (Canadian) on any airport meal before leaving, 'because the in-flight food may not be up to our normal standards'.

Good, old-style thinking, except that the only 'meals' on offer before the departure gate were polythene-wrapped bagels at a bar. I notionally 'dined' on two packets of peanuts, an apple and a Bloody Mary, and left the notional change. The cabin stewards – serving below-normal-standards cheese and biscuits – were surly all the way home. But the captain wasn't on message with his farewell 'thank-yous' and 'pleasant trips'. On MasochismAir, we never forget we have no choice.

# TO ENGLAND, THE ASHES

## Richard Williams

A fellow sporting £50,000-worth of pink diamond ear studs and apparently wearing a dead skunk beneath his helmet enabled England to tear the Ashes, cricket's oldest and most coveted prize, from Australia's grasp at the Oval yesterday. Until then Kevin Pietersen's presence in the series had been notable for a few middling scores and a bunch of dropped catches. Now he will be feted as the man whose first Test century came just in time to rescue England from the threat of a collapse that would have turned a summer of rediscovered joys into a very bitter autumn.

So ended seven and a half weeks of steadily mounting tension, which began with a chastening defeat for England at Lord's and will end today with a victory parade through the centre of London. In between times the entire nation learned about the peculiar contents of a 123-year-old brown urn, and was taught how to tell the difference between Freddie Flintoff's reverse swing and Shane Warne's slider.

As it had always looked like doing, the fate of the five-match series remained in the balance until the very last two-hour session. Since day one of the Lord's Test on July 21 there has been little to choose between these two very different sides, one of them in the ascendant, the other appearing to have passed its apogee. Even the luck was equally distributed. Incorrect decisions by the umpires have evened themselves out. When Glenn McGrath, the Australians' great fast bowler, stepped on a stray ball during a warm-up session at Edgbaston and missed two matches, both of which Australia lost, the gods replied by restricting the contribution of Simon Jones, an increasingly significant member of England's four-man pace attack, at Old Trafford. A bone spur on Jones's foot eliminated him from the Oval match.

When Pietersen came to the wicket at 11.15am yesterday, England had lost three wickets for 67 runs and were in the throes of self-immolation. Having started their second innings with a six-run lead, they needed either to bat out the day or to score enough runs to set Australia an impossible target in the time remaining. The loss in successive balls of their captain, Michael Vaughan, and Ian Bell, who failed to score for the second time in the match, had plunged the innings into crisis.

Pietersen is a 25-year-old from Natal who left the land of his birth four years ago to play for his mother's native country because he felt South Africa's racially based quota system had damaged his chances of international selection. Not thought to lack a measure of self-confidence, he disdained the defensive posture with which others might have attempted to while away the day and chose to ride his luck. On his way to 100 – during which he was twice dropped early in his innings, once off Warne's bowling and again by Warne himself – he crashed the great leg-spinner for six with a blow that splintered his bat.

The dismissals of Marcus Trescothick, Flintoff, Paul Collingwood and Geraint Jones shredded the nerves of England's supporters but failed to dent Pietersen's resolve. Joined by Ashley Giles, England's much-criticised spinner, he continued to use up the available overs while raising the total beyond Australia's reach.

Even the Australian players joined the applause for his century, a further manifestation of the sporting attitudes on display from both sides throughout the series, and symbolised a month ago in the image of Flintoff putting an arm around the disconsolate Brett Lee as England won the second Test at Edgbaston.

As Pietersen celebrated his achievement, England's supporters in the 23,000-strong crowd, and the millions around the world following the game via television, radio and internet, began to glimpse the possibility that the old enemy might finally be there for the taking. For much of the day the Barmy Army, as England's hard core of travelling fans call themselves, had filled the air with their adapted football chants, primarily as a means of suppressing their apprehension. 'You fat bastard, you fat bastard, give that man a pie,' they sang as the tubby Warne hopped up and down in front of the umpire Rudi Koertzen, begging for a favourable decision.

Gradually, however, their tone turned to one of genial mockery. 'Can we play you every week?' they implored as Pietersen swung one of Lee's 90mph deliveries for six. The ears of McGrath rang with 'Five-nil, five-nil' as he patrolled the boundary between spells, a reminder of his unwise prediction, on the eve of the series, of an Australian clean sweep.

McGrath, Warne and their colleagues have been the masters of cricket's little world for 10 years. Taking over from the fearsome West Indies teams of the 70s and 80s, they developed a philosophy of all-out aggression that banished for ever the idea of Test cricket as a slumberous activity out of tune with the new digital universe. The finest compliment is that this summer their own tactics have been used to beat them. 'Warney dropped the Ashes,' the Barmy Army sang as the shadows lengthened and the demands on Australia entered the realms of the unfeasible. Then, however, they serenaded him with a new song: 'Wish you were English, we only wish you were English.' As Warne acknowledged the unexpected salute, his team mates turned to stare in astonishment.

By the time Pietersen was finally out, bowled by McGrath with 158 against his name, Australia had recognised the inevitable. Yesterday McGrath and Warne, two of the greatest bowlers of all time, each in his 36th year, walked off into history to the sound of a farewell ovation as Australia faced the impossible target of 342 to win in 18 overs.

Even if it represented the kind of generosity that comes easily to winners, it seems improbable that any cricketer will ever again receive such an affectionate valediction on a foreign field. In the hour of England's greatest triumph, at the end of an unforgettable summer, the spirit of cricket had been renewed.

# 'HERE'S TO TOMORROW': A SURVIVOR SPEAKS.

## Sandra Laville

The diary entry reads: 'D-Day has come. I will walk again and I did it today. I was confronted with 20-foot bars which I knew I would have to walk up and down. I was asked to lift myself up and I took my first steps. It is unbelievable, I'm standing up and I'm walking. Here's to tomorrow.' Two months before Martine Wright recorded this moment she had been on her way to work, on a Circle line tube, when the suicide bomber struck and her legs were trapped in the wreckage. At the Royal London hospital surgeons amputated her legs above the knees, the first of five major operations.

It is only now, in the Douglas Bader rehabilitation unit of Queen Mary's hospital, Roehampton, that Martine can begin the long, painful process of trying to walk again against the odds.

Each day in the gym, which is the hospital's walking school, beads of sweat break out on her forehead as, leaning on tripods and standing four feet tall, she swings one hip forward, then another, to move her metal prosthetic legs across the floor. What remains of her own legs are fitted into a set of prosthetics, known as short rocker pylons – a development on the artificial legs worn by Bader, the second world war pilot.

'They look like something my dad would knock up in the garage,' said Martine. 'But apparently they are really good for getting your balance, they are training legs and then I will move on to something else. The most difficult thing is that you obviously can't feel your feet.

'It's really hard. I have days when I can do two laps and some days when I can hardly lift them at all. If I stand too long it is really uncomfortable. You have to be really fit and I spent time in the gym doing weights and strengthening my stomach muscles. But after lying down in a hospital bed for two months, the day I first stood up was incredible.'

Martine's injuries are rare. Most amputees are able to keep their knees, which makes the process of learning to walk on prosthetics easier, according to her physiotherapist, Maggie Uden. But surgeons had to remove her legs above the knee after she was trapped in the wreckage of the tube carriage, leaving her with injuries that require her to use 280% more energy than a normal person to take a single step.

'When it first happened I was obsessed by watching people cross their legs, I used to watch TV and focus on that. Now I'm obsessed with how other people were injured and whether they have got knees,' she said. 'I am just obsessed by knees. I suppose because I haven't got any. I just stare at people's knees and lower legs.'

Before the bombing Martine was an active thirtysomething, who went to the gym twice a week, swam regularly and enjoyed travelling, to Indonesia, Thailand and the Middle East. Now after two months at the Royal London hospital, she has moved to the rehabilitation unit of St Mary's where her life is restricted to a room on a ward and long hours in the hospital gym.

Physically she fears that she may not be through the worst. She has developed complications involving bone growing into her muscles.

'The doctor has told me I've got complications with what legs I have left and I get really paranoid that they are going to take more of my legs away. I get phantom pains, the sensation of hot pins and needles, and having that constantly is very painful.

'I can feel my heels sometimes, and my feet. It's my brain thinking that I have had legs for 32 years and now I haven't.

'But I have always said I am determined to walk again. I keep writing it in my diary. I AM GOING TO WALK AGAIN. It's on every page.

'My plastic surgeon said she had never met anyone like me in her life because I came out of intensive care smiling and recovered so quickly from the injuries I sustained. But no one can give me answers. No one will give me answers. I wanted someone to tell me whether I could walk again, whether I would be able to walk upstairs, whether I would be able to run and how long it's going to take me.

'In the beginning people would say, "Of course you are going to walk again." Then I met my physiotherapist and she said, "Well your injuries are quite rare and as a result we haven't seen many people walking with these injuries." When I heard that I went down like a stone. But then someone else would come and say, "Of course you will walk."

'One day a specialist came round from another hospital. I kept asking him, "I will walk again won't I? I am going to walk?" He said, "Well, these are very serious injuries. You know with your injuries, I'm not sure Martine, I'm not sure. I think you will basically be walking with two sticks for the rest of your life." Then he said, "Goodbye, nice to meet you." And left.

'After that I just went right down, I was crying and really low. But two hours later my plastic surgeon came back and said, "Martine, take no notice of him, you're definitely going to walk. I have never met anyone so determined in all my life."'

Few will predict exactly when she will be walking on a full-length pair of prosthetic legs, or how able she will be. At some point she will move from the rocker legs on to new prosthetics, but she hopes one day to buy specialist artificial limbs designed for people who have lost their legs above the knee.

'They have a computer chip in the knee joint that calculates your gait so it helps you walk. But they are very expensive, around £20,000, and you can't normally get them on the NHS.'

The cost of the legs, purchasing a ground-floor flat to replace her second floor property, paying for adaptations to her new home and her mother's house – where she will live initially – could run into hundreds of thousands of pounds. But Martine and other victims have yet to receive a penny from the government's criminal injuries compensation scheme and face a delay of up to two years before awards are given out.

Payouts are capped at £500,000, a level that was set in 1996. So far she has been paid £6,000 by the London Bombings Relief Fund, which has raised £8.77m from public donations.

'Money is a huge worry for me at the moment when all I should be thinking about is walking again,' she said. 'I don't have a secure future, I don't know whether I will be able to return to my job, and I need to go out and buy all these adaptations for my mum's house and look for a new flat for myself.

'It is nearly three months on and they [the government] need to sort out how they are going to take care of us.

'We can't sue anyone so we have to rely on the criminal injuries compensation. When I first heard it was capped at £500,000, I thought that's a lot. But it isn't. I was on £40,000 a year and that's 10 years of my earnings. I am only 32 years old.

'We have the criminal injuries and we have the London Bombings Relief Fund. But I don't understand why this fund isn't paying out substantial grants now.

'It is simple maths. They need to see how many people were injured, look at those injuries and say, we've got £8m here, let's give it all out.'

For the immediate future, home will be Queen Mary's hospital, where she is visited regularly by her boyfriend, Nick Wiltshire, and her parents and her brother and sister.

Whatever happens, she is coming to terms with the fact that her life has changed forever, physically and emotionally. The only hint of anger towards the bombers comes in a diary entry she had forgotten she made.

It reads: 'The hole in the ceiling and the floor of the carriage apparently mark the place where the bastard suicide bomber blew himself up.' Otherwise she makes no mention of the four men who attacked London on July 7.

'There are days when I feel sorry for myself,' she said.

'I'm a nice person, I'm a really nice person and I don't think that something like this should happen to a nice person. So I have to believe this happened for a reason, otherwise it is unthinkable. Maybe I was chosen to have no legs at all as opposed to someone who lost one leg because I am stronger than them, because I can deal with it.

'I would love to have a magic wand and be able to go "ting" you've got legs. But that is not going to happen. People say to me I am amazing and they don't think they could do this. But what choice have I got? I either lay down and die, sit in this wheelchair for the rest of my life, or I get up and I walk.

'This changes your whole perspective, your values, what is important. What I am thinking now is that if I could help some other young person with the same or similar injuries in future, then maybe some good will have come out of this.'

# PINTER AT 75: CHUFFED
# TO HIS BOLLOCKS

## Michael Billington

They say that a prophet is not without honour, save in his own country. The same is often true of writers. This weekend the 75th birthday of Britain's most famous living dramatist, Harold Pinter, is being marked by a star-studded, three-day celebration ... not in London, but at the Gate theatre, Dublin. 'A man of 75,' says Pinter ruefully, 'needs a bit of affection and it's nice it's coming from Dublin.'

Meanwhile, in his native land the only visible – or audible – mark of the birthday is the premiere on BBC Radio 3 of a stunning new work, *Voices*: a collaborative venture between Pinter and composer James Clarke that deals with man's inhumanity to man. For the rest, the British theatre seems to have adopted Alan Bennett's cheeky suggestion, on the occasion of Pinter's 50th birthday, that the best way to commemorate it would be with a two-minute silence.

But Dublin will be the centre of Pinter festivities with performances of *Old Times* and an assembly of plays, poetry and prose. Michael Gambon is jetting in from New York where's he been filming with Robert De Niro, while Jeremy Irons is arriving hot-foot from Budapest. Other participants include Derek Jacobi, John Hurt, Stephen Rea and Penelope Wilton. Playwrights Tom Stoppard, Frank McGuinness and Conor McPherson will also be among the guests at a dinner at the Unicorn restaurant. 'It's important,' says Irons, 'to make it the best celebration we can to show our affection and to encourage Harold to go on.'

Michael Colgan, director of the Gate, which has already staged three previous Pinter festivals, denies that this weekend hooley for the Hackney hero is an implicit rebuke to London. 'I just knew when I set it up,' he says, 'that I'd be going it alone. But I also felt that Pinter, like

Beckett, sometimes suffers an unjustified neglect. Both are writers of fierce integrity who have never tailored their work to commercial needs and who are not automatically West End or Broadway friendly. If I stage Pinter, it's because I believe he has totally redefined the nature of drama and because, like Beckett, he appeals to my taste. A Dublin woman once said to me, "All you do is exercise your personal prejudices." I explained that's just what a producer does.'

Pinter himself is, to purloin a phrase from *The Homecoming*, clearly 'chuffed to his bollocks' by the Dublin festivities. 'I'm very moved,' he says, 'by the presence of so many actors I've worked with over the years.' Despite the after-effects of his battles with cancer of the oesophagus, he also hopes to take an active part in proceedings. Asked if he feels aggrieved by the relative silence in London, he says laconically: 'I believe one fringe company is currently staging *The Lover*.'

If the National and other theatres have missed a trick in allowing Pinter's birthday to go unremarked, he remains as globally popular as ever. His agent, Judy Daish, says a new translation of his work has just appeared in Germany, where productions multiply. Cate Blanchett is shortly to direct *A Kind of Alaska* in Sydney. And there is a phenomenal interest in his work in Brazil and Venezuela, where Pinter's overtly political plays are perhaps more instantly appreciated than in Britain.

Pinter's moral detestation of persecution and torture, from whatever source, is, however, at the heart of *Voices*, to be broadcast on his birthday. Introducing a preview of the work for friends and cast – including Gawn Grainger, Roger Lloyd Pack, Anastasia Hille and Indira Varma – Pinter said it is about 'the hell that we all share here and now'. Combining extracts from *One for the Road*, *Mountain Language*, *Party Time*, *Ashes to Ashes* and *The New World Order*, it is more than a collage of human cruelty: it also expresses a deep-felt yearning for tolerant compassion.

What makes it aurally experimental is the way James Clarke's music vividly embodies the text. After a phrase, for instance, from *Mountain Language* – 'tell her to speak the language of the capital' – we hear the distant sound of an Azeri singer that echoes the culture and language being actively suppressed. Even silence, as in Webern and Stockhausen, becomes part of the musical texture.

What is rare is to find a composer so in tune with a writer. 'I studied Pinter for A-levels,' says Clarke, 'saw Peggy Ashcroft in *Landscape* and *A Slight Ache* and have followed the plays ever since. After seeing *Ashes to Ashes* in 1996, I wrote to Pinter suggesting a collaboration. We had lots of meetings in which Harold talked about the way violence can be evoked with a few economical strokes. He came up with a text in 2000 and I set to work. But what struck me all through was Harold's warmth and absolute trust.'

So, one way and another, Pinter's 75th birthday will not go unremarked. It just seems suprising that an English dramatist, for whom London is a living presence, should be more honoured by the Liffey than the Thames. But perhaps, in the end, it's the ultimate tribute. What it signifies is that Pinter's ability to create archetypal images that embody our dreams and nightmares transcends national frontiers.

# INSIDE THE ASBO CAPITAL OF BRITAIN

## Eric Allison

Manchester has earned itself the dubious soubriquet of being the 'Asbo capital' of England and Wales. Gorton, to the east of the city centre, where Channel 4's *Shameless* is filmed and where I happen to live, is believed to issue more orders than any other area of the city. According to the *People* newspaper at least, this makes the area the centre of antisocial behaviour.

Recently, a reporter and photographer from the *People* went to Gorton to test the hypothesis. They parked an old BMW in one of the area's 'grey desolate streets'. Within minutes, the paper breathlessly reports, 'the car was surrounded by tearaways looking to plunder it of anything worth stealing'.

In the car, the journalists had left behind several items, including 'alcohol, mobile phone, CDs and laptop computer bag'. Approximately 47 minutes after the car was parked (what took so long?), a youth cycled by, spotted the items and left. He returned on foot, with a scarf hiding his face, forced the car window, stuffed the items under his jacket and scarpered. Six minutes later, the youth (by now a 'yob') was back. He hotwired the car and accelerated away, with a 'screech of tyres'.

What a story, what a strike for the sword of truth! Somebody leaves a haul of goodies on show in a motor in a deprived area and the car gets broken into. What would have happened, I wonder, if the car and contents had been left untouched? Would the paper have run a story praising the honesty of Gortonians?

Reading the piece, I was torn between anger and amusement. But it really wasn't a laughing matter. The newspaper also ran a comment piece, which opined that Gorton needs a massive influx of police to tackle the yobbos. Actually, that is the last thing this area needs: the first is the provision of recreational facilities for the young.

The story left a nasty taste in my mouth – and it wasn't put there by the young miscreant. I would bet good money that if that honeytrap of a motor had been left unattended in Sloane Square for an hour the result would have been the same. So why pick on a blighted area to demonstrate that there are thieves about?

Of course crimes are committed in Gorton. There is burglary, vandalism, drug addiction and all the other signs of urban deprivation. But there are also many decent, hard-working parents who struggle to raise their kids in an area that seems designed to encourage children to behave badly. Yet instead of helping these families, by providing their kids with something to do and somewhere to go, those in power talk tough and issue more Asbos.

This spectacle of mainly privileged politicians demonising the children of grossly underprivileged parents ought to be a matter of shame for a government publicly committed to reducing inequality. But it seems that, like my fictional near neighbours, our leaders are devoid of shame.

The Labour party conference is in Manchester next year. I offer my services as a tour guide of the 'Asbo capital' to the visiting ministers who – in the words of a local kid I recently spoke with – 'care jack shit about us'.

October 22 2005

# THE DREADED MOMENT: KIDNAP

## Rory Carroll

We finished the interviews, deep in the Baghdad slum known as Sadr City, and our two vehicles started heading back to the hotel. The street was deserted until three cars, including a police Land Cruiser, sliced around a corner and into our path. Gunmen piled out and surrounded us.

One pistol-whipped Safa'a, the driver, spraying his blood on to my lap. Another wrestled the translator, Qais, out of the door on to the ground. Another pumped three bullets into the windscreen of the follow-up vehicle, narrowly missing the driver, Omar.

It was 2.15pm on Wednesday, and a moment I had dreaded since moving to Iraq nine months earlier had arrived: kidnap. A potential death sentence for Iraqi staff as well as the foreign correspondents who are the targets. Since hostages started having their heads sawn off we have all been obsessed by it.

In agreement with my Iraqi colleagues, the plan, if cornered, was for me to leg it. With a gun at my head that was not an option. I was bundled out and thrown into a Honda. I glimpsed Omar sprawled on the ground, an AK-47 trained on him.

We sped away, the Land Cruiser leading. A man in police uniform in the front passenger seat pointed a pistol while my neighbour in the rear seat handcuffed my wrists behind my back and shoved my head into his lap. 'OK, OK,' he said. It was not OK.

Angling my head it was possible to see sagging powerlines, crumbling houses, sheep grazing on rubbish, traffic. I waved a foot to try to catch the attention of a trucker. It was rammed back on to the floor. The driver, stocky and stubbly, turned with a toothy grin and said, 'Tawhid al-Jihad'. Otherwise known as Abu Musab al-Zarqawi's al-Qaida in Iraq, the beheaders of Ken Bigley. I stopped breathing.

We pulled off the road and, within sight of traffic, had a 10-minute pitstop to change. A different car and different clothes. I stripped naked and was handed a brown T-shirt and a pair of stonewashed fake Versace jeans with no button. 'More Iraqi, good, good,' said one man. I was left barefoot. We rejoined the traffic. Documents and a copy of Iraq's draft constitution poked from the pocket of the front seat, suggesting this was a newly stolen car. The kidnappers relaxed. One lit a cigarette and flicked through my documents.

'Irish. Journalist. Not British?' He shrugged. American helicopters buzzed overhead but however hard I visualised it, no Rangers came shimmying down on ropes.

The front passenger turned and indicated his colleagues. 'Ansar al-Sunna'. The bad news was that that was the group that killed an Italian journalist. The good news was that this contradicted the driver. I suspected – hoped – they were winding me up.

The headcutters are Sunni extremists but Sadr City is Shia, a rival Islamic sect, and the fiefdom of the radical cleric Moqtada al-Sadr. We had gone there to follow Saddam Hussein's trial on television at the home of a family persecuted by his regime. The kidnappers had learned of our presence and lain in wait.

We pulled into the walled driveway of a smart two-storey house. The vehicles left and the house owner, a medium-built man in his late 30s, took over. A portrait of a Shia imam gazed down from the wall of the living room, which was bare save for rugs and cushions.

As the man I would come to call Haji, a term of respect for Mecca pilgrims, sifted through possessions taken from my car, I asked about my colleagues. He examined a notebook spattered in blood. 'They OK, no problem.' He said I was to be exchanged for a Shia militiaman jailed by the British in Basra, the spark for last month's violent protests. I wanted to believe that but feared being sold to the highest bidder. There was a rumour that Sunni groups were back in the market after a lull in hostage-taking.

A separate set of metal cuffs clicked on to my wrists and I was led into a hallway. Beneath a stairwell there was a black cavity, an entrance to an unlit concrete passageway five metres long, one metre wide. A rug and a pillow were laid out. The door clanged shut and a lock turned. Pitch blackness and silence. Going by previous hostage cases, this could be home for months. Still, no bag over the head, not chained to a radiator – could have been worse.

I sat down and tried to remember why I volunteered for Iraq. Curiosity, ambition and hoping to clear my head after a broken relationship, among other things. It wasn't feeling clear now. No story was worth this. In any case I'd missed the story – Saddam could have broken down and pleaded guilty for all I knew.

Hours passed. I pictured news of my abduction reaching family and colleagues. Not a happy image so I thought about my cat, Edward. Insects crawled up my leg. Dusty Springfield crooned in my head. Who invited her in?

Sounds of domesticity reverberated through the concrete. A woman's voice. Children running and laughing. Pots walloping in the kitchen. The television blared. Egyptian comedies, it sounded like. Haji's family laughed long and loud.

After fitful sleep the door banged open. 'Morning, Rory,' smiled Haji. After being allowed to use the toilet and shower, with cuffs removed, a younger man provided pitta bread, jam, cheese and sweet tea in the living room. 'You on al-Jazeera, BBC, everywhere,' announced Haji, chuffed. I was a celebrity. Great, get me out of here.

Cuffed again and back in the gloom, it occurred to me that the British government's official position was not to negotiate with terrorists. Fingers crossed for the Irish government.

Children banged on the door and took turns at holes in the chipboard to peer at this exotic, valuable pet who could not be allowed to stray.

Unleashed for supper, feeling stiff and sore, desperate to lengthen my time out of the tomb and provoke dialogue, I obtained permission to stretch and do press-ups. Haji grinned and took a photograph. The children loved it. The pet does tricks!

Momentarily more host than captor, Haji fetched an English-language version of *What is Islam*, a summary of the faith by the late ayatollah Muhammad Shirazi. He appeared not to have read up on 60 Things Forbidden by Islam, pages 38-41, which include a ban on imprisoning someone unjustly.

Back into the passage for a second night. Then, Haji's mobile rang. A murmur, then laughter. Minutes later the door swung open. I was going home, he said. In the boot of his car. A moon hung high over Baghdad as I clambered in.

After 20 minutes of bouncing over potholes I feared I was en route to another gang of kidnappers, my buyers. I found an oil spray can. The plan: zap their eyes and sprint.

We stopped. The boot opened to reveal a police pick-up truck with a mounted machine gun. Real police. Haji shook an officer's hand, nodded at me and drove into the night, apparently a free man.

Ahmad Chalabi, the deputy prime minister, waited with a smile at his palm-fringed compound. Elements of Moqtada al-Sadr's movement had snatched me, ostensibly to gain leverage for friends detained by the British in Basra, he said, though some wanted to sell me to jihadists. He said his lobbying had clinched the release. 'We got you out just in time.'

It was over. I slumped into a seat. An aide fished a can of beer from his jacket pocket. 'I think you'll be wanting this.'

# THE X-FACTOR

## Charlie Brooker

So winter's virtually upon us. The nights are cold and dark. The skies are bruised and drippy. Bird flu victims litter the pavements. It's depressing. No wonder all you want to do is stay indoors swaddled in your duvet, drinking tea and watching *The X-Factor*. Who can blame you?

After all, some of this year's contestants can genuinely sing – by which I mean they invest their performances with genuine passion and soul, instead of just doling out the usual technical wibbly-wobbly note-bending you see in contests like this (you know – the sort of hark-at-me Mariah Carey bullshit that only the very thickest breed of moron could possibly enjoy).

Yes, some of this year's contestants are the best yet. And some very very much aren't.

Take Chico – or to give him his full name, Chico Time. Chico can't really sing at all – not even the wibbly-wobbly way. All he can do is yelp like a dog getting its prostate examined. By a vet with sandpaper hands. That's a drawback in a competition like this, and Chico knows it.

Fortunately, he's hit on a way to compensate for his lack of vocal expertise: leaping about like a ninny. He also grins, flashes his pecs and shrieks 'it's Chico time!' quite a lot.

Chico's performances are so rubbish, they quickly plunge beyond 'crap', 'rotten' or 'abysmal', drop off the bottom of the chart, and reappear at the top, next to 'brilliant', 'visionary', and 'epoch-making'. He inadvertently borders on greatness. As such, he thoroughly deserves his place in the contest.

Unlike Journey South, a pair of excruciatingly earnest male Gillette models who specialise in shouting and looking slightly pained. I say 'slightly' pained – I mean 'extremely'. Each time they hit a particularly sincere section of the lyric, they go all red-faced and funny-looking, like they've been stuck in a lift for three hours and need to go to the toilet, but can't because there are ladies present. They creep me out.

And as for their name – they're not fooling anyone with this 'we're two northern lads who got in a caravan and headed down to London to seek our fortune, hence Journey South' bullshit. It's a euphemism for cunnilingus. I know it, you know it ... hell, even Kate Thornton knows it, and she probably doesn't even have a vagina – just a smooth Barbie-style bump. Journey South. For God's sake. I mean, come on.

Who else is in it? Well, there's Shayne (good voice, pleading eyes, looks like every male Hollyoaks cast member ever, rolled into one), Phillip (so off-key last week he seemed to be showcasing a new avant garde vocal style that takes utter disregard for melody as its starting point), Maria (top-heavy Mariah Carey type), the Conway Sisters (a Poundstretcher version of the Corrs), and Chenai (so blub-prone she's in danger of crying all the fluid out of her body).

Which leaves us with three genuinely excellent performers. There's Nicholas (who last week managed to cover Marvin Gaye's 'Let's Get It On' without desecrating it in the slightest), Brenda (sassy Aretha Franklin type with a voice the size of Jupiter) and finally, 41-year-old Andy, who according to the official *X-Factor* website 'works as a Dustbin Man' – not a 'binman', you'll note, but a 'Dustbin Man' – which makes him sound like some kind of waste-disposing superhero. They keep banging on about him being a binman as though it makes him part of a different species, which is a touch patronising, and probably a little depressing for any binmen watching at home, hunched before the screen in their Dickensian hovel. Anyway, whatever he is, he can certainly bloody sing.

In my book, those final three make equally deserving winners. Simon, Louis and Sharon might as well call the contest off now and manage one each. But sod it, like I said, it's almost winter, and bird flu's on the way. They should stay on air. Cooped up in our hatches, we're going to need all the telly we can get.

November 7 2005

# EXPLOSION IN THE SUBURBS

## Naima Bouteldja

In late 1991, after violent riots between youths and police scarred the suburbs of Lyon, Alain Touraine, the French sociologist, predicted: 'It will only be a few years before we face the kind of massive urban explosion the Americans have experienced.' The 11 nights of consecutive violence following the deaths of two young Muslim men of African descent in a Paris suburb show that Touraine's dark vision of a ghettoised, post-colonial France is now upon us.

Clichy-sous-Bois, the impoverished and segregated north-eastern suburb of Paris where the two men lived and where the violent reaction to their deaths began, was a ticking bomb for the kind of dramatic social upheaval we are currently witnessing. Half its inhabitants are under 20, unemployment is above 40% and identity checks and police harassment are a daily experience.

In this sense, the riots are merely a fresh wave of the violence that has become common in suburban France over the past two decades. Led mainly by young French citizens born into first and second generation immigrant communities from France's former colonies in north Africa, these cycles of violence are almost always sparked by the deaths of young black men at the hands of the police, and then inflamed by a contemptuous government response.

Four days after the deaths in Clichy-sous-Bois, just as community leaders were beginning to calm the situation, the security forces reignited the fire by emptying tear gas canisters inside a mosque. The official reason for the police action: a badly parked car in front of it. The government refuses to offer any apology to the Muslim community.

But the spread of civil unrest to other poor suburbs across France is unprecedented. For Laurent Levy, an anti-racist campaigner, the explosion is no surprise. 'When large sections of the population are denied any kind of respect, the right to work, the right to decent accommodation, what is surprising is not that the cars are burning but that there are so few uprisings,' he argues.

Police violence and racism are major factors. In April, an Amnesty International report criticised the 'generalised impunity' with which the French police operated when it came to violent treatment of young men from African backgrounds during identity checks.

But the reason for the extent and intensity of the current riots is the provocative behaviour of the interior minister, Nicolas Sarkozy. He called rioters 'vermin', blamed 'agents provocateurs' for manipulating 'scum' and said the suburbs needed 'to be cleaned out with Karsher' (a brand of industrial cleaner used to clean the mud off tractors). Sarkozy's grandstanding on law and order is a deliberate strategy designed to flatter the French far-right electorate in the context of his rivalry with the prime minister, Dominique de Villepin, for the 2007 presidency.

How can France get out of this political race to the bottom? It would obviously help for ministers to stop talking about the suburbs as dens of 'scum' and for Sarkozy to be removed: the falsehoods he spread about the events surrounding the two deaths, and his deployment of a massively disproportionate police presence in the first days of the riots, have again shown his unfitness for office.

A simple gesture of regret could go a long way towards defusing the tensions for now. The morning after the gassing of the mosque, a young Muslim woman summed up a widespread feeling: 'We just want them to stop lying, to admit they've done it and to apologise.' It might not seem much, but in today's France it would require a deep political transformation and the recognition of these eternal 'immigrants' as full and equal citizens of the republic.

November 8 2005

# IT IS AN AMPUTATION –
## ON WIDOWHOOD

### Katharine Whitehorn

'She wanted to be a widow. If you didn't marry, people called you an old maid. If you did, your husband beat you. So being a widow was best.' Whoever said that – I can't remember where it comes from – had plainly never been married, or if she had, only to a vicious millionaire 60 years her senior, for being a widow is not best. It is awful.

I'm not talking only about the obvious agony of the young mother whose husband is killed in an accident, or the soldier's wife who is told her brave man has been shot and will she kindly move out of married quarters in a month. Such tragedies are reasonably rare, but the common lot of women – you only have to look at life expectancy – is to live longer than their men.

My husband, Gavin Lyall, was 70 when he died nearly three years ago. We'd been married for 45 years, since we met on *Picture Post* in the 50s, drifted across Europe on the pay-off money when it folded, and came back engaged. I stayed with journalism; Gavin, after a few years, gave it up to write successful thrillers; in due course we acquired a house and two sons.

'It is an amputation,' said one of the letters I got when Gavin died – a good analogy. Nothing can put back what's gone, but sooner or later the person who has lost a leg learns to walk with a crutch, the woman with only one hand left somehow manages to cope – even if there are phantom pains in the limb that's no longer there.

To begin with you go from raging misery to total numbness, which is just as well as there's so much to be done at that stage everyone's being solicitous and kind. It's when the drama is over and you face the grey mudflats of the future that the real widowhood begins. There's a pointlessness to life. 'I think, why am I doing all this for just me?' said

41

Liz Shore, the widow of Sir Peter. Why cook, when there's no one waiting to be fed? Who's going to notice if you haven't made the bed or cleaned the sink (never mind that your ever-loving husband probably wouldn't have noticed anyway)? 'Nothing seemed worth doing,' said another widow. 'I didn't have proper meals – it would be 5 o'clock and I realised I hadn't had lunch. I'd eat a lot of chocolate – if I was a stone extra, what did it matter?'

The death takes longer than you might think to sink in – sink in at all levels, that is. Joan Didion wrote that she found it very hard to give away her husband's clothes: wouldn't he need them when … ? I remember, too, that I once commented to one widow that another seemed unduly bowed down still, since it was a year since her husband had died: 'Oh no,' she said sadly, 'that's when you realise it's for ever.'

In some ways, life stays the same: I haven't moved, I'm still working, and we never did breakfast together except on holiday (breakfast, we felt, being no time for human relations). The cats have reluctantly realised that I am now all they've got and are as demanding as ever. But when Gavin was alive, the television was on most of the time. Now I scarcely watch any, except for the news. I'm inclined, too, to say 'yes' to any event on offer, even boring talks (some of them given by me). Gavin would never go out three evenings in a row and made a serious fuss if it was even two. I see a fair amount of my eldest son Bernard and his family, less of Jake, who lives in California, though we talk endlessly on the telephone. They are both marvellous, but you can't live through your sons and heaven help you if you try.

I had hoped that after a while the good memories would drive out the ghastly last weeks of Gavin's life, and to an extent they did, but never completely. What does happen is that the good memories become a source of pleasure and comfort, tinged with the same autumnal ache, the same regret one feels about having once been young, of the unreturning years. A phrase can bring them back, a smell. Proust may have talked of his madeleines, but in my case – sorry about this – it's the smell of gin on a cold day: it brings back the Thames boat where we were always happiest and where we scattered Gavin's ashes.

Real friends are a godsend, and not just by being a shoulder to cry on.

Even from the earliest days they can distract you or do things with you or at least pour the alcohol, without which I don't see how anyone gets through this. But many women find that acquaintances shun them, cross the street to avoid them 'because they don't know what to say'. Even some friends change the subject with clumsy speed if death, or the husband's name, comes up, though we mostly ache to talk about him.

Mrs Torrie, who founded the Cruse Clubs for widows, said that people have an atavistic fear that bad luck is catching. She also said: 'To a man, every widow represents a dead man.' It's understandable, too, that people are unsure as to what on earth to say. In Virginia Ironside's excellent book about the rage of bereavement, she excoriates every one of the usual platitudes that people use – I particularly disliked people who said: 'I know how you feel. When my brother died… when my aunt died …' I wanted to snarl: 'It isn't the same at all.'

Somehow you have to start living again. As one friend put it: 'I always thought when Mark died my life would be over. The trouble is, it isn't.' And some widows are amazingly valiant. I know one who took over her husband's firm without knowing a thing about it. She said: 'It was pride that did it – I wasn't going to be bested by these bloody men.' Another, who had always been cooked for in the far east, taught herself to cook proper meals, as a discipline. Another learned, against all advice, to drive her husband's enormous Citroën, in a matter of weeks after his death.

But it isn't easy. In Keith Waterhouse's hilarious book *Good Grief*, he is deadly accurate about the way a widow is too often treated. His heroine goes into her husband's office: they make a fuss of her, offer her tea. She pays a second visit and is cold-shouldered all round: plainly they're not up for her making a habit of it.

One trouble so many widows have is that their bereft state conflates with all the normal problems of growing old. You may be ruefully glad that there's no witness to the gradual decline and fall of your curves. But there's no one to fasten your bra if you've broken a wrist, drive you back from your cataract operation or bring you soup and newspapers if you're laid up: lucky if you have a friend or family, awkward to the point of tears if you're quite on your own. Widows, too, often can't afford many of the things that might help, like a journey or a course in something new: the generations that had no pensions of their own may have little or nothing from their husband's, just the state pittance to live on.

And too many widows are lonely: maybe their grown children live nowhere near, or their friends turn out to have been mostly their husband's friends, the leftover half of a couple who have always 'kept themselves to themselves' is particularly bereft. Even popular women can feel alone: Felicity Green expressed it well: 'I have plenty of people to do things with – I just have no one to do nothing with.' Some women, of course, find another mate, or want to, but there are too few men in the age group, and those there are tend to go for someone younger.

After a while, the things that wracked me were not the good memories; it was the bad bits that snagged at my mind: the things that went wrong that I could never now explain, make amends for or change. One counsellor-friend told me of a woman who seemed to be incapable of tackling her misery at all. My friend assumed she must have loved her husband exceptionally, until the woman suddenly blurted out – 'I 'ated the little bugger' – and then they could move on.

Losing your husband has two separate aspects: there's missing the actual man, your lover; his quirks, in Gavin's case his kindness, the extraordinary Aladdin's cave of his mind. But marriage is also the water in which you swim, the land you live in: the habits, the assumptions you share about the future, about what's funny or deplorable, about the way the house is run – or should be what Anthony Burgess called a whole civilisation, a culture, 'a shared language of grunt and touch'. You don't 'get over' the man, though you do after a year or two get over the death; but you have to learn to live in another country in which you're an unwilling refugee.

Soon after the memorial service for Prue Leith's husband, Rayne Kruger, she and her sons found themselves having lunch in the garden at 3pm. 'Father would never have allowed this!' said Prue lugubriously, and her son said: 'Look, Ma, there's not much of an upside, but you might as well enjoy what there is.'

There are widows who can find nothing to cheer them at all, but for most of us, after a time, there are a few upsides – lifelines to be grabbed at. To have been in some way answerable to someone else for half a lifetime was not wretched, but to be released from that does have something to be said for it.

So much depends on whether you do enjoy doing things on your own. Two and a half years after Gavin died I found myself kicking around Nice for a long afternoon and early evening, sitting for the odd coffee or drink, and I suddenly thought: 'When I was young this was one of my favourite things – and I haven't done it for decades.' It was some sort of a milestone.

The misery of losing the person you love will never change, but the social consequences of being on your own, are, I think, getting better. As more and more women have worked at some point in their lives, fewer are going to feel utterly lost without their husbands. The sort of life you had outside the marriage may well determine how well – or, at least, how soon – you can manage to live, now that you're on your own. And come to feel, as I do, more glad that he lived than wretched that he died. In the words of Siegfried Sassoon: 'I am rich in all that I have lost.'

# A TALE OF TWO BBCS

## Simon Jenkins

Question. How can one institution, the BBC, make something as good as *Bleak House* and as bad as *Rome*? How can the panjandrums who order these things preview their best-ever Dickens and their worst-ever toga saga and cry 'Darlings … wonderful!' at both? The place must be out of control.

*Rome* is a mystery. A rambling plot, weighed down by Troy-like dialogue and devoid of suspense, is interrupted – as if for commercial breaks – by inserts of copulation and throat-slitting. The director of the first parts, Michael Apted, has disowned the editing, said to have shortened what was merely bad to what was incoherent. If the BBC denies directors access to the editing suite, what price its much-vaunted artistic integrity?

But Apted and his producers must surely take responsibility for the plot, the script, the acting, the ludicrous sex and violence. The BBC suborned every outlet, even Radio 4's *Today* programme, to give *Rome* hyperbolic plugs, not least for claims to 'historical accuracy'. As Robert Harris has pointed out, it is as accurate as depicting Clemmie Churchill having sex with Ribbentrop and poisoning Chamberlain before the second world war. If this is what you get for a compulsory licence fee, give me subscription television any day.

Much has been made of *Rome* being a £60m co-production with America's HBO, to which the BBC contributed £9m. Something apparently went terribly wrong when the elephantine production went on location in Italy. Hannibal had the same trouble. But what is the virtue of a public service co-production if artistic control is abrogated, assuming it was? The fact is that the BBC blew millions on a turkey. Its executives are the highest-paid group in the public sector. If they were not protected by a charter, heads would roll. What with *Up Pompeii, Caligula* and now this, the Roman empire is taking a terrible revenge on us northerners for what the Goths did to it back in AD410. It must be time to call it quits.

Cut to Andrew Davies' *Bleak House*. It is as good as could be. Literary critics have nit-picked over turning 1,000 pages into nine hours of television. They have objected to Tom's accent, Skimpole's plausibility and the absence of fog. Philip Hensher, in the Guardian, refused to watch lest the pictures distort his imagination as conveyed by Dickens's prose. I assume he must also tear out the Phiz illustrations from his book. It is hopeless to compare the form and content of a film against a Victorian novel. It may or may not evoke the original, but it cannot conceivably be 'faithful' to it. Film is a different medium. Is Verdi faithful to *Othello*, or Shakespeare to his crib, Cinthio's *Hecatommithi*? Is Keats faithful to a Grecian urn, or Mendelssohn to *A Midsummer Night's Dream*?

I did not like Davies sensationalising *Middlemarch*, not for his lack of authenticity but for wrecking its delicacy. I recall him altering Lydgate's chaste kiss on each of Rosamund's tears into a jaw-crushing mouth-to-mouth resuscitation. *Bleak House*, so far, has no such fault. I can dispense with fog which was, to Dickens, a literary metaphor (and surely the longest passage without a main verb in fiction). The camera achieves the same claustrophobia with its nervy close-ups, dark sets and costumes and intense facial expressiveness. The pictures are fast and impressionistic. So is the novel. So was Dickens.

Each character on screen demands to be the focus of the plot. Tulkinghorn embodies something more awful than evil itself, he embodies the law. Esther Summerson is not just another goody two-shoes but a moral fulcrum, and mercifully plain. Beauty was never so fallen as in Lady Dedlock. The lesser characters mesh in and out of gear, bringing clarity to a convoluted thriller by the sheer power of their acting. Burn Gorman's Guppy is beyond compare, as if he had all the mysteries of Chancery wrapped round his little finger.

*Bleak House* recalls the days of television excellence, the golden age of the BBC's Henry James adaptations in the 1970s and Granada's *Brideshead*. That the medium should be so parasitic on past genius for inspiration may be a poor comment on its creative juices. But as a genre, these works are superb. The quarry of English literature is not sacred. No damage is done by mining it for new interpretations and new enjoyment. Shakespeare has survived all the rocks hewn from his slopes. I delighted alike in Mel Gibson's *Hamlet* and Kenneth Branagh's *Much Ado*. Deborah Moggach's recent version of *Pride and Prejudice* may not be the novel, but it has inspired a glorious film. Much that is 'lost in translation' is gained in immediacy for those unfamiliar with the original language. I do not care if Dickens would have approved or disapproved of *Bleak House*. He is dead. But if his work can inspire entertainment of this quality – and drive thousands back to read his work – something of him lives.

I sense that the difference between these two sagas is the difference between two present-day BBCs. *Rome* is the first, frantically trying to ape Hollywood. It is all big hotels, Armani suits, Roman temples, bed-hopping and back-stabbing. It regards art as for Greeks. Real Romans eat ratings. Any critic of *Rome* is warned that 6.6 million people watched the first episode. Too bad if a thousand artists were thrown to the lions. Tessa Jowell, the Atia of culture, wants numbers. This BBC throws legions steeped in blood and porn into battle against Pompey and Sky, Americans and Gauls. The other BBC is *Bleak House*. It is a place of murk as dense – and meetings as interminable – as Jarndyce and Jarndyce. Its executives inhabit a Chancery 'mistily engaged in one of ten thousand stages of an endless cause, tripping one another up on slippery precedents, groping knee-deep in technicalities'. Gloomy corridors and dank basements are served by a myriad Guppys, Flites and Krooks. They will suck blood from Jarndyce and Jarndyce until the crack of doom, when the entire estate is eaten up by costs.

This BBC still has about it the cobwebs of a glorious tradition. On high are its governors, Tulkinghorns, Dedlocks and Chadbands. Below in Tom-all-Alones, a ragged girl called art does sometimes emerge, terrified, before a ghostly scheduling committee. She is allowed a moment, a desperate whirling dance before the lights, before returning to her hovel. This Chancery can still sponsor great work. But it is soporific with subsidy, groaning for money to build more *Rome*s in a day. As Kenge loftily explained on the high court steps at the climax of

Jarndyce: 'If the public have the benefit, and if the country have the adornment, of this great Grasp, it must be paid for in money, sir.'

Fair enough, but the one thing that this saga blows apart is the BBC's claim that British public service broadcasting needs one overarching coordinating genius, one monopoly supplier: namely, itself. If it can dole out public money equally to quality and tosh without a shred of critical control, who needs it? Why not give the same power, and the same money, to a broadcasting commissioner or a television council to distribute as it chooses? What is unique about the BBC, the 'great Grasp'?

# I WAS AT A PARTY WHEN
# I GOT THE SUMMONS

## Catherine Bennett

A few months ago, Cherie Blair summoned me for an audience. She was a guest of honour at a party. 'Cherie wants to meet you,' said the emissary who had been sent to bring me to her presence. Off I went.

Cherie, bringing her face very close, said she wanted to know why I'd written horrible things about her. It was an impressively straightforward opening pleasantry, and how I wished, in the following bout of *esprit d'escalier*, that I had responded with equal honesty, itemising 1) her exploitation of her husband's public position for private gain, 2) her undignified enthusiasm for anything gratis or discounted, 3) her worrying reliance on individuals of extreme flakiness, and 4) the Blairs' numerous taste issues – including the deployment of their family life for promotional purposes, and apparent delusion that they constitute some sort of royalty, a point that could not have been better illustrated than by Cherie's presumably recently acquired habit of sending for her subjects.

But this was a party, an embarrassing place for a confrontation with a stranger, and it seemed more tactful, if cowardly, to settle on a less contentious but still controversial aspect of Mrs Blair's behaviour, which might more smoothly be converted from personal criticism into a tepid debate about her public role. What explained her zealous interpretation of the duties she attributes to 'the prime minister's consort' (as she put it in her 'I am not Superwoman' speech)? Given what she has achieved in her own name, why does Ms Blair QC, devote so much of her time to trailing around after her husband as if she had no status of her own and nothing better to do? Wasn't it, I ventured, rather 1950s?

At once, Mrs Blair was all feminine incomprehension. Not be with her husband? But she loved him! Of course she wanted to be at his side.

She looked at me as if I'd just turned a garden hose on the pyre upon which she was about to commit suttee. What kind of loving wife would ask such a question? Why, Mrs Blair said, didn't I, too, feel that way about my own… yes, just what, exactly, was my situation? The answer prompted a triumphant, dawning glint. 'Now I understand,' said Mrs Blair, happily.

Moreover, our consort insisted, she was no different from previous consorts. Look at Denis, she said. For a learned QC, it was not, perhaps, the most masterly piece of ratiocination. Denis? Yes, let's look at Denis, shambling about in the background. How often did we see him sporting free watches donated by a foreign premier, or doing the lecture-tour hokey-cokey at £30,000 a pop? How many times, for that matter, did we ever get a really good eyeful of Mary Wilson, or of Audrey Callaghan, or even Norma Major, who was only recognised as an important asset after Cherie had guest-edited an upmarket knitting magazine? How much did we ever learn about Ffion Hague, when she, too, was instructed to compete against the mighty Liverpudlian?

The painfully reluctant emergence, this week, of Doreen Davis, the latest political wife to be assessed for consort potential, only emphasises what the Blairs have done to transform the traditional job description for prime minister's spouse – lurking supportively about in the background without actually drawing attention to oneself – into a demanding, almost full-time occupation, requiring a press office, bulletproof tank, hair and make-up, and an eye-catching make-over for every significant appearance. In fact, Tory suspicions that David Cameron is a barely-disguised Blairite are confirmed by Mrs Cameron's very modern willingness to pose in her kitchen, to ascend platforms for public hugging, and even to volunteer as a rival fertility goddess, having her pregnant tummy stroked by the new, young face of Conservatism. Doreen Davis, on the other hand, is depicted as an obscure, pitiful and in almost all respects disappointing figure, who must learn to do better. 'All of this – the media attention – is not natural for me,' she told the *Daily Mail*, adding, as if her husband's pretensions required nothing less, on her part, than a Madonna-like combination of exhibitionism and self-discipline: 'But if it's what needs to be done, then I'll do it.'

Although it has been orchestrated by a feminist, this recent upgrading of the female consort's job – from silent goldfish to performing seal – can hardly constitute much of an advance for future women incumbents when they have to choose between this showy form of servitude or being depicted as unfashionably meek. While it would be churlish to deny that Cherie's intense commitment to her duties – right down to the long silk train she wore this week – has made her an almost impossible act to follow, there must be a sense that eight years of this peerless comedy is probably enough. Or, at any rate, that it's time someone less suttee-minded got a chance. And the next time she sends for me, I shall certainly say so.

# DOWN WITH DECAF

## Lucy Mangan

'Do you have any decaf?' Ah, those five little words that mean so much. Specifically, that somewhere along the way you have dropped your guard and become involved with the kind of po-faced gimp who thinks that ingesting a few micrograms of the mildest stimulant know to man is akin to injecting eight gallons of crystal meth into your eyeball and following it with a heroin chaser. 'I'm sorry,' you reply. 'I only have beverages whose raison d'etre has not been removed in order to accommodate the self-indulgent witterings of morons. Would you like some water instead, or will its reckless combination of hydrogen and oxygen induce some kind of convulsion?'

Fortunately, the favourite utterance of fools may soon be consigned to oblivion. Researchers for the US National Institutes of Health have found that drinking caffeine-free, rather than unadulterated, coffee increases the levels of 'bad' cholesterol in the blood, which can lead to grotty arteries and heart disease.

The researchers (that's scientists funded by an agglomeration of proper public health bodies, all you decaf doilies who are trying to raise your papery hands in protest) described the findings, which were based on people drinking three to six cups a day, as 'very surprising'. But for those of us who are sick of being harangued by Quorn-filled, carb-less freaks intent on using their rapidly diminishing physical resources to suck the little remaining joy from the lives of anyone acquainted with them, the results were better described as 'very delightful'.

It is enough merely to acknowledge this development. But it does open up a world of counterintuitive possibility – a world in which saturated fat may one day be proved to sluice out instead of stop up arteries, refined sugar is revealed to be just the thing for buffing up tooth enamel and complex carbohydrates are instrumental in purging the body of cellulite.

Or, even better, a world in which muesli causes deep vein thromboses, carrot sticks and hummus give you BSE and brown rice makes your head explode.

Perhaps if we get enough scientists to put their heads down and concentrate, the greatest triumph of all will come to pass. The headline will read: Pork Scratchings Cure Cancer – Sunflower Seeds Do Sod All.

November 21 2005

# IN PRAISE OF ... AUSTIN

## Leading article

Most days for the past 16 years, the *Guardian* has printed a pocket cartoon by Austin on page one and another inside. They were often admired, and they frequently won him awards. Yet only those who watched David Austin at work could have been fully aware of the depths of his ingenuity and his talent. Each evening, Austin – only his surname was ever revealed – would present the duty editor with a choice of nine potential cartoons, after which he would refine the two that were selected. For those who made the choice, the difficult bit was not picking two to adorn the newspaper, but having to discard at least three or four others which would also have been sure to give pleasure.

A pocket cartoonist needs to be that rare combination, a workhorse gifted with vast and fluent powers of invention, able to come up with something tart and topical even on days when the news is thin. In the circumstances, those who pursue the trade would have more right than most to fret and complain. Yet whatever the tensions, Austin remained at all times peaceable, courteous and self-effacing, greeting praise not just with gratitude but with apparent surprise.

With his death at the age of 70, an astonishingly rich production line is finally halted. Yet the best cartoonists, though working in a form that seems transient, are also, over the years, historians of changing fashion, taste, attitude and zeitgeist. In that sense, David's amused and faithful chronicling of the way we live now will long survive him.

WINTER

# A DEVASTATING SLOWING
# OF THE FLOW

## Ian Sample

The powerful ocean current that bathes Britain and northern Europe in warm waters from the tropics has weakened dramatically in recent years, a consequence of global warming that could trigger more severe winters and cooler summers across the region, scientists warn.

Researchers on a scientific expedition in the Atlantic Ocean measured the strength of the current between Africa and the east coast of America and found that the circulation has slowed by 30% since a previous expedition 12 years ago.

The current, which drives the Gulf Stream, delivers the equivalent of 1m power stations-worth of energy to northern Europe, propping up temperatures by 10 degrees celsius in some regions. The researchers found that the circulation has weakened by 6m tonnes of water a second. Previous expeditions to check the current flow in 1957, 1981 and 1992 found only minor changes in its strength, although a slowing was picked up in a further expedition in 1998. The decline prompted the scientists to set up a £4.8m network of moored instruments in the Atlantic to monitor changes in the current continuously.

The network should also answer the pressing question of whether the significant weakening of the current is a short-term variation, or part of a more devastating long-term slowing of the flow.

If the current remains as weak as it is, temperatures in Britain are likely to drop by an average of 1 degree celsius in the next decade, according to Harry Bryden at the National Oceanography Centre in Southampton, who led the study. 'Models show that if it shuts down completely, 20 years later, the temperature is 4 to 6 degrees celsius cooler over the UK and north-western Europe,' Dr Bryden said.

Although climate records suggest that the current has ground to a halt in the distant past, the prospect of it shutting down entirely within the century are extremely low, according to climate modellers.

The current is essentially a huge oceanic conveyor belt that transports heat from equatorial regions towards the Arctic circle. Warm surface water coming up from the tropics gives off heat as it moves north until eventually, it cools so much in northern waters that it sinks and circulates back to the south. There it warms again, rises and heads back north. The constant sinking in the north and rising in the south drives the conveyor.

Global warming weakens the circulation because increased meltwater from Greenland and the Arctic icesheets, along with greater river run-off from Russia, pour into the northern Atlantic and make it less saline which, in turn, makes it harder for the cooler water to sink, in effect slowing down the engine that drives the current.

The researchers measured the strength of the current at a latitude of 25 degrees N and found that the volume of cold, deep water returning south had dropped by 30%. At the same time, they measured a 30% increase in the amount of surface water peeling off early from the main northward current, suggesting far less was continuing up to Britain and the rest of Europe.

Disruption of the conveyor-belt current was the basis of the film *The Day After Tomorrow*, which depicted a world thrown into chaos by a sudden and dramatic drop in temperatures. That scenario was dismissed by researchers as fantasy, because climate models suggest that the current is unlikely to slow so suddenly. Marec Srokosz of the National Oceanographic Centre said: 'The most realistic part of the film is where the climatologists are talking to the politicians and the politicians are saying "we can't do anything about it".'

Chris West, director of the UK climate impacts programme at Oxford University's centre for the environment, said: 'The only way computer models have managed to simulate an entire shutdown of the current is to magic into existence millions of tonnes of fresh water and dump it in the Atlantic. It's not clear where that water could ever come from, even taking into account increased Greenland melting.'

Uncertainties in climate change models mean that the overall impact on Britain of a slowing down in the current are hard to pin down. 'We know that if the current slows down, it will lead to a drop in temperatures in Britain and northern Europe of a few degrees, but the effect isn't even over the seasons. Most of the cooling would be in the winter, so the biggest impact would be much colder winters,' said Tim Osborn, of the University of East Anglia climatic research unit.

The final impact of any cooling effect will depend on whether it outweighs the global warming that, paradoxically, is driving it. According to climate modellers, the drop in temperature caused by a slowing of the Atlantic current will, in the long term, be swamped by a more general warming of the atmosphere.

'If this was happening in the absence of generally increasing temperatures, I would be concerned,' said Dr Smith. Any cooling driven by a weakening of the Atlantic current would probably only slow warming rather than cancel it out all together. Even if a slowdown in the current put the brakes on warming over Britain and parts of Europe, the impact would be felt more extremely elsewhere, he said.

# THE DAY THE SKY FELL IN

## Matthew Engel

The significant dates of this crisis are lodged in my head like the dates of the second world war. And the day the sky fell in was April 20 2004.

I still have a clear memory of Laurie that morning, standing by the car in his green school sweater and black trousers. I remember being struck by how tall he was getting. It was the first day of his summer term and he had just promised me – to appease my preference for more cerebral games than football – that he would have a try-out for the under-12s cricket.

First he had to attend what appeared to be a routine hospital appointment. He was getting close to his 12th birthday and, in his entire life, had never suffered anything worse than athlete's foot until, just after Christmas, he had begun to complain, quite literally, of a pain in the arse.

'Piles!' I said. 'The Engel curse!' Indeed, I casually wrote in my diary one day: 'L's piles are killing him.' This turned out to be the most bitterly ironic sentence I have ever written.

Anyway, the GP said my diagnosis was nonsense. It was an abscess: common enough, and treatable with a simple operation, a thought that so terrified Laurie that, on the February morning when he headed to Hereford for the op, I had to tell him to stop fussing and remember there were children in hospital who were really ill. And that was the most bitterly ironic sentence I have ever uttered.

The operation was said to have gone fine, and a succession of doctors insisted there was nothing to worry about. But the pain did not go away. And by April a strange swelling had appeared round his groin.

We were, I suppose, up until this point, a thoroughly enviable family, living comfortably on an old farm in a beautiful corner of England: myself, my wife, Hilary, Laurie, our home-baked son, and Vika, our five-year-old daughter, adopted, after many adventures, from a Russian orphanage. We were not quite as happy as we bloody well should have been. But Laurie was the least of our worries.

We had just come back from two years in America, which had been a triumph for him. Thrust into an unfamiliar environment, forced to change his name (becoming Larry, because Americans think Lauries are girls), he had emerged from an uneasy start to become a star inside the classroom and out. He was popular, self-assured, funny and charming. Prone to be opinionated and cocky. But, as they say in Yiddish, he was turning into a *mensch* – a man in the best and fullest senses of the word.

He did not, however, turn into an American. Within days of returning home, he shrugged off his accent, rejoined his old friends and was breezing through Year 7 at his Herefordshire secondary school. He wanted to win Wimbledon, or be a sports journalist, at least one of which was thoroughly plausible – he was pretty good at tennis, but he was developing an absolutely lovely writing style. The world seemed at his feet. Unfortunately, all hell was breaking loose inside his body.

That April 20, I was on my way to Latvia to write a piece for the Guardian about the enlargement of the EU. I never got there. I first heard the word 'tumour' from Hilary down an uncertain mobile line while on the train to London.

Ward 15, the oncology ward, at Birmingham Children's hospital, is a modern addition to a Victorian institution. Oncology was a word I had never previously encountered, even in Scrabble. But it's a serviceable euphemism: 'the study of tumours'. The ward was opened in 1991 – post-Thatcher, early Major – and it shows: the construction was cheapskate. The adolescent bay comprises four beds, separated by thin curtains. Theoretically, it probably isn't cramped, but in practice each child has a parent sleeping alongside them, in camp beds. And it is normally full, as is the whole ward, so that the doctors often have to take charge of a dozen or more 'outliers' on the general wards, amid the broken legs and appendectomies.

There is little natural light in the bay: the window is directly under a walkway. The air conditioning is primeval, producing more sound than air. In high summer, the place is a hellhole. And it's noisy even in winter, with four competing TVs and/or PlayStations, and families shouting above them. (That assumes you can score a functioning Playstation – mad rules prevent patients bringing in their own on 'electronic safety' grounds.) It's not somewhere one would choose to be ill.

There are a couple of isolation rooms, usually reserved for patients who are too sick to enjoy the privilege. Beyond them, there are double doors leading to the high dependency unit, a place mentioned only with a shudder. When we arrived, it was being swabbed down: someone had died from MRSA, according to rumour. There were a lot of rumours in Ward 15. None the less, it was not an especially sociable place: the children were often too ill, and the parents too harassed and defensive. Laurie would be in and out of Ward 15 (and wards 7, 8, 10 and 16) for the next year.

Something, however, needs to be said right now. Laurie's disaster had already happened. His cancer could and should have been picked up sooner. Had a sample been sent for biopsy following his minor op, the disease would have been discovered 10 weeks earlier, which might have saved him. Had we still been in America, that would have happened. We were assured it would have happened in Birmingham, too.

But most children in Ward 15 seemed to have been misdiagnosed. British medical students are told if they see a bird on their lawn, they should presume it's a sparrow, not a lanceolated warbler. Paediatric cancer is rare, and non-specialists don't look for it. ('You know,' one doctor told me, 'a GP could go through their entire career and never see anything like what Laurie's got.' 'But the surgeon missed it, too,' I protested. 'The same,' he said.) Several mothers told us they were written off as paranoid, or their children as moaning wimps. Once the problem is identified, however, the NHS roars into action.

The surroundings may have been tatty, but I have no reason to believe that Laurie could have had better care anywhere in the world. No one in Birmingham ever mentioned scarce resources. No one questioned the price – at least not to us. Decisions were made with due regard to international standards, and those dictated a treatment for Laurie that must have cost the taxpayer a million or more. That's my guess: we never had to think about it.

Those first few days seem in retrospect like a phoney war. The doctors made reassuring noises even when we were taken into the second most dreaded place in Ward 15: a softly furnished spot known to everyone as 'the bad news room'. Yet the news was not that bad: paediatric cancer, they assured us, was not like adult cancer. The recovery rate was very good: 70, 80, even 90% was mentioned. We met the consultant assigned to Laurie, Dave Hobin, whom we were encouraged to call Dave. He was a jolly, rather Pickwickian figure. I said I wanted to take Laurie to watch Liverpool play. Go right ahead, he said smilingly, carry on as normally as possible. Amid his tears and fears, which were already real enough, there was even a part of Laurie, so Hilary divined, that was a little bit excited about being so special.

If that was true, it was beaten out of him soon enough. The first MRI scan was both forbidding and excruciating: the pain in his bottom – whatever it was – made lying still on it a torment. Then came the first operation, to insert what is known as the Hickman Line, the central line or, to the more baby-talk-minded paediatricians, 'wiggly'. This is a brilliant invention, designed to avoid injections and ease into the patient's system all the necessary blood and drugs – and Laurie would need gallons and gallons.

But still there was some hope that it was all a false alarm. One night I passed Philip Gornall, the surgeon who had first pressed the panic button. He was staring at the mysterious images of Laurie's innards. 'There's something strange about these pictures,' he said. 'This isn't developing the way I would expect it to develop.' It might not be cancer after all, he hinted. 'If it's a virus of some kind, we'll find the antidote and zap it,' he said.

We soon discovered why he thought that. The suspicion was that Laurie was suffering from rhabdomyosarcoma, a rare but identifiable and usually treatable cancer that attacks the soft tissues, though only of people under 20. In fact, as Hobin explained to Hilary, Laurie and me the next day, this was its evil twin: rhabdomyosarcoma alveolar, even rarer, more aggressive and much more likely to recur. Maybe a dozen British youngsters a year get this.

He obviously felt uneasy: jolly-seeming people do when delivering blunt messages. He kept repeating the phrase 'to be honest with you' as a verbal crutch. The tumour had already reached stage three of the four possible stages. The chances of recovery, he said, are 'middling'. What does that mean? 'Fifty-fifty.' My head spun, and I was very close to fainting. Laurie burst into understandable floods of tears.

Thankfully, Hobin would never be that blunt with Laurie again. And sensibly Laurie was not invited a week later when we were called in for what I thought was a routine technical discussion. 'You're not about to sandbag us again, are you?' I asked lightly. There was no answer, because he was.

Hobin had looked at the pictures again, more closely. The cancer had spread further than he first thought: it was already metastasising up towards the aorta. This was, in fact, stage four. He gave us a new piece of paper, detailing a new chemotherapy protocol. 'I'm not going to take any chances with this,' Hobin said.

I think of the summer of 2004 as the *Book of Job* period. Our old world disintegrated. Each week contained unimaginable horrors, for Laurie above everyone. Not taking any chances meant giving Laurie a course of high-dose chemotherapy, which could not possibly be repeated. His body could not take more. If it failed, there would be no ammunition left. We understood that, or Hilary and I did.

Early-21st-century chemotherapy will be regarded by future doctors with the contempt today's doctors reserve for leeches. The drugs are blunderbusses. They kill the cancer cells all right; they also kill everything else within range, especially the body's other fast-growing cells – the follicles of the scalp, for instance. Which is why the patient's hair falls out, as Laurie's soon did, in ugly hunks, one summer's afternoon. And they reduce the blood count, rendering already sick people vulnerable to every available infection. So just as the patient is recovering from a bout of chemo, they may well have to be yanked into hospital for a week of transfusions and antibiotics – at least half a dozen times, in Laurie's case.

The other effects are less predictable, though the hospital thought they had all the possible ones listed on a leaflet they gave us. In fact, all his senses reeled. Laurie's taste buds rebelled, as in an extreme version of pregnancy. Ever after, he would eat only intermittently, and if he said he fancied something, we had to rush out and find it at once, in case the moment passed.

His sense of smell went berserk. He could not bear to be in the same room as a cup of coffee or a dab of perfume. A roast in the oven or chicken soup on the stove constituted torment. A rare meal he was relishing one evening went uneaten because he got whiff of a sprig of mint. His hearing actually became more sensitive, so that, from the first dose onwards, he hated loud noises. He was never again to get pleasure from music. And the music that resounds clearest in my head is the tinkling of Ward 15's drip-machines, warning the nurses that it was time to take action: 'Dee-dee dee-dee dee-dee'.

Then there was the pain. Laurie was immediately put on morphine to ease the hurt from the original tumour. But no one told us morphine causes constipation, which was worse. To stop his weight loss, the doctors inserted a feeding tube through his nose and we set up a whirring contraption at home so this pink gunk could enter his stomach through the night. Laurie loathed it with a passion. When he was nauseous – which, with the chemo, was a regular occurrence – he would puke up the tube and have to go to hospital for them to reinsert it, very painfully. (Eventually, he just refused and we forgot about it.)

Meanwhile, we had Vika to contend with. From where she sat, being ill looked an effective way of gaining attention at her expense. She wanted to be poorly, like Laurie. On May 22 2004, the eve of her sixth birthday party, she got her wish. Bouncing on our trampoline, she cracked a bone in her ankle and ended up in plaster – to her mild satisfaction, and to the horror of the teachers at her then school (we soon moved her), one of whom announced that she could not cope.

Somehow, we had to. At first, the phone rang constantly. I believe now that everyone we knew wanted to say and do the right thing, it's just that some had a better sense than others of what that was. We weren't exactly consistent ourselves: if people called for news, we grew impatient with them; if they didn't call, we resented it. An old university friend of mine, a former golf champion now in a wheelchair, summed up the situation perfectly: 'You don't want sympathy,' he said, 'you want empathy.' Some people tried to tempt us into alternative remedies, none of which seemed remotely relevant to Laurie's disease. Some tried to be reassuring, telling us about friends of theirs who had conquered cancer. There are at least

200 different forms of cancer, so that was as helpful as saying they knew someone who had fought off a nasty cough. Some acquaintances were solipsistic: 'I'm sorry about your news. I'd hate it to happen to my son.'

What we needed most was practical support. Before April 20, Hilary was worried that Laurie hardly needed her any more: at that age, he was more my boy. Now she reverted – instinctively, with a quiet heroism – to a form of motherhood as intense as breastfeeding. This meant we were desperate to get help with Vika, if I was to do any semblance of work. We kept failing.

It's hard to find a nanny to work in a crisis-ridden household situated in deep countryside. One left after three weeks, saying she was going to work in the US; she was still working nearby, in a less troubled home, a year later. The next quit after 10 days, having been asked to 'wash up a plate that wasn't Vika's'. A third never arrived.

Then there was Colin, who helps us with the garden; he was stung by our bees, had an allergic reaction and nearly died. I think that was the week the dog had a stroke, lay inert by the front door and was carted off to the vet where, it was assumed, she would be put out of her misery.

A neighbouring farmer, Bob, told me not to worry. He had been a rancher in South America and once went through a phase like ours. Both he and his horse were desperately ill. When the horse died, the local Indians told him to be happy: 'He has died for you, señor? Now you will live.' Bob recovered. But so did our dog, which, under the circumstances, made me distinctly uneasy.

Laurie also showed signs of recovery. The original tumour started to shrink. Hobin pronounced himself pleased. In early August, Laurie endured the final chemo dose of the first phase, after which they had promised him a break. Things appeared to be stabilising. We even made tentative holiday plans.

Hobin assumed that I would have been on the web, checking up on him. In fact, it was months before I could face doing any such thing, whereupon Google told me I was misspelling alveolar. Nor did we ask what that original 50 – 50 chance had now become. I later discovered the official position was 'a 20 – 30%' chance. But those kind of figures, familiar to everyone who knows a cancer patient, are based solely on mathematical calculations of past performance. They do not take into account a doctor's gut feeling.

Whenever things seemed to be going OK, I would sometimes pump Hobin or another doctor in the hope of reassurance. But I never got it. They always conveyed the impression that they didn't really believe Laurie would pull through. On the other hand, they never seemed to contemplate surrender.

In August, Hilary and I did. This sub-crisis began the night of the 2004 Olympics' opening ceremony, and I was on Birmingham duty while Hilary was back home – always a sign that Laurie was up for male bonding, not just the constant nursing and reassurance that only Mum could provide. There was every chance he would be home in a day or two. After a while, he said he was sleepy, and I went out for a lone drink in some dismal Brummie pub. I returned to find him in agony. Within a few hours, every imaginable organ was wired up to something. And, unimaginably, he had a catheter fitted at 3am. Even more unimaginably, the thick double doors swung open, and Laurie was wheeled into the high dependency unit. Later that day, the duty consultant took me into the bad news room and said he had veino-occlusive disease, a rare side-effect of chemotherapy (and, we learned later, unknown after the particular drug Laurie had just had – would we mind if they wrote it up for the journals?). Essentially, his liver had packed up and he was retaining fluid.

Yes, it could be treated. In the meantime, his liquid intake had to be restricted: no more than 300ml a day, barely a half-pint. From infancy, Laurie had always been a big drinker – juice, usually – and this had survived his general loss of appetite. It was the cruellest torment yet. Here was our big, brilliant son, lying in an oxygen mask, hairless, with a swollen belly, and tortured by thirst. That was the first moment of complete despair.

But he battled back. The morning they said the 300ml could go up to 600 was one of glowing victory. And the high dependency unit actually turned out to be the luxury wing, where the best nurses gave almost one-to-one care in the nicest rooms. I argued like crazy when they turfed him back on to the ordinary ward. By then, the Athens Olympics – an event

I was supposed to be reporting – was over. We had hardly noticed it.

By September 2004, our lives had regained a little equilibrium: 'the new normality', I called it. Laurie returned home, and even went back to school for a time, while the doctors considered the situation and pronounced that surgery – the normal strategy for sarcomas – was impossible because of the site of the tumour, and that the next stage would be radiotherapy and 'maintenance chemotherapy', much lower doses to keep any recurrence at bay.

The radiotherapy was under the control of Dr David Spooner, a tall, shambling, rather elusive figure who was a great enthusiast for his branch of the trade. The Americans, he explained, had much better success rates than the Europeans with this cancer, because they went hard on radiotherapy, and worried less about side-effects: possible, probable and certain, which he then listed in grim detail. I could only nod very weakly. He was not reassuring either. 'I have great respect for rhabdo alveolar,' he said. Six months earlier, I would have assumed he was talking about a Swedish Nobel prize-winner.

This treatment took place at another Birmingham hospital, the Queen Elizabeth. It took two months – five minutes a day, five days a week, not a convenient regime when you live two hours away, but made tolerable by the Rhys Daniels Trust, a charity that provides flats for families in this situation, and by the hospital's flexibility with our appointments (late on Mondays, early on Fridays). One radiotherapy treatment was nothing, of course. But, as with x-rays, there is a reason why radiographers run.

But Laurie's life did become a little more tolerable. So did Vika's, as the blessed Andrea came into our lives and helped look after her part-time. And there were even small moments of pleasure, as Laurie began to take short walks (never his favourite activity), regained his enthusiasm for whipping his mates on video games, and even got back some appetite. The day he asked for more Chinese chicken wings was one of pure joy.

Christmas and New Year were OK, actually, spent amid friends and laughter. There followed two whole months when Laurie was never once rushed back to hospital with a raging fever. All his pain now was palpably the result of the treatment rather than the tumour. And in March, Hobin called a halt to the chemo with one course to go, to avoid further side-effects. 'He's had a good whack,' said Hobin. 'What do we do now?' I asked. 'We watch,' he said, 'and we wait.'

Laurie regained strength with the springtime. His hair reappeared. He went back to school – not full-time because he tired so easily – developing a skilful way of working the timetable so that he never quite managed to be well enough for maths. He tried valiantly to join in at football. He returned to tennis, hitting the ball as neatly as ever without yet being able to run much. He weighed himself daily, and each kilo regained was a cause for cheering. On May 21, we organised a joint birthday party for the two children – aged 13 and 7 – and invited all the neighbours, loads of them, who had helped us through the grim times. There was a secret subtext: we knew the good times might be brief. We didn't knew how brief.

A week later, we went on holiday to Devon, with our friends, the Watkins family, whose son Arthur had been Laurie's pal since they were toddlers. They rushed out to the tennis court, as of old. That was May 28, Laurie's actual 13th birthday, and we celebrated with a cake and a small party. Late the following evening, I was lying in the living room of our rented cottage, a little bit pissed. And I remember the thought passing through my mind that, for the first time in over a year, I was rather mellow. At that very moment, there was a piercing yell from the next room: Laurie had touched the side of his head, and felt a bump.

The next day, a glorious Bank Holiday Monday, was spent at the hospital in Exeter, where local doctors fingered his head and made hurried phone calls. I was called into a private room to speak to the duty registrar in Birmingham. He was sure the cancer was back. That evening, Hilary and I took a long, melancholy walk through the fields, while trying to maintain a vaguely upbeat front for Laurie.

Yet when Hobin returned to work on the Tuesday, he broke with all precedent and cheered us up. He wasn't so sure. 'This isn't what I would expect,' he said. 'If it's going to come back, it's very unlikely to be so far from the original site. It could be anything.' He told us to enjoy our holiday, and not to panic.

Even when he examined the bump a week later, he was uncertain: 'I don't know what it is,' he said. But Hilary knew: she knew the night Laurie said to her, 'Mum, I've got a pain in my kidneys.' And Hobin knew once he saw a scan showing tumours not just on Laurie's head, but on his back and side as well. The trip to Birmingham would be too dreadful, so I had asked Hobin to phone with his findings. It was Monday June 13. 'This is not a good news call, I'm afraid,' he began. He was careful not to say that Laurie would die. He merely said there was nothing he could now do to prevent it.

The final phase lasted more than three months. Hilary and I took two decisions, which we never regretted. First, Laurie was to die at home, surrounded by his family, not in a hospice, and certainly nowhere near Ward 15. Second, we would do our utmost to shield him from the whole truth: he must never, ever, be entirely without hope. This was resisted by several healthcare professionals – some of them good friends – who thought he should have the chance to prepare himself.

We thought that was wrong where a 13-year-old was concerned, certainly this one with all his zest for life. Hobin said if Laurie asked him point-blank, he would have to tell the truth, which was fair enough, but another reason to stay away from Birmingham.

Hobin prescribed a new course of oral chemotherapy, to be taken at home, designed for 'stabilisation', not cure. Now I did work the web, frantically hunting a lifeline. But the friends who had talked of alternative cures had gone silent in the face of the sheer brutality of Laurie's cancer. I tracked down the professor at the University of Utah leading the research into rhabdo alveolar. He replied politely, but said this was a 'mean' form of cancer and that a cure was nowhere in sight. He said Laurie had had the right treatment, and offered no miracle, no experimental drug, no last hope.

Slowly, very slowly, Laurie began declining. He more or less stopped eating again. The doctors began disappearing from our lives, to be replaced by nurses. His death was not in dispute, but there was a strange vagueness not only about when, but how. Morphine patches kept the pain at bay, but made him ever sleepier. Visits from friends became uneasy as he lost heart for PlayStation duels and his last great craze, Japanese Yu-Gi-Oh! cards. But Arthur's mother, Ruth, would soothe him by massaging his feet. He remained beautifully polite, always thanking people for coming to see him and asking how they were.

But he couldn't watch football or the Ashes series that was gloriously unfolding: too tense. He took refuge in his old TV favourites – *The Simpsons, Friends, South Park, Little Britain* – where the unexpected occurred within predictable parameters. One day he stopped laughing even at these. He stopped reading. Eventually, he more or less stopped speaking. I began to break down regularly, as I had in the early days. I no longer knew what was selfishness (my own self-pity) and what was selflessness (my hatred of his suffering). Then I began to think the inability to distinguish was perhaps a definition of love.

But we don't believe he was conscious of his fate, and are grateful for that. At the end of August, he refused to watch the US Open tennis because, he said, 'It's too painful to watch my favourite sport, when I know it will be months before I can play it again.' If only. Still, he battled, and occasionally would surprise us. Hilary was with him almost constantly, barely aware of the rest of the world. Once, in the middle of the night, Laurie begged to hug Vika, and I fetched her from her bed and they embraced instinctively, neither fully conscious.

Outside, the September days were tauntingly sunny and warm. And still he would not give in, until – with the sun rising on yet another golden autumn day, September 22 2005 – Hilary went to have a bath, I lay down beside him and dozed while Vika played at the foot of the bed, and he quietly slipped away. Peacefully, as they say.

We held what we decreed was not a funeral but 'a celebration of his life'. Three hundred people stood on our lawn on a sunlit afternoon, looked out on to the Black Mountains, and we sang and laughed and reminisced. I asked them to remember him not as 'Laurie, who died, but as Laurie, who lived'. People said they will never forget the occasion, and if that means they will never forget him, it will have served its purpose. Then we buried his husk in the village churchyard.

His friends in Washington said they intended to plant a tree for 'Larry'. So on the spur of the moment we flew over for the weekend two weeks later. Not many people get a ceremony on both sides of the Atlantic: I told the gathering that this meant he ranked with Churchill and JFK, and that Laurie's response would have been: 'Cool.'

The death of a child is like no other. I've lost my best pal, and half my hopes and dreams. Hilary and I will never 'get over it'. We don't want to get over it. The challenge is to ensure that we can accept Laurie's death into the narrative of our lives without destroying everything else that we touch.

This is an expurgated version of the story. It cannot remotely convey all Laurie's suffering, all his anguish, all his despair – nor the vibrancy of his personality. He hated pain, and he had heaps of it. He loved life: 'I want to go shopping, play football and eat doughnuts like everyone else,' he said at one point. It cannot convey our own inadequacy in comforting him.

It cannot convey the sheer desolation we feel now – the stabbing pain that hits us both when we contemplate the things Laurie could, would and should have done, or notice something associated with him: a half-deflated football in a forgotten corner or our Monopoly set or a packet of Skittles. My eyes well up whenever I hear Liverpool have scored, because I can't tell him.

It cannot convey the slow realisation that has overtaken Vika, as it seeps in that he will never be there again, either hugging her or biting her head off, as older brothers do. It may be decades before she grasps the profundity of her loss.

After Laurie died, someone asked me if there were any positives to come out of the experience, a question that took me aback. I couldn't think of any at the time, but I have been trying. I have a more relaxed view of my own death now, I suppose, but that may not be a positive. And I have a more relaxed view of other people's foibles.

The crisis brought out the best in almost everyone. Towards the end, we sometimes had traffic jams on the drive caused by neighbours bringing us hot dinners. We had to haul my sister-in-law Liz (to take just one example) off a plane to Spain because we needed her help at home. What mattered is not that she said yes, but that we knew she wouldn't even hesitate.

I can't say either of us has found God, but I am at least looking in that direction: I want a word. But if there is meaning or purpose or logic in this, we can't see it. In the early stages of the illness, I thought – superstitiously, maybe – that I was being punished. I thought of all the shitty things I'd done, the beggars and *Big Issue* sellers I had walked by. But Laurie never walked by a beggar: he was the softest touch in the world. He was punished with all the pain.

There seems no medical reason to explain it either: our families have both been pretty robust. I can only believe it was blind chance that brought Laurie a disease of such rarity and cruelty. We had always tried to be cool-headed parents: even when a motorised sniper was terrorising Washington, I told the kids that they were far more likely to be run over by a car than shot from one. But here we were brought down by a true chance in a million: something so rare that most doctors have never heard of it. A lottery win in reverse.

We have received hundreds of lovely letters (and I apologise if anyone is still awaiting a reply). Some people – journalists, mostly – admitted they could find no words. Others tried to find comparisons. One seven-year-old told Vika about her dog dying. For some societies – pre-20th-century Britain, Africa now – the death of a child is not such a desperately rare occurence. Ours, happily, is different, and I find myself clinging to the handful of friends who have first-hand appreciation of our situation. One letter stood out. It came from a friend who had himself lost his son. It read as follows:

'This much I'm reasonably certain of, that there are much worse emotions to have to live with than sadness, however vast and deep that sadness might be. It can be uplifting, invigorating, strengthening, motivating and, above all, a powerful reminder of how much Laurie still matters, and always will. It can be other things, too, but don't let it.'

I am still awaiting the uplift, invigoration and strength. But we have found the motivation to start the Laurie Engel Fund. What we discovered is that the problems we faced were not unique. Cancer among older children has been rising fast. Their cancers tend to be rare, so are especially prone to misdiagnosis. The symptoms can be falsely attributed to growing pains, sports injuries or (sometimes) drug abuse. The death rate is unnecessarily high.

And the treatment – in the broadest sense of the word – is often inappropriate: even the tone of voice on Ward 15 was sometimes infantile. The alternative for most older teenage sufferers is to be placed alongside adults, which can be worse. So we are working with the Teenage Cancer Trust and aiming to raise £100,000 in a year to fund a state-of-the-art private bedroom, which Laurie would have loved, in a new specialist unit aimed specifically for older children, in Birmingham, if the health authority ever gets its act together and agrees to build one. Laurie wanted to make a difference: and if he can achieve that, it will be a positive.

There was another small thing. After the celebration of his life, I realised that the 300 pairs of feet that had stood on our lawn had scared off the moles that had been digging up the cricket pitch where Laurie and I did battle. But then again, I have no further use for the cricket pitch.

Update: The fund actually reached £250,000 in its first year, thanks largely to the generosity of *Guardian* readers. Construction of the new Birmingham unit is expected to start in early 2007. Teenage Cancer Trust Laurie Engel Fund, Fair Oak, Bacton, Herefordshire, HR2 0AT.

www.laurieengelfund.org

# ENOUGH OF THIS LOVE-IN

## Jonathan Freedland

The honeymoon's over – or at least it should be. After all, we've had two months of it. Ever since David Cameron wowed the Conservative party conference in Blackpool, the man has been carpet-bombed with love. First, the Tory faithful swooned for him when he delivered a speech without notes, then the media fell even harder. (Some suspect it was the other way round, with Conservatives only realising they had been swept off their feet when the TV correspondents told them they had.) Since then the bouquets and perfumed letters from the press have not stopped coming. The love-in has had no let-up.

It's not hard to see why. After the baldheads and retreads that have preceded him in the post, Cameron is exciting. He speaks fluently, has Tony Blair's knack for expressing potentially boring, political points in loose, human language and is, as you will now have read a zillion times, fit and young.

Crucially, he understands the importance of shedding his party's culturally conservative baggage – the Norman Tebbit inheritance that made the Tories seem perennially nasty and out of touch. Yesterday he said all the right things, condemning the Conservatives' dominance by white males as 'scandalous' and insisting that he loves this country 'as it is, not as it was'. In one of his best lines, used before, he faulted Labour's top-down habits while simultaneously taking on the great she-elephant herself, declaring: 'There is such a thing as society, it's just not the same thing as the state.'

So there are plenty of reasons why Tories should be excited. Even Labourites can allow themselves a small smile of satisfaction. If the measure of Margaret Thatcher's success was the extent to which she changed the Labour party, then it is a tribute to Labour that the Tories feel they have to walk and talk like centrists to stand a chance of power.

But that should be the limit of it. Progressives should start telling the media: enough of the infatuation – it's getting embarrassing. For a 'compassionate conservative', as Cameron styles himself, is not a new creation. We have seen one before – and his name was George Bush.

He too knew how to talk nice – 'No child left behind' he promised in 2000, usually surrounded by plenty of telegenic black and female faces – but once he had installed himself in power, he was as ruthless a rightwinger as any Republican in history.

Cameron is no chum of Bush – and the president is unlikely to alienate Blair by getting too cosy with him now – but the parallel is not entirely bogus. For one thing, Cameron too is surrounded by ideological neoconservatives, his campaign manager and shadow chancellor George Osborne chief among them. Cameron strongly backed the Iraq war while his allies, Michael Gove and Ed Vaizey, last month founded the Henry Jackson Society, named after the late US senator who is the patron saint of neoconservatism.

It's all of a piece with a new Tory leader who wants to look and sound kinder and gentler, but is actually truer and bluer. Europe hardly featured in the leadership contest, but one of Cameron's few specific promises was to pull his MEPs out of the European People's party grouping in the European parliament – leaving them instead to rub along with a few ragtag nationalists and hardliners on the fringes. Even IDS rejected that move as too batty.

But it is domestically where Cameron comes into clearest focus. Labour strategists are torn on whether to run against the new man as woefully inexperienced – or as a veteran of a discredited era. He was an aide to Norman Lamont on Black Wednesday and at Michael Howard's side in the dog days of the Major administration.

That won't necessarily make much impact in itself – but it might, once Labour points out that Cameron remains true to the ideology of that unlamented age. In four years in the Commons he has voted against every extra investment in schools, hospitals and the police. He voted against the increase in national insurance that went on the NHS. He wants to abolish the New Deal and undo Britain's adherence to the

European social chapter, the document that ensures a variety of rights and protections for British workers.

Again and again, Cameron may talk left, but he remains a man of the right. The work-life balance is a favoured theme, constantly advertising his own hands-on involvement in family duties, yet in 2002 he voted against a battery of measures that would have extended maternity leave to 26 weeks, raised maternity pay and introduced two weeks' paid leave for fathers as well as leave for adoptive parents. Most striking, given his own circumstances, he voted against giving parents of young or disabled children the right to request flexible working.

On schools, he has advocated a voucher system that would send resources to private schools at the expense of state comprehensives. On health, he has argued for a 'patients' passport', which would enable individuals to jump the NHS queue, partly using public money to go private.

It is on the economy, though, that the gloss should wear off fastest. Cameron talks of 'sharing' the fruits of growth between investment and tax cuts. Sounds reasonable, everyone likes sharing. Trouble is, that diversion of funds to tax cuts would bite deep into planned spending: losing £12bn this year and £17bn next, according to Gordon Brown. That will allow the chancellor to use the same tactic against Cameron that destroyed each of his predecessors. Which services will be cut? Which school playground won't be renovated, which hospital ward will be shut?

What it amounts to is a long list of contradictions, if not hypocrisies. Cameron told the nation that 'everyone is invited' to his new Tory party. Yet he was the chief author of a manifesto that played on fears of immigration and asylum in a way that could only make relations between the races more tense. He was 'fed up with the Punch and Judy politics of Westminster, the name-calling, backbiting, point scoring'. Yet his closest ally, Osborne, launched a wholly personal attack on Brown that called names, bit backs and scored points.

Labour will have to decide how to deal with this, and soon. Within three months in 1997 William Hague was branded a baseball-cap-wearing loser. In the same period in 1994, Blair was deemed a JFK-style winner. Labour will have to decide its theme and stick to it. Brown signalled it: Cameron is a rightwing wolf in compassionate sheep's clothing. He is the same old Tory, just rebranded and with a full head of hair.

We will have to weigh Brown's record against Cameron's panache – and choose. What really matters most in politics, style or substance? We are about to find out.

# CAMERON'S COSY EMBRACE

## Simon Hoggart

David Cameron had told us that he wanted the House of Commons to stop sounding like Punch and Judy. Instead what he offered us was Richard and Judy – cosy and warm, perfect with tea and a biscuit. Though perhaps the questions were more challenging, and took less time to ask.

The new Tory leader, leading at his first prime minister's questions, was anxious to demonstrate that he was beyond old-fashioned name-calling. Instead he wanted to show his willingness to cooperate with the government where it was deserved. He wished to help Mr Blair on education. He yearned to be at his side over climate change. He needed to be in the prime ministerial embrace.

Mr Blair was less enthusiastic. He was like one of those handsome young men on the Dick Emery show, pursued by the star in drag. 'Ooh, you are awful. But I like you!' his female character would purr, as she tried to twine her arms round him. A look of panic would cross the young man's face as he attempted to flee.

The new Tory leader arrived in the House before Tony Blair, who was fashionably late getting to his seat. Mr Cameron looked nervous. He fiddled with his chin, tried a nervous smile and let his lips work as one eating an imaginary doughnut. His wife, Samantha, was up in the gallery. She is to give birth in two months' time. They say that babies in the womb respond to their mother's anxieties. This will be born as if he or she had just drunk eight cups of strong coffee.

Prime minister's questions is a horrible experience for anyone who might be described as a human being. Mr Cameron did have the great advantage: most of his own side were actually on his side. For Tory leaders, that is a help.

He had to wait for a while. By tradition, the opposition leader can only speak after at least one Labour MP has asked a question. Jeff Ennis asked how Mr Blair would be able to deal with a young, handsome, charismatic and intelligent politician – 'such as myself!'

Wacky question planted by the whips? I expect so. Mr Cameron was finally able to get to his feet, to huge (his favourite word) cheers from his own side. 'Thank you. Thank you. Thank you, Mr Speaker,' he said, nervously. 'The first issue the prime minister and I are going to have to work together on is getting the good bits of your education reforms through the Commons and into law.'

Hilary Armstrong, the Labour chief whip, started shouting, as she often does. She is the Commons' bag lady, railing against anyone who hasn't given her 20p. Mr Cameron broke off. 'That's the problem with these exchanges. The chief whip on the Labour side shouting like a child. Now, has she finished?' he yelled at her. 'Have you finished? Right!'

It was a terrific *coup de théâtre*. He was ostensibly offering to help Labour. But he had to please his own side too. So he picked on the weakest member of the government, now in deep trouble for incompetent whipping. He had spotted the wounded zebra, and was giving it a good gumming.

Mr Cameron's offer of support on education left Mr Blair startled. He must have expected assaults over Gordon Brown's massaged statistics, or the EU rebate. Maybe he had not expected this sneaky attack – not a Trojan horse so much as an entire Newmarket stud.

What Mr Cameron was offering, in the guise of cooperating for the good of the nation, was a deal by which Tony Blair could force his policies past his unwilling party with the help of Tory votes. If he accepted the hand of friendship, it would be pushed behind his back to make the half-nelson of revenge. No Labour prime minister could cope with that. Do Liverpool cooperate with Everton, agreeing on a draw before the match?

Mr Blair flannelled. He couldn't agree with schools having the right to decide admissions. And what about investment? He had to find something that made him sound different from the Tories: almost anything would do.

Later, when Mr Cameron ('I want to talk about the future. You used to be the future, once') raised the environment, Mr Blair jabbed his forefinger at him. 'Sorry I'm pointing my finger, breaking up with new consensus,' he said apologetically.

But there is not new consensus. Just the old battle pursued by other means. All we now know is that Edward Scissorhands is wearing boxing gloves.

# A FACE TRANSPLANTED

## Julian Baggini

If you had a different face, would you be a different person? It sounds unlikely. After all, Isabelle Dinoire, the French woman who received the world's first face transplant last month, was not the victim of body-snatchers. Our identities run deep, while appearances are merely superficial.

But maybe when it comes to who we are, appearance and reality are not so easy to distinguish after all. William James argued that 'between what a man calls me, and what he simply calls mine, the line is difficult to draw.' I talk of my body and my face as though there is a separate I that owns them. But strip away all that is mine – my memories, my personality, my short, fat, hairy legs – and what is left of me?

This thought led James to make this outrageous suggestion: 'In its widest possible sense, however, a man's Self is the sum total of all that he can call his, not only his body and his psychic powers, but his clothes and his house, his wife and children, his ancestors and friends, his reputation and works, his lands and horses, and yacht and bank account.' 'Love me, love my American Express Gold Card' turns out not to be a vulgar injunction but a stark statement of the facts.

James was certainly flying in the face of philosophical orthodoxy. Most philosophers have been rather down on material things, especially the fleshy bits. Rene Descartes, for example, conceived of the self as pure mind, utterly distinct from the body, though condemned to mingle with it during our earthly lives.

But then Descartes was a man, and as recent feminist philosophers such as Genevieve Lloyd have argued, cool reason is historically code for the noble masculine, while hot flesh is code for the base feminine. Men are therefore prone to deny the essential embodiment of the self, even while their own brains are located in their underpants.

But if the self really is necessarily embodied, then how we look could well be a part of who we are. Would Marilyn Monroe have become the person she was if she looked like Anne Robinson? The answer seems obviously to be no. But we are more reluctant to reach similar conclusions about ourselves. Do we then spend millions on breast enhancements, hair restorer, slimming and body-building products and so on in order to remain exactly the same people we already were? Appearance is not all, but how we look seems to be none the less part of who we are.

December 15 2005

# HOW NOT TO WEAR THAT DRESS

## Hadley Freeman

Even in the frippery-laden world of fashion journalism, there are several immutable laws to which all members of the corps know they must adhere. Number one is that you must grit your teeth and smile when you are asked, as you will be at least 10 times a day, 'What's in fashion these days?' by acquaintances when they learn what you do for a living. This is closely followed by the equally fixed commandment: Thou shalt not wear a high street copy of a designer dress when meeting up with said designer.

Most of you are probably familiar with Roland Mouret's Galaxy dress, a supremely sexy little number that has been worn by pretty much every female celebrity in town, running the gamut from Rachel Weisz to, er, Carol Vorderman. Despite the approximate price tag of £1,000, demand far exceeded supply, adding further to its appeal, and when Mouret himself announced last month that he was leaving his label, the dress took on collector's item status, culminating in it being dubbed dress of the year or, as most fashion magazines had it, That Dress.

I, however, do not have a clothing budget that stretches to collector's items. I can afford to shop in Topshop, though, which is precisely where I found myself earlier this week, buying a near-as-dammit copy of the Galaxy dress for literally a 20th of the original's price. So excited was I about my fabulous high street find that the second immutable law slipped out of my dizzy head as I proudly wore the new item that night to the birthday party of a fashion editor.

Things did not start off brilliantly when I walked in, tootled on up to the hostess to give her a birthday kiss only to see that she was wearing (the original) Galaxy dress (though to her eternal credit she smiled gracefully at my fashion faux pas). At this point, I was still too dazzled to consider what I should obviously do (ie, leave), but when Roland

Mouret himself walked in and took one look at my cheap knock-off with an expression best described as 'mild displeasure', my head cleared pretty quickly. It was as though I was doing a karaoke version of 'Like a Prayer' and Madonna walked in, and Mouret's face looked pretty much how I imagine Mrs Ritchie's would if she ever heard me try to hit her notes. And so, and not before time, me and my dress got the hell outta there.

The next day, my professional reputation was in predictable tatters. 'Soooo, I heard about you and Your Dress …' began pretty much every conversation I had that day. (NB: 'Your Dress'. Very different from 'That Dress'.) And so I coped the only way I know how: I went back to Topshop and bought another Mouret 'homage' in another colour. Because the third immutable law is this: one can never have too many dresses.

# I, REG, TAKE THEE, DAVID

## Patrick Barkham

There were two feather boas, a motorised leopard-skin sofa and a spangly silver jacket but the man affectionately described by his fans as a 'raving queen' sprang a surprise yesterday. Leaving high camp to the crowd, Sir Elton Hercules John registered his civil partnership with David Furnish wearing an impeccably restrained dark suit.

Civil, understated and in the shadow of Windsor Castle, it was a partnership the Queen would probably approve of. The house of Windsor could also learn a trick or too from the celebrities that increasingly eclipse it. Bowing before his audience like a portly stationmaster pleased to have won a tidy platform award, Sir Elton blew kisses and waved back the crowd's affection.

The middle-aged women clutching Marks & Spencer's bags en route to their Christmas shopping agreed it was a spectacle far superior to the royal wedding, when Charles and Camilla had grimaced and gurned before fleeing their fans gathered on the narrow high street.

The entertainer formerly known as Reg Dwight showed the royal family how to work a crowd. 'Thank you so much everyone,' he said. 'Thank you. Fantastic.' No protesting voices were raised outside the highest-profile of the 678 civil partnership ceremonies held by gay and lesbian couples across England and Wales yesterday. Instead, Sir Elton's determination to have a low-key private day was politely sabotaged by a mob of curious, accepting and terribly genteel onlookers who made room for each other on stone doorsteps. 'We came for the fun and a little bit of razzmatazz,' said Carole Hewett from Maidenhead, surveying the grey hulk of Windsor Castle behind the 17th-century Guildhall, where Sir Elton 'married' Mr Furnish, his partner of 12 years. 'This is living in the 21st century.'

In many ways, it was media-made celebrities doing royalty better than the family born to it, and a popular acceptance of 'gay marriage' – or celebrity gay marriage at least – that even stretched to teenage boys. 'I thought it was really good,' said 13-year-old Drew Freezer. 'His car looked pretty nice and I reckon he's got a really nice lifestyle. I hope he has a good life,' his 11-year-old brother, Luke, added solemnly.

This was largely a girls' day out. 'My husband is totally against it,' said Mrs Hewett. 'When we got up at six this morning he said "you're mad". He knows I'm here but he doesn't want anything to do with it.'

'I'm not into his music but I like his style,' said Bob Charles, 66, who with Roy Williams, his partner of 39 years, was one of the few gay couples outside the Guildhall. 'He's just a typical raving queen.' They agreed that as gay activists in the 1960s they would never have imagined a day like this would come. 'If old Quentin Crisp had been alive now – and I remember sitting with him in the 60s – he would have been over the moon,' said Mr Williams.

The lack of kitsch disappointed some. 'I like reading about him – his wobblies and tantrums,' said Kelly Trevisani. 'I thought he would wear a more flamboyant suit, all glittery and white, but it doesn't matter,' said Melanie Freezer. 'It was better than Prince Charles' wedding. He just seemed to get in the car. Elton wanted to be here.'

Despite the understatedness of the £560 ceremony, showbiz is an irresistible force of human nature. He peered at a pyramid of photographers from behind purple shades and sported a glitzy brooch on his jacket.

Out of sight of the crowds, the couple first went into the mayor's parlour to sign the register. Then they entered the Ascot Room, where the ceremony took place before the registrar, Clair Williams – who married Charles and Camilla – seven guests and one beast: Sir Elton's mother, Sheila, and stepfather, Fred; Mr Furnish's parents, Jack and Gladys; the artist Sam Taylor-Wood and art dealer husband Jay Joplin; publisher Sandy Brant; and Sir Elton's black and white spaniel, Arthur. Boasting an address book that would be the envy of many a royal, Sir Elton chose Ms Taylor-Wood to take his wedding photographs and shower the couple with confetti. 'It was very normal,' she said. 'There were tears. They kissed at the end. It was very, very happy. It was like any other couple getting married,' added Mr Joplin.

For a man who once nursed a £4,000-a-week fresh flowers habit, the white roses and lilies twinned with green leaves were tastefully low-key and left behind for the second gay couple of the day, who registered their partnership in the afternoon.

Outside, Sir Elton and Mr Furnish bowed and waved regally and accepted a cake and a kiss from two girls desperately promoting their local Ben & Jerry's shop. Sir Elton surveyed his audience and puffed out his cheeks in amazement. 'God bless,' he whispered into the darkening sky and ducked into the black Rolls-Royce: groom and groom, bound for home and the serious business of celebrating.

# LET'S CELEBRATE THE UTTER BLOODY GOODNESS OF THE WORLD TODAY

## Polly Toynbee

At the turn of the year miserablism is in the air. Pessimism, disgust with everything, ennui, cynicism, all these are enemies of progress: thirst for improvement requires optimism and belief. Yet the desperate (and comical) disease of nostalgia for the past and distaste for the present is in danger of spreading from the dottier pages of the *Telegraph* and *Mail* into the bloodstream of the nation.

Nostalgia, usually a disability of the old, is infecting relatively young people too, as thirtysomethings bewail the mass culture of the moment as somehow more mass and more crass than it was. Where is 'authenticity', the cry goes up, as people hunt in vain for things so rare no one else has found them. 'Decadence' is all around. Everything is worse, values are gone, rudeness is rife, Britishness is in peril, the future is in the hands of fat kids fixated on PlayStations while bingeing yob culture rules and we're all going to hell in a handcart. (Which antique expression only shows how long people have thought society doomed.)

Look at the recent strange crop of moral doom books, some on the bestseller lists. *Is It Just Me, Or Is Everything Shit?*, by thirtysomethings Steve Lowe and Alan McArthur, blasts away with a splenetic nihilism at most of the things most people like best. In *Talk to the Hand – The Utter Bloody Rudeness of the World Today*, Lynne Truss is funny and self-aware enough to know her diatribe is ahistorical, but what the hell, she slams into modernity with the same gleeful outrage. Utterly predictable is Digby Anderson's collection of his fellow *Telegraph* stable of effete moaners shaking their fists under the pompous title *Decadence*.

Let's get one thing clear. This is the golden age – so far. There has never been a better time to be alive in Britain than today, no generation more blessed, never such opportunity for so many. And things are getting better all the time, horizons widening, education spreading, everyone living longer, healthier, safer lives. Unimaginable luxuries and choices are now standard – mobile phones sending pictures everywhere, accessing the universe on the internet and iPods with all the world's music in your ear. Barring calamity, there will be better. Acknowledging steady progress is the only way to prove what more could be done, if we tried harder.

Decadence is an empty word, an emotional spasm over a feared falling away from some better era. A Latin word, the Romans felt themselves in perpetual decline from their own mythical beginnings. Plato bemoaned decline long before that. Drop into history anywhere and find this fear that people were once more civil and more civilised, usually at some time set just beyond living memory. In 1431 Christine de Pisan complained about the decline in manners in *The City of Ladies*. American universities teach a course in 'the rise in the culture of American rudeness'. This fear of things forever getting worse is irrational: for how can it always have been true? Since when, exactly?

It is doubtful people really are ruder now. There was no more disgusting and vulgar rudeness than the way the upper and middle classes treated their battalions of servants in bygone times: see old diaries and novels *passim*. Nostalgia is unsurprisingly rare among those with any memory of working-class roots. That is because nostalgia is almost always thinly disguised snobbery among those choosing to identify with the upper classes, longing for days when people knew their place, you could get good service and a huge underpaid class lived in dread of losing their job or failing to get a reference on the passing whim of the well-heeled if ever they answered back. Read Dickens to see if people were really nicer or politer. For decadence, look no further than the poisonous snobbery of 'polite society' Edwardians. As for drunkenness, bingeing was OK for upper-class youth: read Evelyn Waugh.

Is mass culture so deplorable? Shopping is the number one leisure activity – nothing wrong with that. A cornucopia of affordable pleasures invites the eye at Ikea. (It is mostly men who inveigh against retail therapy, but is sport any more elevating?) The self-defeating search for the 'authentic' is just another kind of snobbery: nothing is worthwhile if everyone else can have it too. 'Authentic' is as empty as 'decadent', an inchoate, yearning word. What is inauthentic about wearing clothes someone designed for a chain store instead of for a 'designer' shop? Nothing wrong with food from a supermarket, those modern miracles of splendour and choice: the old corner shop selling beans, Oxo and white sliced died because it was worse. Meanwhile, more people listen to classical music, buy books and attend blockbuster art exhibitions than ever before. Culture high and low was never more accessible and it thrives. Television was never better either: memory compresses the good bits. As for pop music, we aficionados of Radio 2's *Sounds of the Sixties* with yer old mate Brian Matthew are weekly reminded of the excruciating dross that rubbed up alongside the Greats. It is human to miss things fondly remembered from youth, but it is folly to imagine those things as necessarily 'better'.

This disease breaks out in a virulent rash at certain times. Why now? If this year was the worst it gets economically, with only a minor lessening in 10 years of unbroken good growth, maybe there is a vertiginous sense that such a run of good fortune can't last. Or maybe affluence brings with it other expectations: it allows the great 'what's it all for?' to loom.

There is plenty to be angry about: poverty, ignorance, helplessness, social injustice, environmental depredation (or the walloping million-pound bonuses paid to City bankers in this bad year). The progressive endeavour is to persuade people to want and believe things can always get better and fairer. What has been dismal since the election is Labour's failure to raise those hopes: instead it has swum with the tide of gloom, demanding 'respect' from those who receive none themselves. More children stay on at school and achieve, but Labour echoes the mood of the moment – things are worse, youth is worse with much to fear and little to celebrate. Tony Blair's lack of inspirational leadership may now be bizarrely exposed by the Conservatives as Cameron overtakes on the inside, claiming climate change, redistribution and Africa. (It won't last: wait until Bob Geldof and Zac Goldsmith demand things no Tory party could agree.)

But Cameron's clever artifice has rightly identified the great lacuna in Blair's leadership: Blair has triangulated away the big issues that engage the heart, while deliberately hiding the redistributive good Labour has done. This current phoney mood that yearns for yesterday is partly a longing for things Blair has always avoided. People – or at least enough of them – enjoy affluence but they want to be asked for altruism too. Craven politicians offering only better management demand nothing noble of the voter. The 'better yesterday' syndrome is partly a symptom of Labour's lack of much vision for better tomorrows. New year needs new resolutions from Labour.

# HAS CHARLES KENNEDY'S 'PROBLEM WITH DRINK' DESTROYED HIS POLITICAL CAREER?

## John Sutherland

Nowhere does the British class system operate more clearly than in the wet world of alcohol. It's ingrained in the terminology. Charles Kennedy is not, perish the thought, a 'binge drinker'. That contemptuous term is reserved for the lumpen-drunken, those toss-pots who defile our city streets every weekend night with human waste, screamed obscenity and vomit. Kennedy is not a 'celebrity drunk', like George Best or Gazza. He is not a public-performance drunk, like Jeffrey Bernard of 'unwell' fame. He is not a slob, like those celebrated on Moderndrunkardmagazine.com, who regard alcoholism as one of the inalienable rights of man. Kennedy is not a 'lush', like Carol in Coronation Street. Above all, he's not an 'addict', like the (recovered) Mother Teresa of the soccer pitch, Tony Adams.

Charles Kennedy, privy counsellor that he is (and will continue to be, even now he has resigned as leader of the Liberal Democrats) has what is delicately termed a 'problem with drink'. His drinking, like his advice to the sovereign, is a privy and high-toned thing. Alcoholics, of course, invariably have a problem with drink. It's how to keep the stuff coming after everyone else has stopped, gone home, or passed out.

It's in the nature of problems to have solutions. In his public admission, Kennedy reassured us that his drink problem was 'essentially resolved'. He hadn't touched a drop for two months (not, alas, something for the *Guinness Book of Records*). Solution, resolution: same thing. End of problem, move on. Those close to him were evidently unconvinced by his latest new leaf. Resolutions, even essential resolutions, are cheap, particularly so early in the new year.

What next for the ex-leader? Will he succumb again to what the press likes to call his 'demons', or will he win his 'battle with the bottle'? Cliches won't help. There are two moments in the drinking career when recovery is most hopeful. One is AA's classic 'touching bottom' – when you've lost everything: job, family, place in society, health, self-respect. AA is full of such down-and-out, where-else-can-I-go? alcoholics.

The other moment is when, before that final plunge into the depths, you realise all your safety nets have gone. If you don't do something instantly, you'll be over the edge. The 'moment of clarity' (more AA-speak) does not return. The path of such alcoholics in recovery (I was one such) is easier, and – in non-drinking career terms – more hopeful. Assuming, that is, they can pull back.

If he stays sober, Kennedy can climb to the top of the slippery pole again. He's got the years to do it, and the political talent. His brain doesn't seem to have suffered any obvious alcoholic rot. He'll have time to do the rounds of the chatshows, and endear himself to the electorate. He's ambitious and loves power: the party had to stamp on his fingers to make him let go of the leadership.

If he plays his cards right, Kennedy could be the first British politician to integrate 'recovery' into a revived and even more successful political career than he aimed at when ostensibly sober. His aim should be not merely recovery but spectacular recovery.

Showbusiness shows how it can be done. The industry is star-spangled with performers who have 'battled booze', come clean about it, done something about it, and come back, stronger than before. Kristin Davis, for example, who plays Charlotte in *Sex and the City*, is a publicly confessed, spectacularly recovered drunk. She gave it up 14 years ago ('It was leading me down a dark road'). She drinks on screen brilliantly. Like the spectacularly, and equally publicly, recovered Jack Osbourne, Davis obviously had her moment of truth early in life.

Who, if one was casting *Kennedy the Movie*, would one pick for the lead from the ranks of the spectacularly recovered? Robert Downey Jr? Too spectacularly recovered, perhaps, and too prone to spectacular relapse. Charlie Sheen? The pudgy cheeks are perfect, but the complications of sex addiction wouldn't fit with the Scottish presbyterianism. Christian Slater? Too darkly good-looking. Nick Nolte? Too old and too obviously ravaged. Ben Affleck? Yuk. Tim Allen? Perfect.

Kennedy will have a lot of time on his hands in the next few weeks. He should walk to Leicester Square one afternoon, when the debates pall, and catch the Johnny Cash movie *Walk the Line*. As played by Joaquin Phoenix (whose family knows a lot about addiction and its perils) the singer is portrayed as a hero of spectacular recovery. Had he not come through the fire – drinking and drugging – Cash might, on the strength of his early songs, have been remembered as a great country artist, but not the greatest: a verdict which, the film suggests (and most fans would agree) depends on his later, cleaned-up career.

Sadly, many who overdrink never come back. Many who do recover jog along sober, but with duller lives than they had before. But a significant proportion rise above their wretchedness and, in sobriety, get to places that, arguably, they couldn't have, without the experience of addiction and the self-knowledge it can bring.

So the prescription for Kennedy is: work hard, regain the trust of your colleagues and constituents (two years before the next election is enough time), rebuild your career, aim higher than before, don't drink, and listen to your Johnny Cash CDs.

# GEORGE GALLOWAY:
# NO RESPECT IN THE HOUSE

## Zoe Williams

It's rare to come across a TV programme, indeed a cultural experience of any sort, that manages to bring together two points of view you absolutely hate, and pit them against each other. Rarer still for that programme to be *Celebrity Big Brother*, which normally contains no ideas at all, even by accident. These notions have alighted like ugly sparrows upon the head of George Galloway.

The first is this: that young people, in order to be 'engaged' with politics, need to be spoken to in language they understand, via media they have a track record of taking an interest in. Post-internet, post-PlayStation, post-reality telly, traditional campaigning simply won't reach them. This has become orthodoxy. More young people vote in *Big Brother* than in elections, ergo, politicians must appear on *Big Brother*. It's daft. I've been to Sainsbury's more often than I've been on a protest march; it doesn't follow that I will only turn up to a march if someone along the route will sell me tomatoes on a two-for-one offer.

The second argument is very rarely openly framed, yet is visible in all kinds of political discourse. It is that anyone with passion, with a judgmental moral code, with an idea in his or her head beyond 'let's all stay calm, and make more money', is inherently foolish, and that such an individual's arguments are only valid if they are totally blameless from every conceivable angle, and in the unlikely event that they prove impossible to decimate with flimsy personal attack, can be laughed at for having anything so old-fashioned as a set of beliefs.

As soon as *Celebrity Big Brother* started, the *Guardian* tried to get hold of the Bethnal Green MP through constituency channels. A bit mischievous, this. A surgery had been held on Friday, and of course no MP returns a call in a day – I'm still waiting for Diana Johnson to email me back from November.

In any case, the idea was reinforced that 'Gorgeous George' is all style and no substance and is in love with his firebrand image, and that any cause he associates himself with is just an excuse for his attention-seeking. But if this were an MP with a reputation for being jolly – Boris Johnson for instance – no such inquiry would have been made.

This makes it a mug's game to be the person with the trenchant beliefs, as by modern standards you will never be worthy of them. Channel 4, while it denies having any agenda, manifestly intends to excise Galloway's political views. Since day one, when it cut several of the contestants agreeing with the MP about the Iraq war, the *Big Brother* edited highlights have yet to show him saying anything about politics. And in E4's round-the-clock version, the MP is repeatedly bleeped.

Is he going on about sex and using coarse language? Or is he being censored in a more serious way? Precisely because he claims to have principles, they are deemed worthy of less respect than those of someone who slept with Sven-Goran Eriksson. And here is the real reason for the disenchantment with politics among 16- to 24-year-olds: idealists, who might inspire passion or loyalty, or even interest, are cut down for something totally trivial.

Galloway, though, is guilty of falling in with that standard line of 'I want to connect with the millions of people – most of them young – who are turned off by conventional approaches. It's the Gen-X factor'. Not so. It doesn't take blathering populism to hook them, but the very opposite: it takes conviction.

Galloway has conviction as well as *Big Brother* membership. He emerges from this business more sinned against than sinning. His detractors should be held accountable for political inertia in this country. Yes, the *Big Brother* machine does get a lot of votes. But let's not become so confused by the word 'vote' that we seriously believe 16-year-olds want to run the country this way.

January 12 2006

# IRAN: THE NEXT BIG
# TEST OF THE WEST

## Timothy Garton Ash

Now we face the next big test of the west: after Iraq, Iran. As the Islamic revolutionary regime breaks the international seals on its nuclear facilities, and prepares to hone its skills in the uranium enrichment that could, in a matter of years, enable it to produce nuclear weapons, we in Europe and the United States have to respond. If we mishandle this, it could lead not only to the edge of another military confrontation but also to another crisis of the west.

The European policy of negotiated containment, mistrustfully backed by America and ambiguously accompanied by Russia, has failed. It was worth trying, but it was not enough. Everyone seems to agree that the next major step is for the matter to be referred to the UN security council. Even the Bush administration, so contemptuous of the UN during the Iraq crisis, now regards that as Plan B. What then? The security council raps Tehran over the knuckles. President Ahmadinejad says go to hell. The security council comes back with sanctions, which would be limited by the geopolitical and energy interests of oil-hungry China and energy-rich Russia, and the economic interests of Germany, Italy and France.

Iran continues (overtly or covertly) with uranium enrichment, while those sanctions produce a growing siege mentality in the country. The regime will tell its people that they are being unjustly and hypocritically punished by the west, merely for developing nuclear energy for peaceful use, as Iran is entitled to do under the nuclear non-proliferation treaty. Compare and contrast Washington's treatment of nuclear India! Many will believe that propaganda – which, like all the best propaganda, contains a grain of truth. External pressure, in this form, could thus consolidate rather than weaken the regime.

What's our Plan C? For the hawks in Washington and Tel Aviv, Plan C would be to bomb selected Iranian nuclear facilities, in order to slow down Iran's progress towards the bomb. Despite all the famous pinpoint precision of state-of-the-art US bombing, one can be quietly confident that this would take the lives of innocent civilians – or, at least, of people whom Iranian television could credibly claim were innocent civilians. A recent trip to Iran convinced me of two things: first, that there is a large reservoir of anti-regime and mildly pro-western feeling in Iran; and, second, that this reservoir could be drained overnight if we bombed. Instead, you would almost certainly have a wave of national solidarity with the regime. At the moment, the extremist Ahmadinejad is playing into the hands of the neoconservative extremists in the west; but at that point, the extremists in the west would have played into the hands of Ahmadinejad.

So what should Europeans and Americans do on the edge of this Persian precipice? Here are a few things for starters. First, Europeans should take the threat of an unpredictable, fragmented Islamic revolutionary regime obtaining nuclear weapons very seriously indeed. Europeans led the movement against nuclear arms escalation by the superpowers in the 1980s; today's threat of nuclear proliferation is probably more dangerous. Americans, for their part, should not confuse European warnings about the need to proceed cautiously with cowardice, euro-weeniness, and all those other failings of 'cheese-eating surrender monkeys' attributed to us by red-blooded American anti-Europeans.

Second, we should share all the information, knowledge and intelligence that we have. The US secretary of state, Condoleezza Rice, has observed that Iran is unique among the countries of the world in that the US has so little direct contact with it. The US has had no diplomats there since the end of the embassy hostage crisis a quarter-century ago. It has very few businesspeople or journalists there. And, if James Risen's *State of War* is to be believed, the CIA managed to shop its whole network of agents in Iran to the Tehran authorities by inadvertently sending a list of them to a double-agent. So they don't even have any spooks there. The Europeans, by contrast, have diplomats, businesspeople, journalists and possibly also spooks aplenty in Iran, and so should be better informed.

Ahmadinejad is the president, but not the ultimate boss. The boss of this theocratic regime is the supreme leader, Ayatollah Khameini. Without his say-so, the nuclear seals would not have been broken. But he is constrained by strong interest groups, such as the Revolutionary Guards, and by other ayatollahs, such as the president's fudamentalist guru, Ayatollah Mohammad Taghi Mesbah-Yazdi.

As important is the dynamic within Iranian society. I feel deeply uncomfortable when I hear the American neoconservative Frank Gaffney calling for a revolution in Iran. It's so brave of him to risk other people's lives. Iranians would do well to remember what happened to their fellow Shias in the south of Iraq when the last President Bush encouraged them to rise up at the end of the Gulf war. But it is the case that Iranian society is potentially our greatest ally – indeed, probably the most pro-western society in the Middle East outside Israel.

# ARE YOU GAY-ADJACENT?

## Oliver Burkeman

If this sounds, at first, like the kind of question you can't answer without asking your next-door neighbours some overly personal questions, think again. Instead, we're about to enter the murky if all too familiar world of the Spurious Demographic Category, that broad-brush archetype so beloved of the marketing industry. The term is in the spotlight this week thanks to Sony, which, as well as launching a record label dedicated to gay artists, is trialling a national radio show targeting gay and 'gay-adjacent' listeners. But what does it really mean?

The earliest published source appears to be the *Advocate*, the American gay news magazine, that used the phrase in 2002 to describe a 'hunky bartender' working in a gay club in the MTV series *The Real World*. The implication seemed to be that the character would make the show more appealing to gay audiences, but since then the meaning has been completely reversed. Now it's joined a cluster of terms describing the adoption of traditionally gay culture by straight people – 'metrosexual' being far and away the most popular, with 'just gay enough' trailing in second place (and now seemingly as defunct as *Talk* magazine, which coined it).

Fundamentally, as with most marketing-speak, 'gay-adjacent' is just an attempt to have it both ways, if you'll pardon the expression: to stop commercialised gay culture losing its edge (so that its core audience doesn't desert it) while rendering it more inviting to straight but non-homophobic consumers (who none the less might feel excluded by anything labelled 'gay'). The result? Everyone's happy – especially, as so often, the entertainment industry's shareholders.

But the phrase didn't really hit the big time until the end of last year, when Stephen Colbert, of the satirical US TV programme *The Daily Show*, reflected upon the claims made by certain bigots about Hurricane

Katrina – that the tragedy had been divine retribution for New Orleans' thriving gay culture. In fact, the French Quarter, the heart of that culture, was largely spared. 'If anything,' noted Colbert, 'the lesson of Katrina is: God loves gays, but hates the gay-adjacent.'

January 13 2006

# ARCTIC MONKEYS:
# *WHATEVER PEOPLE SAY I AM,*
# *THAT'S WHAT I'M NOT.*
# THE REAL DEAL – FOR NOW

### Alexis Petridis

In a few weeks' time, it seems likely that 'When the Sun Goes Down', the third single by Arctic Monkeys, will follow its predecessor straight to number one. The teenage quartet have become fixed in the national conscience with such speed that it's hard to react to this prospect with more than a shrug. In the past six months, the media have parroted the tale of their rise to stardom so often that there can be hardly anyone who is unaware of its salient points. The only surprise was that it didn't turn up in the Queen's Christmas speech: 'At this time of yarh, one's thoughts turn to the Commonwealth, and also to Arctic Monkeys, who cultivated a fanbase by making MP3s available on the internet, and before they had even released a proper single, managed to sell ite London's Astoria.'

And yet, ignore the hype and the idea of 'When the Sun Goes Down' topping the charts appears a deeply improbable scenario: the biggest-selling single in Britain might soon be a witty, poignant song about prostitution in the Neepsend district of Sheffield, sung in a broad south Yorkshire accent. You don't need to be an expert in pop history to realise that this is a remarkable state of affairs.

Their debut album suggests there is plenty more that is remarkable about Arctic Monkeys. In recent years, British rock has sought to be all-inclusive, cravenly appealing to the widest audience possible. Oasis started the trend, hooking mums and dads with familiar-sounding riffs and 'classic' influences, but it has reached its apotheosis with Coldplay, who write lyrics that deal only in the vaguest generalities, as if anything too specific might alienate potential record buyers. Over the course of

*Whatever People Say ...*, you can hear the generation gap opening up again: good news if you think rock music should be an iconoclastic, progressive force, rather than a branch of the light entertainment industry.

Alex Turner can write lyrics that induce a universal shudder of recognition: Britain's male population may grimace as one at the simmering domestic row depicted in 'Mardy Bum' ('You're all argumentative, and you've got the face on'). For the most part, however, anyone over 30 who finds themselves reflected in Turner's stories of alcopop-fuelled punch-ups and drunken romantic lunges in indie clubs should consider turning the album off and having a long, quiet think about where their life is heading.

Meanwhile, Arctic Monkeys' sound is based entirely on music from the past five years. The laconic, distorted vocals bear the influence of the Strokes. The choppy punk-funk guitars have been filtered through Franz Ferdinand, the frantic rhythms and dashes of ska come via the Libertines. Turner's refusal to tone down his dialect probably wouldn't have happened without the Wearside-accented Futureheads.

Thrillingly, their music doesn't sound apologetic for not knowing the intricacies of rock history, nor does it sound wistful for a rose-tinted past its makers were too young to experience. Instead, Arctic Monkeys bundle their influences together with such compelling urgency and snotty confidence that they sound like a kind of culmination: the band all the aforementioned bands have been leading up to.

You could argue that, musically, there's nothing genuinely new here. But you'd be hard-pushed to convince anyone that *Whatever People Say...* is not possessed of a unique character, thanks to Turner, who comes equipped with a brave, unflinching eye for detail (in 'Red Light Indicates Doors Are Secured', a taxi queue erupts into violence amid anti-Catholic invective), a spring-loaded wit ('Fake Tales of San Francisco' advises hipsters to 'gerroff the bandwagon, put down the 'andbook') and a panoply of verbal tics that are, as he would put it, proper Yorkshire: the words 'reet', 'summat' and 'owt' have never appeared in such profusion outside of the Woolpack.

He's also capable of more than one-liners. 'A Certain Romance' is an insightful, oddly moving dissection of the chav phenomenon. It keeps spitting bile at a culture where 'there's only music so there's new ringtones', then retracting it a few lines later – 'of course, it's all OK to carry on that way' – as if the narrator is torn between contempt and class solidarity. Eventually, the latter wins out: 'Over there, there's friends of mine, what can I say, I've known them for a long time,' he sings. 'You just cannot get angry in the same way.' It certainly beats guffawing at Chavscum.com.

At moments like that, *Whatever People Say...* defies you not to join in the general excitement, but it's worth sounding a note of caution. We have been here before, a decade ago: critics and public united behind some cocky, working-class northern lads who seemed to tower effortlessly over their competition. The spectre of Oasis lurks around Arctic Monkeys, proof that even the most promising beginnings can turn into a dreary, reactionary bore. For now, however, they look and sound unstoppable.

# THE FLAWED CULT OF THE CENTRE GROUND

## Seumas Milne

No one can doubt that we are in the endgame of the Blair era. Even if the sense of crisis that gripped Downing Street in the run-up to Christmas – when John Prescott lashed out at the government's plans for schools and Gordon Brown signalled his dissatisfaction with Blair's European rebate deal – has passed, the prime minister's authority is manifestly draining away. He has already been defeated by his own MPs on the flagship terror bill, he has lost control of Labour's national executive and was unable even to get his candidate elected as general secretary, and he now faces a string of backbench revolts, culminating in the prospect of defeat on education reform without a climbdown on selection and local council powers.

Assuming he swallows that indignity, the next crunch is likely to come with the May local elections. They are almost certain to be a gruesome experience for Labour, especially in London, for which the prime minister will find it difficult to pass the buck. And while it's true that Blair relishes nothing so much as the war without end on his own party, an increasingly public cabinet struggle over the timing of his departure can only undermine the government's electoral prospects, as the media darling David Cameron drives all before him.

But instead of opening up an unrepresentative political system after years of New Labour control freakery and spin, the prime minister's loss of grip seems to be closing it off still further. The forces that dominate British politics have responded to Blair's enfeeblement by rushing to occupy that narrow strip of territory now taken to be the centre ground. In the case of the Tories, Cameron has presented himself as Blair's natural successor, even as marginally to his left, appearing to challenge business and police privileges, prioritise global poverty and the environment and, in the ultimate pantomime of spin, redistribution and social justice. And whoever wins the Liberal Democrats' leadership election, there is no question that the Young Turks with their little orange books and neo-liberal nostrums are the rising power in the party.

Gordon Brown has been heading in exactly the same direction. Presumably convinced he has party votes for the leadership succession in the bag, Brown has turned to the right. Declaring himself a Blairite at last, his attempts to woo Rupert Murdoch, the *Daily Mail* and the corporate world have become ever more shameless: boasting of his role in privatising air traffic control, the exorbitant Private Finance Initiative, the disastrous partial sell-off of the London tube, all the while wrapping himself in an imperial union jack and banging the drum for a US labour market model that has seen American workers' hours rise by nearly 40% over the past two decades. Blair's response to the Cameron challenge has been to insist that only by sticking with the centre ground – and himself as long as possible – can the new Tory threat be seen off.

There are two very obvious flaws in this cult of the centre presided over by the political elite. If only mathematically, it is clearly essential for any political party or alliance that wants to win office to straddle the centre ground (though in a first past the post system, its importance will depend on the balance between the other main parties). But that in no way excludes the necessity of representing the majority of voters who are outside that political space. For all New Labour's claims about its big tent politics, the party has been less of a genuine political coalition under Blair than at any time in its history. The result has been a crisis in political representation which has fuelled a wider alienation from mainstream politics. And the price for Labour was spelled out at last year's general election, with more than a million votes lost to the superficially left-leaning Liberal Democrats and smaller parties and a low turnout in its traditional areas.

The other flaw at the heart of the current centrist mania is its cockeyed location of the centre ground. The assumption that the broad Blair-Cameron consensus – social liberalism combined with free market economics, privatisation, low taxes on the rich and a welfare safety net – reflects the centre of gravity of public opinion is completely unfounded. On the contrary, opinion polls have long recorded large majorities against privatisation and the commercialisation of schools and hospitals, support for stronger workplace rights and higher taxes on the well off – as well as opposition to the war in Iraq and kowtowing to Washington, all positions usually regarded as well to the left of centre in official politics. What is described as the centre ground in fact reflects the dominant views of the political class and media and corporate elite – hence the weight it is given across the political establishment.

But for Labour MPs, trade unions and all those who want to maximise the chances of a more progressive government after Blair has gone, the real centre ground of British politics is a pretty useful starting point. And key parts of an alternative agenda to address public concerns ignored by the Blair administration are in fact already Labour policy. In the last couple of years, Labour's previously docile conference has voted to halt the privatisation and commercialisation of the NHS, keep the Post Office in the public sector, bring rail back into public ownership, restore the pensions-earnings link and end the ban on Gate Gourmet-style workplace solidarity action. Blair and his fellow ministers have of course rejected all this. But along with withdrawal from Iraq, they are all policies that command public support and could be used to help shape the terms of a post-Blair leadership contest. Now Labour MPs have started to take things into their own hands there is a real basis to challenge New Labour's control of the government's direction. If Blair's legacy is not to be a Cameron administration, that will have to go much further.

# REVOLUTION IN THE ANDES

## Richard Gott

One of the most significant events in 500 years of Latin American history will take place in Bolivia on Sunday when Evo Morales, an Aymara Indian, is inducted as president. People of indigenous origin have, on occasion, risen to the top in Latin America. But Morales's overwhelming election victory took place on a tide of indigenous mobilisation that is especially powerful in Andean countries. Elections in Peru and Ecuador this year might also bring success to indigenous movements.

The heirs to pre-Columbian civilisations have conquered their distrust of white 'democracy' and are again moving to the front of the historical stage. They do so as one of Kondratiev's long economic waves has been sweeping through the continent like a tsunami. The terrible impact of neoliberal economics is reminiscent of the slump of the 30s that brought revolution to many countries of Latin America.

Morales's victory is not just a symptom of economic breakdown and age-old repression. It also fulfils a prophecy made by Fidel Castro, who claimed the Andes would become the Americas' Sierra Maestra – the Cuban mountains that harboured black and Indian rebels over the centuries, as well as Castro's guerrilla band in the 50s. His prophecy exercised US governments in the 60s. Radical elected governments were destroyed by the armed forces – guardians of the white settler states – supported by Washington. Countries such as Brazil, Chile, Argentina and Bolivia were prevented from following anything that might have resembled the Cuban road.

Today the rules have changed. The cold war no longer provides an excuse for intervention, and the US is stretched in other parts of the world. The ballot box, for the first time in Latin America, has become the strategy of choice for revolutionaries and the poor majority. The result in Bolivia is a president who invokes the memory of the silver

111

miners of Potosi and Che Guevara, who dreamed of a socialist commonwealth of Latin America.

The 'axis of good' – as Morales terms it – of Cuba, Venezuela and Bolivia, is a huge threat to US political, economic and cultural hegemony. It is also a challenge for Latin America's traditional left, which has never had much success in coping with indigenous populations. Now the representative of Bolivia's farmers, tin miners and coca growers of indigenous ancestry is to wear the presidential sash and seek their incorporation into political life. They will be joined by more overtly socialist groups that derive their legitimacy from half a century of union work – an alliance that will be at least as problematic for the president as US hostility and international companies seeking to exploit Bolivia's oil and gas. These won't be nationalised but will certainly have to pay higher royalties.

False dawns are common in Latin American history, but the strength of the radical tide suggests that this time it will not be dammed, still less reversed.

# THE DAY LONDON WENT
# WHALE-WATCHING

## Owen Bowcott

'It went that way,' said a policewoman, gesticulating upriver with her radio. Beyond the arches of Lambeth Bridge a police launch manoeuvred awkwardly midstream. A spout of water erupted from the sunlight glimmering on the Thames.

A sprint over Lambeth Bridge. A taxi hailed and instructed to 'follow that whale'. Then the point where crowds were congregating on the Embankment. On the parapet's far side, straining against the ebb tide and under the eyes of hundreds of astounded sightseers, was a northern bottlenose whale. The species inhabits the Atlantic, where it can dive to depths of 1,000 metres hunting squid, and remain submerged for up to two hours. Its appearance in London is unprecedented.

This creature's blowhole sounded like someone trying to clear their mouth under the shower – but much, much louder. A sleek dorsal fin surfaced each time it arched its back. Between 4.5 and 6 metres long, it was making slow progress.

A pod of two or three had been spotted on Thursday out in the Thames estuary. The first report from the capital was around 8.30am yesterday, when a passenger on a train called to say that, unless he was hallucinating, he had just spotted a whale's spout.

By 9.45am, the lifeboat from Tower Pier had been scrambled. '[The whale] wasn't stuck,' said the helmsman, Kevin Maynard, 'but the current was so strong at Westminster Bridge.' By mid morning, a police launch had joined in efforts to herd the whale out to sea. For more than an hour, between Lambeth and Vauxhall bridges, it dodged pursuers. Below the MI5 building, it demonstrated sophisticated counter-surveillance skills, diving deep and resurfacing far upstream.

At one point, the beast swam in close to a pontoon. 'It looks tired and scared,' suggested one woman. A grey scar, or growth, was visible on the left of its bulbous, black head. 'I've seen porpoises and dolphins up here,' said the skipper of the *Thames Moonclipper* as it pulled away from the shore, 'but I've never seen a live whale up here.' Passersby snapped photos on their mobiles. On the mudbank below the MI6 building, a crowd gathered. Aspiring James Bonds were visible on the balcony, ever vigilant.

'It's gone to ask for directions,' joked one watcher as the whale veered towards the police launch. 'A friend I called said it was bound to be a female – because it was lost,' said Katherine Chapman, who had come out of her office to peer over Vauxhall Bridge.

On the shingle below Battersea power station, the whale beached. It thrashed around in the shallow waters, beating its tail. Men from the harbourmaster's launch jumped out and splashed about to scare it into deeper water. A 'hurrah' went up as it swam back out.

By 1.35pm, it had passed the Peace Pagoda in Battersea Park, before doubling back and grounding a second time. One London paper nicknamed the creature 'Pete' but conservationists were more sombre. 'No one has given it a name,' said Mark Simmonds at the Whale and Dolphin Conservation Society. 'It would be too painful if it passes away. It's not a good prognosis.'

January 21 2006

# PIMP CHIC BRITAIN

## Katharine Viner

Although you might not know it from the headlines about legalising brothels, the government announced a crackdown on prostitution this week. That is certainly welcome, as far as it goes: prostitution is booming and official Britain has now acknowledged that the buying of sex is not just a fact of life but an expression of men's power over women, which would not exist in a free and equal society.

And yet the impact of prostitution goes far wider than kerb crawlers and red-light districts. Its influence now permeates our culture, from music and the media to advertising and fashion, with the result that selling sex has become normalised in public life. Former prostitutes write sex columns in newspapers, men's magazines promote the sex industry, 'pimp chic' is fashionable. If the legislation is to work, a broader challenge to the way we have come to see prostitution is needed.

The government's proposals – apart from the misguided notion of legalising small brothels – are sensible. A national campaign against kerb crawling and a drive against street prostitution are necessary because many more men now visit prostitutes: a study published last month showed that in 2000, more than 9% had paid for sex, a sharp increase on 5.6% in 1990. Sex tourism, often under the cover of stag weekends, is widespread, and the surge in sex traffic has meant that Britain is now flooded with desperate women tricked or forced into prostitution. The services women are expected to provide for their clients have expanded, with previous taboos such as kissing and anal sex becoming mainstream. And the government has at last acknowledged that prostitution is not a crime without a victim, and that men who pay for sex are abusers – 'scummy men', in the words of the Arctic Monkeys song.

But what about areas of life beyond legislation? The sudden increase in men paying for sex is reflected in, and in many ways facilitated by, our wider public culture. The sexualisation of British life has been rapid and comprehensive and in the process the sex industry has been made to seem ordinary, presented as an acceptable late-night or between-meetings occupation for men – and just another career choice for women.

So we now have two Sunday newspapers featuring 'sex columnists', whose qualification is that they buy or sell sex. The *Sunday Telegraph* offers its middle England readers sex tips from 'Belle de Jour', an ex-prostitute who also gained a blog prize from the *Guardian*'s website, and a book deal. The *Observer* presents the greasy-gloved Sebastian Horsley, a man who claims to have slept with 1,000 prostitutes and is given to saying things like: 'What I hate with women generally is the intimacy', 'The whore fuck is the purest fuck of all' and 'The problem is that the modern woman is a prostitute who doesn't deliver the goods.' It's as if those who buy and sell sex are the best at it – as if sex was nothing to do with intimacy, emotion, or a physical connection between people. What defines good sex is that money has changed hands.

Meanwhile, lads' magazines continue their assault on British women with articles that aggressively blur the line between girlfriend/boyfriend and prostitute/punter relationships. *FHM*, the biggest-selling men's magazine, asks its readers to calculate a 'pay per lay' by working out how much money they've spent on their girlfriends – all those flowers, meals, fine wines – and dividing the figure by how much sex they got. Less than £5 per coitus is 'too cheap – she's about the same price as a Cambodian whore'. Why bother forging relationships when you can just buy a 'Cypriot tart' off the street? James Brown, the former editor of *Loaded* who has since made a career out of advising media companies on appointing editors, said this week: 'I think sex on a first date is fine as long as you get a receipt.'

We are also witnessing an ugly and bizarre glorification of pimps. Pimps earn their money by pocketing the cash women earn by having sex with punters, and are usually violent, yet MTV's biggest hit TV show is *Pimp My Ride*, which takes people's rusty cars and turns them into vehicles that – well, look like they belong to a pimp. Our own Saturday *Guide* explained the phenomenon thus: 'Everyone wants to look like a pimp these days. Or at least drive a car that a pimp might have lent them for the weekend.' This show is deemed family entertainment. Mimicking gangsta rap stars such as Snoop Dogg, Selfridges' advertising campaign this Christmas portrayed a man made to look like a pimp, holding a goblet of champagne and draped with two half-naked women dressed like prostitutes. 'Get your Christmas booty,' ran the strapline. The rapper Nelly launched a drink called Pimp Juice. Virgin Atlantic ran an ad campaign for their upper class service called Pimp My Lounge.

This passion for prostitution has infected so many areas of public and cultural life. Selling your body is dressed up as a highbrow literary endeavour, not only by Belle de Jour but also in Tracy Quan's bestselling *Diary of a Manhattan Call Girl* – described as 'a cross between *Bridget Jones's Diary* and *Pretty Woman*', and soon to be a movie in which the heroine, like the author, becomes a prostitute at 14. Victoria Beckham wears a T-shirt saying 'Pillow talk is extra', teenagers sport tops bearing the word 'Whore', schoolgirls carry pencil cases with the Playboy logo, celebrities such as Wayne Rooney and Jamie Theakston visit brothels, city firms take clients to lapdancing clubs, gyms offer pole-dancing classes, men go to websites to review prostitutes in the way you might review books on Amazon.

Somewhere along the line, paying for sex has lost its stigma.

In many ways, the increasing acceptability of prostitution reflects our sacrifice of morality and equality on the altar of capitalist ethics. Sex has been resolutely commodified, and it is hard to argue against anything if you are making money, as the making of money has become an acceptable moral justification in itself.

Meanwhile, women are being killed (since 1990, more than 70 prostitutes are known to have been murdered in the UK) they are being beaten and raped (60% of prostitutes say this has happened to them in the last year) and they are exploited because of their drug addictions (95% are dependent on heroin or crack). Former prostitutes report severe levels of trauma.

Paul Holmes, the former head of the Metropolitan police vice unit at Charing Cross, said: 'In my 32 years working in vice, I can count on one hand the number of working girls who were not coerced or abused.' The men who visit prostitutes are deluding themselves if they think what they're doing is just an another harmless commercial transaction, like shopping for gadgets.

It is a relief that the government did not give up on women and stepped back from legitimising prostitution as an acceptable commercial practice, as had been feared. But the law is not enough. If the normalisation of prostitution is to be reversed, we have to go further and make the buying and selling of women unacceptable in our national culture. We need a zero-tolerance approach to the use of prostitution in media, fashion and advertising, and to the promoters of the sex industry who pervade our public life. These people paint themselves as liberators, but in reality they undermine the social advances women have made, and degrade those they profess to respect.

# WHY BRITAIN IS IN LOVE
# WITH JOHN LEWIS

## Jess Cartner-Morley

Not long ago, a painfully hip American style website rang and asked me, as a London fashion editor, for a quote about my favourite shop in London. I told them it was Dover Street Market, which, for the uninitiated, is a high-concept, fashion-as-art emporium in Mayfair, packed with deconstructed limited-edition cross-brand-synergy utility-meets-vintage pieces, inspired by Japanese animation and hand-buried in cedar chippings over the summer solstice for a bespoke distressed finish. You know the sort of thing.

This was a total lie. I was just thrown into a panic by the Manhattan drawl of this other journalist who, you could tell, was some Chloë Sevigny lookalike hipster babe, so I tried to think of somewhere that made me sound cool. I know, I know: I'm pathetic. Dover Street is marvellous, if you like that sort of thing, but no way is it closest to my heart. That dubious honour does not go even to Harvey Nichols or Selfridges. Even Topshop is pipped at the post. There is only one store for me, and that is John Lewis.

Yesterday I made the happy discovery that I am far from alone in this predilection. A consumer satisfaction study by Verdict found that John Lewis is the nation's favourite store, praised for value for money, range of products, and well-informed staff.

It might seem baffling how such an untitillating store could inspire such affection. But that is the point. John Lewis is the antidote to the Zara-fied shopping world of near-disposable clothing. Whereas in Zara you are duped into unwise purchases by the prospect that since that dress probably won't be in stock next week, you had better buy it now, even if you don't like it that much, John Lewis nurtures shoppers who do a 'recce' (and call it a recce) before making a purchase.

After a Zara or Topshop spree, John Lewis is an oasis of refreshing wholesomeness. This is a world of explicit rationalism, where shop assistants know where things are and people spend their free time on actual hobbies – tapestry, for goodness' sake – rather than frittering their life away in changing rooms.

John Lewis is shopping without the guilt. On my last trip there I bought photo albums, child's swimming armbands, mothballs, a meat thermometer, Egyptian cotton pillowcases, church candles, fine-knit wool tights. I spent quite a lot of money, come to think of it, but so sensibly that I'm sure it didn't actually count as spending, although admittedly I have not checked this against my bank statement. And, of course, I bought buttons, because I always do when I'm there. For that half-hour, I truly believe that one day I will replace all the missing buttons in my wardrobe. Too much cross-brand-shopping utility-meets-vintage shopping, I guess: I'm seduced by a fantasy of being sensible.

London bombing victim Martine Wright at Queen Mary's Hospital, Roehampton. Martine is learning to walk again after losing both legs. (DAN CHUNG/GUARDIAN)

*Overleaf:* Ruth Kelly, education secretary, presents a white paper on education to the cabinet. Tony Blair, John Prescott, Charles Clarke and Geoff Hoon are all clearly visible. (MARTIN ARGLES/GUARDIAN)

The first female couple in Britain to get married, Grainne Close and Shannon Sickles proudly show off their wedding bands at Belfast City Hall. (MARK PIERCE/PACEMAKER)

David Cameron and his wife, Samantha, at the Conservative party conference, Blackpool, where Cameron's speech wowed his audience. (MARTIN ARGLES/GUARDIAN)

January 30 2006

# 'HUMAN ENHANCEMENT': WHAT PRICE HUMANITY?

## Madeleine Bunting

My daughter is 10. Fast forward 25 years, and she is having her first child – early by the standards of all her friends, but she's keen on 'natural'. Of course, she did pre-implementation genetic diagnosis, and she and her husband (yes, very old-fashioned, they married) had some agonising days deciding on whether to modify a genetic predisposition to depression and whether to splice in a gene for enhanced intelligence. In the end, they felt they had no option but to give their baby the best possible start in life.

Five years later, my little granddaughter is starting school. Again her parents have talked over the pros and cons of cognitive enhancement. A pharmcogenetic package is now routinely offered on the NHS after the government decided that, given international competition in the global knowledge economy, there was no option but to ensure the nation's schoolchildren had better powers of memory and concentration. I had my doubts, but I have to admit that my little granddaughter is proving a wonderfully clever creature – a constant source of amazement to me.

My doubts were in part assuaged by the fact that I had already started stronger doses of the same cognitive enhancement drugs. They've helped hugely with my forgetfulness (I'm just hitting my 70s). They are part of a cocktail of drugs I'm now taking to postpone many of the effects of ageing. I dithered a bit but in the end there was no option. I'm doing the childcare for all my five grandchildren and I need to be strong and fit for them. My age expectancy is now 110, so the plan is that I can help out a bit with the great-grandchildren too.

What we've been unhappy about is that my daughter has been very tired trying to hold down her job and be a mum, and she's come under a lot of pressure from her boss to get help. What they mean is that she should go on to Provigil. They point out that if she was taking it, she could miss several nights of sleep without any problem. Her colleagues call her a bio-Luddite for refusing. She's already the only one not to have taken her company's early diagnosis – she said she didn't want to know whether she was going to get Alzheimer's disease in 30 years' time.

The other thing that concerns us is that many of the children in my grandchild's school have had much better enhancement programmes. The cleverest went to China for the latest technology. I can see that my grandchild is never going to keep up. At the moment, she doesn't mind that she's bottom of her class, but she'll be lucky to get to a good university. The one hope I've got is that they might introduce quotas for 'naturals' or 'near-naturals' like her. Anyway, to cheer her up I bought her the equivalent of what we called iPods in the old days – the chip inserted behind her ear gives her 24/7 access to stories and music. She downloaded a book I loved when I was her age, *Little House on the Prairie*. She thinks it's magical.

This is the most conservative of a range of scenarios about the possibilities of 'human enhancement' that have prompted fierce debate in the US and are exercising many a scientist's mind around the world. The pace of development in four distinct disciplines – neuroscience, biotechnology such as genetics, computing and nanoscience – is such that many envisage dramatic breakthroughs in how we can modify ourselves, our physical and mental capabilities. We could live much longer and be much stronger and cleverer – even be much happier. A whole new meaning to 'Be all you can be'.

To the real enthusiasts – they call themselves transhumanists – humanity is on the point of being liberated from its biology. In their advocacy of our 'technological rights', they believe that human beings are on the brink of a huge leap in development, leaving behind the sick, quarrelsome, weak, fallible creatures we have been up to now. We will be, as their slogan goes, 'better than well'.

This is the prospect that horrifies the so-called 'bio-conservatives' such as Francis Fukuyama, who argues that transhumanism is the most dangerous ideology of our time. There are plenty who share his concerns, pointing out that the implications for human rights, indeed for our understanding of what it is to be human, are huge. What place will equality have in this brave new world? What place will privacy have when brain imaging can read our thoughts and transcranial magnetic stimulation can manipulate our thoughts? What powers over our brains will the state demand in the war against terror?

A point well made by *Better Humans*, a pamphlet launched next week by the thinktank Demos, is how far advanced public acceptance is of many of the principles that underlie these technologies. So we're not talking about radical new steps, only an acceleration of existing trends. For example, if you can have Viagra for an enhanced sexual life, why not a Viagra for the mind? Is there a meaningful difference? If we show such enthusiasm for 'improving' our noses and breasts with cosmetic surgery, why not also improve our brains? As computers continue to increase in power and shrink in size, why shouldn't we come to use them as prostheses, a kind of artificial limb for the brain? If we have successfully lengthened life expectancy with good sanitation and diet, why can't we lengthen it with new drugs? Ritalin is already being traded in the classroom by US students to help improve their concentration.

There's no available stop button. Much of the research that could be ultimately used for human enhancement is urgently needed to counter such neuro-degenerative diseases as Alzheimer's. But it's all too possible to envisage how fast, in a competitive, unequal world, we could hurtle towards some horrible futures. The one I outlined above for my descendants was the most benign I could imagine. There's no point in sci-fi style panic. The best hope lies in the strength and quality of public debate and democratic institutions to regulate and direct the use of these powerful technologies.

# HELMAND PROVINCE: THE WILD FRONTIER

## Declan Walsh

Last October Major Shaun Pendry, leader of a British advance team in Helmand, got his first serious taste of life in the wild south of Afghanistan. He was out with an American convoy when it was ambushed: tracer bullets and machine-gun fire zinged off the armour-plated Humvees as they sped through a high-walled village. They were attacked again four miles down the road, this time with rocket-propelled grenades. At least 10 rockets whooshed past, according to a captain in the last vehicle. Fortunately, they all missed. 'Welcome to Afghanistan,' an American officer told him.

Over the next few months, 4,200 more British soldiers will be deployed in this sprawling province wedged against Afghanistan's border with Pakistan. The British will be spearheading a Nato force that will attempt to take control of the volatile southern provinces and, in doing so, allow around 4,000 American soldiers to return home. (Counting the British troops already on the ground in Afghanistan, and a further deployment of 1,300 to the Kabul region in May, Britain will have 5,700 troops in the country by July. This compares with 8,500 currently in Iraq.)

The defence secretary, John Reid, admitted that the south is a 'more demanding area' than the north or west of Afghanistan, the regions in which British troops have been deployed so far. This is a considerable understatement. Afghans have an unsettling tendency to welcome foreigners initially, then expel them violently, as the British learned to their cost in the 19th century and the Russians in the 20th. This remains an extremely volatile region – and Helmand is one of its most unruly corners.

The Nato mission comes at a critical point in efforts to rebuild Afghanistan. Four years after American bombers and their Afghan allies toppled the Taliban, success hangs in the balance. Some things have gone well – two peaceful elections, a growing network of smooth roads and a record number of girls in school, for instance. Three million refugees have returned from Pakistan and Iran. The reopening of parliament last month was an eye-popping sight: crusty warlords, turncoat Taliban, fresh-faced women and former communists all gathered together in one chamber to talk about a future.

But in several key areas, reconstruction is stumbling dangerously. The Taliban, buoyed by brash new tactics, have stubbornly refused to die away. Until last summer suicide bombs were an exotic rarity in Afghanistan. Now there are several a week. The tactical twist carries unnerving echoes of Iraq: on Christmas day, Afghanistan saw its first videotaped beheading of a coalition 'collaborator' released on the internet.

Meanwhile, despite all the talk of clean government, President Karzai has appointed several former warlords to powerful positions, and the booming drug business – now worth £1.6bn per year, and providing 87% of the world's heroin – has slithered into the new corridors of power. It is estimated that 17 of the 249 new parliamentarians are drug smugglers. Another 64 are believed to have links to mafia-like armed groups. Drugs, thugs and insurgency are an old scourge in these parts, of course. But now they are blending together into what Chris Mason, a former US State Department official, calls 'a perfect storm'. A drugs war is looming, one that will pit foreign forces against the burgeoning drugs mafia. And Helmand is to be at the heart of the fight.

Its geography is as daunting as its violence. Craggy peaks touch 3,000 metres in the mountainous north where the one-eyed Taliban leader, Mullah Muhammad Omar, took shelter after 2001. The south is carpeted in vast, lonely deserts. Summer temperatures average 47C (117F). The cocoa-coloured River Helmand cuts between these two zones, flanked by a green belt of land as it twists sluggishly towards Iran.

The fertile riverbanks were once the site of an ambitious American dream. During the cold war, Washington poured millions into building a giant hydroelectric dam and a web of irrigation canals. Today, these canals help nurture a far more lucrative crop than the wheat they were intended for: poppies.

Poppy and its more lucrative derivatives opium and heroin, grease every wheel of the local economy. In Lashkar Gah, the provincial capital, new mansions, complete with gondola-shaped roofs and mirrored green windows, peek over the high walls in the wealthiest suburbs. Businessmen rip around the city in top-of-the-range 4x4 jeeps. Provincial officials and police chiefs have curiously expensive cars and houses. And at night the southern desert roars with the sound of high-speed convoys – jeeps crammed with itchy-fingered gunmen and Class A narcotics – whizzing across the hardened sands.

'Drugs permeate everything here. It's like asking people in Iowa not to grow corn,' says Lieutenant Colonel Jim Hogberg, the provincial US commander. His first discovery here, he says, was the paramount importance of the tribe and its subsidiary streams: honour, money and bloodshed. 'Being commander in Helmand is like being in an episode of the *Sopranos*,' he says. 'You never know who will be at the dinner table next week because there's always someone getting whacked.'

The token international presence has given the Taliban carte blanche to terrorise at will. A mafia-style assassination campaign against Afghans linked to western aid has stepped up alarmingly in the past six months. In June 2005, five men working for an American contractor were executed at the side of the road. Last month, gunmen walked into a mosque in Laskhar Gah, singled out a man named Engineer Mirwais from the rows of worshippers and shot him in the head. He worked for a Bangladeshi aid agency providing clean water.

Teachers, as elsewhere in the south, have been particularly targeted. In recent weeks 'night letters' – menacing tracts pinned to mosque doors and shop windows – have warned those teaching girls to stop. Defiance carries a heavy price. On December 15 2005 the Taliban dragged Laghmani, a teacher from Nad Ali district, from a classroom of teenagers and shot him at the school gate. The bloodshed has left many Helmandis, influential tribal leaders in particular, hedging their bets, Hogberg says. 'People are straddling the fence. They do not want to commit to the government yet.'

Hogberg met the local ulema, or council of religious leaders, to build bridges. He initially got a frosty reception. 'The governor didn't want me to meet them. When I did, they wouldn't even shake my hand. They just sat down and raked me over the coals for three hours. They said there was no longer any discipline in Helmand – they preferred to cut people's hands off,' he says. But after a local public television station was inundated with requests to repeat its broadcast of the meeting, the sides met again. 'I'd rather have them shouting at me than shooting at me,' says Hogberg.

The meetings also kindled an unusual friendship. After some discreet phone contacts, the American commander started meeting the ulema head, usually late at night. 'It helps build trust,' says Hogberg. But when the pair returned to the public meetings the ulema head criticised Hogberg as strongly as the other mullahs. 'Once the cameras are rolling, he goes at me real hard,' he shrugs. 'It's triangulation, like Jedi mind games. But that's how you make it work with these guys.'

Politics, power and narcotics are intimately interconnected in Helmand. The governor's men take a generous cut of the action, according to narcotics experts. So do the police, who either pocket smugglers' bribes or do the work themselves. The rot is so deep-rooted that US aid officials have given up chasing heroin money and are now trying to attract it. The latest anti-drugs programme run by the US contractor Chemonics involves persuading local 'businessmen' to invest millions of dollars in three new plants to process dried fruit, wheat and vegetables. Their funding, officials admit, comes from narcodollars. 'We'd like to get people to invest in legitimate enterprises,' says director Ray Baum.

The US has a queasy friendship with many drug lords across Afghanistan. Although the State Department has given up to $900m a year to fight the racket, the military on the ground has preferred a hands-off policy, because some of the drug kingpins provide intelligence in the hunt for wanted Taliban and al-Qaida operatives. But Britain, which has led international anti-opium efforts for several years, operates under different strictures. Reid's speech suggested that the Brits are going to try to tackle the powerful smuggling networks head on. If they do, they're going to have to travel south, towards the truly anarchic southern border.

On a freezing December morning, Hogberg leads a convoy through the desert to Khanishin. The isolated village is as far south as US forces dare to venture in Helmand; even so it is a three-hour drive north of the Pakistani border. 'If it's not the end of the earth, it's pretty damn close,' says Hogberg.

Khanishin looks like the outpost of an ancient empire, and in some ways, it is. A giant crumbling fort, which locals claim was built by slaves 450 years ago, dominates the town centre. Men in shalwar kameez with dyed beards and casually slung guns hunker on the crumbling ramparts.

There are precious few signs of the new government, or the west's $8bn reconstruction kitty, down here. It has a handful of schools, no hospital and a ramshackle police force. Two-thirds of the irrigation canals are blocked and useless, the elders complain, and the US-funded wheat seeds that were promised were never delivered. Corrupt officials in Lashkar Gah are suspected.

The only way to make a buck, the people explain, is through poppy, the crop growing in happy abundance just outside the fort walls. The planting season started a month ago. 'Now it's about this big,' says one policeman, raising a little finger. A year ago, one large farmer tried to grow wheat, but made terrible losses, a farmer called Haji Nazarullah says. 'If you want us to stop growing poppy then give us jobs first,' he tells Hogberg.

Khanishin stands at the crossroads of an ancient smuggling route, where narcotics are spirited towards the unpatrolled Pakistani border or west to Iran. It is impossible to nab the criminals, complains the assistant police chief: they have the latest Land Cruisers, small satellite phones and well-oiled machine guns. What is more, a new alliance appears to be developing between the drug lords and the Taliban in the area. The British will have their work cut out down here – if they make it this far.

The auguries are not entirely hopeful. The last time British troops were in Helmand was during the second Anglo-Afghan war in 1880, and it was a disaster. The Afghans sent the British packing after a bloodbath at the battle of Maiwand, halfway along the perilous present-day road between Lashkar Gah and Kandahar. Writing from his sick bed afterwards, one embittered officer blamed the boardroom generals commanding the operation from faraway India. 'Playing chess by telegraph may succeed, but making war and planning a campaign on the Helmand from the cool shades of breezy Simla is an experiment which will not, I hope, be repeated,' he said.

# THE DEATH OF *SMASH HITS*

## Alexis Petridis

And so, it has come to this. Britain's brightest pop magazine has gone, as it once would have put it, down the dumper. *Smash Hits* is to close on February 13, after almost three decades. Circulation and advertising revenue has, apparently, been haemorrhaging since its late-80s peak.

Once it was a magazine so important that even Mrs Thatcher deigned to be interviewed for its pages, albeit disastrously: she announced her favourite record was not by Duran Duran or Madonna but Lita Roza's 1953 novelty 'How Much is that Doggie in the Window?' ('obsessed with free-market economics even as a child,' the interviewer, Tom Hibbert, later wryly noted).

Today, *Smash Hits* is a lost cause that has somehow contrived to shed 840,000 readers in the past 17 years. Eulogies have a tendency to be lachrymose and overblown but I don't think it's overstating the case to say that a part of British pop music has died with it. *Smash Hits* exists in the popular imagination as an ephemeral magazine that asked pop stars what colour socks they wore. As anyone who actually read it will tell you, that's desperately wide of the mark. At its best, British pop music has always been about irreverence and irony, individuality and wit. Americans like their pop stars to be just so; the British like theirs to be a bit wonky. It's the difference between David Cassidy and Dave Hill of Slade, between Justin Timberlake and Robbie Williams and between blonde, bland, perma-grinning Jessica Simpson and Nicola Roberts, the ginger Girl Aloud who permanently wears an expression that suggests she'd be happier working on the tills in Woolworths.

*Smash Hits*, with its impertinent tone and peculiar sense of humour (as one former writer pointed out, the magazine's standard line of questioning was never, 'What's your favourite colour?' but 'What colour is a Thursday?') seemed to understand that perfectly. Its death knell may not have been sounded by the rise of the internet or the popularity of mobile phones, but by the fact that the music industry has spent the past few years trying to rid British pop stars of precisely the factors that make them interesting.

I devoured *Smash Hits* fortnightly from the age of eight. In its early days, it was a very different magazine. It had interviews with the Sex Pistols and Ian Dury and the Clash. It carried a specialist disco page, Steppin' Out With Bev Hiller. Even more esoterically, it ran a specialist indie page: this when 'indie' didn't mean Oasis filling stadiums and the Arctic Monkeys breaking sales records, but music of an unbelievably arcane stripe. I can still remember reading the chart every fortnight, bewildered and thrilled at the names it contained: 'Poor Old Soul' by Orange Juice, 'Let's Build a Car' by Swell Maps, 'There Goes Concorde Again' by And The Native Hipsters, even 'I'm in Love with Margaret Thatcher' by The Notsensibles (released, unbelievably, by a record label called Snotty Snail). Here was a world fascinatingly beyond my ken. It's one of the weirder side-effects of *Smash Hits'* existence that it got me hooked on indie music without ever actually hearing a note.

But *Smash Hits* was about to change: out went the marginal stuff and in came blanket coverage of teen pop, then undergoing a massive revival in fortunes. The period between the rise of Adam and the Ants and the collapse of Stock, Aitken and Waterman's 'Hit Factory' empire may prove to be the last truly great pop era, in that it produced not just great pop music, but great pop stars. While the traditional music press, most notably the *NME*, became ever more verbose and sullen and rarefied in response – this was a time when it couldn't review the new Shakin' Stevens single without mentioning Roland Barthes, Wyndham Lewis and Ingmar Bergman's *Sommaren med Monika* – *Smash Hits* truly understood what pop music was about. Its tone was never fawning or respectful, but impudent, wry and occasionally merciless. Any kind of pomposity was held up to endless ridicule.

Most of the pomposity seemed to come from the mouth of Paul Weller, barely out of his teens and already giving a convincing impression of being the most humourless man ever to pick up a guitar. When Weller surveyed the glitz and glamour of early 80s pop with the withering phrase 'it's like punk never 'appened', *Smash Hits* seized on it, and used it at any opportunity. Every fortnight, it seemed, a picture of rouged-up young hopefuls – Blue Zoo, perhaps, or Cava Cava or Classix Nouveau – would appear with the caption: 'It's like punk never 'appened.'

Memory fails as to which unfortunate first uttered the phrase 'success is, like, a double-edged sword' to a *Smash Hits* journalist, but that too became a catchphrase, rigorously applied any time a pop star began protesting about the pressures of work, as in: 'Boy George stormed out of a TV show complaining of being exhausted and that success is, like, a double-edged sword' etc.

Further hilarity was caused by Weller setting up his own publishing house, Riot Stories, to put out something he dispiritingly dubbed Youth Poetry. *Smash Hits'* response was a cartoon, featuring Weller receiving the Nobel prize for literature with the words, 'Fangyew, fangyew, I'd like to read my latest poem, "Teen Angst Part 4,968".'

Its reviews were equally biting. I can't remember which ill-fated combo decided to do a synth-pop cover of Hoagy Carmichael's 'I Get Along Without You Very Well', but I can remember *Smash Hits'* one-word response: 'Ditto.' In their review of David Bowie's 1983 album *Let's Dance*, there was no sense that the journalist was trying to be reasonable, or to justify his views intellectually. It was something rather more potent and familiar, the genuine disappointment of a let-down fan: 'Well… dull. DULL DULL DULL DULL DULL. But so what? Everyone makes a dull record occasionally.'

As the 80s went on, so *Smash Hits* became bolder, eventually inventing its own argot, affectionately mocking the hyperbolic language of pop. Any pop star whose career was failing was held to be 'down the dumper': by contrast, any pop star who returned after a period in the wilderness was invariably 'back, back, BACK!!!!!' A female singer who overdid the sexiness was automatically a 'foxtress', and a rock star who overplayed the social conscience bit was addressing 'ver kidz'. It may have been like punk never 'appened, but you caught a whiff of the movement's scorched earth puritanism in the mocking disdain with which *Smash Hits* addressed rock-star hedonism. Any ageing rocker who surrounded himself with nubile females was referred to as 'Uncle Disgusting'. Any remarks Uncle Disgusting made about the comeliness of said nubile females were countered in print either with an onomatopoeic representation of someone vomiting (which, if memory serves, went 'SPEEEEEEEOOOOOOW!') or with the phrase 'pass the sickbag, Alice'.

Alcohol was 'rock'n'roll mouthwash' – *Smash Hits* themselves alleged toasted success with 'a cup of milky tea and a cream horn'. Pop stars had their names mangled beyond repair. Having noted both his resemblance to Britain's most famous missing aristocrat and his flexible attitude to sexuality, Freddie Mercury's name was altered by degrees to Dame Frederick Of Lucan. For reasons never fully explained, Stephen 'Tin Tin' Duffy was always Stephen 'Tea Towel' Duffy. The latter was responsible for a genuinely telling *Smash Hits* moment that revealed both something about the brilliance of the magazine and the cultural richness not of 80s teen pop, but of 80s teen pop stars. In an interview, Duffy, possibly tired of being referred to as Tea Towel, announced his intention to form a folk-rock band. 'But isn't that incredibly boring?' asked the interviewer. 'That depends on whether you think Nick Drake is incredibly boring,' countered Duffy.

I stopped reading *Smash Hits* a long time ago, on the grounds that continuing to do so in my 20s and 30s would make me look like our old friend Uncle Disgusting. Occasionally, however, our paths crossed, and when they did, it appeared to be doing much the same job as ever: pricking pop stars' pomposity, dealing in irreverence, making people laugh. A couple of years ago, I found myself watching, awe-struck, while a *Smash Hits* journalist grilled McFly by bellowing entirely unconnected questions at them. 'IS THERE AN AFTERLIFE?' he thundered. Just as McFly would get going on the possibility or otherwise of God's existence, he would interrupt them. 'HAVE YOU EVER MET THE CHEEKY GIRLS?'

*Smash Hits* may not have changed, but pop stars did. In the past decade, rounded, interesting, flawed human beings have vanished entirely from teen pop. Record companies, cleaving to the American model of perfection, began media-training their stars – 'media-training' being a technical term for surgically depriving someone of their personality. Pop music in 2006 is no better or worse than it was 25 years ago – the tracks on Girls Aloud's recent *Chemistry* album are every bit as thrilling as Adam And The Ants' 'Stand and Deliver' – but the people who make it have been focus-grouped out of existence. They are witless automatons, smiley conduits for the groundbreaking work of pop production teams. The spirit of golden-era *Smash Hits* may live on in the flippant, surreal questions asked by the brilliant Simon Amstell on Channel 4's *Popworld*, but stars who appear on the show have displayed a marked tendency to take offence and storm out in a huff. It's no surprise that *Smash Hits* couldn't survive any longer. So let's raise a cup of milky tea and a cream horn to its memory.

# OUT OF THE ORDINARY

## Jon Ronson

I've ended up on a strange cc list. A group of physicists working – sometimes up on high – within the CIA and US military intelligence email each other, often 30 times a day, and one of them has mysteriously decided to copy the emails to me. Mostly they drone on about 'Q*<–>(X)' and so last week I wrote to say, 'Thank you for sending me all these emails, but I haven't got a clue what you're talking about, so you should probably stop.'

The physicist emailed back, 'It appears that Colin Bennett was right after all, and you are an idiot.'

I have no idea who Colin Bennett is, nor why he's telling a CIA physicist that I'm an idiot. I really don't know how I ended up on this list. But the emails are still coming, and I always scan them, just in case. How often does one get sent private conversations between physicists working within US intelligence?

Today, one of them emails the others to say he's had an awful idea. How about this, he writes: 'An Iranian terrorist takes a trip to neighbouring Turkey. He grabs a bird with bird flu. He sticks it in a room with a number of fellow terrorists who've infected themselves with ordinary flu. The virus mutates. The terrorists go to airports and they cough.

'The result,' he continues, 'might be millions and millions of dead infidels. Just a bunch of people flying around, breathing.'

'Oh my God,' I think with mounting horror. 'That could happen.'

I form a nightmarish mental picture of cruel-eyed, fluey terrorists angrily ordering one another to get closer to the chicken. Then I think, 'Hang on – surely all this is asking a virus to do an awful lot?'

The physicists start emailing each other furiously. One suggests that's nothing. Who cares about bird flu when 'the US will launch a nuclear attack on Iran within three months. You have less than three months to decide what to do with your life.'

So what, another ruefully reasons – America is, for all intent and purpose, dead anyway: 'Kids go home from school and, rather than do their homework, they watch MTV, have group sex and get high. [Take] the appearance of the new high school super slut, who makes a decision to copulate with at least 100 guys before she graduates.'

Are these physicists sharing their nightmare fantasies with their CIA employers? Could all this be having an impact on the war on terror?

I consider myself an unusually neurotic person. I once convinced myself that my son had Premature Ageing Syndrome because a few people told me he looked old for his age. I am, I now realise, far, far less paranoid than a bunch of scientists working high up within the CIA. This is not good.

February 4 2006

# MUSLIMS AND CARTOONS: INSULTS AND INJURIES

## Leading article

No newspaper in this country has published the Danish cartoons depicting the prophet Muhammad in ways that have angered many Muslims across the world. The *Guardian* believes uncompromisingly in freedom of expression, but not in any duty to gratuitously offend. It would be senselessly provocative to reproduce a set of images, of no intrinsic value, that pander to the worst prejudices about Muslims. To directly associate the founder of one of the world's three great monotheistic religions with terrorist violence – the unmistakable meaning of the most explicit of these cartoons – is wrong, even if the intention was satirical rather than blasphemous. Their most likely effect will be to encourage Islamist extremism, already finding fertile ground in Iraq. The volatile context of this issue, with its echoes of the furore over Salman Rushdie's book *The Satanic Verses* cannot be ignored.

Back in 1989, when Ayatollah Khomeini issued his notorious fatwa authorising the murder of the British author, the doom-laden phrase 'clash of civilisations' had not been uttered. But since the 9/11 attacks, through to and beyond last July's London bombings, it has become part of all our lives. In this country concerns about Islamophobia have been accompanied by increased sensitivity to the feelings of Muslims. Issues such as Iraq, Palestine and Afghanistan are now viewed to a large extent through the prism of Muslim sensibilities – too much so, for some. The extraordinary unanimity of the British press in refraining from publishing the drawings – in contrast to the Nordic countries, Germany, Spain and France – speaks volumes. John Stuart Mill is a better guide to this issue than Voltaire.

Yet it takes two civilisations to clash, and debate about the images cannot exclude discussion of Muslim reactions from Indonesia, Pakistan,

Gaza or Luton. For the protests, boycotts, flag-burnings and bomb threats seem out of proportion to any slight, real or imagined. It was the editor of a Jordanian magazine who asked (rhetorically) what created more prejudice against Islam, these poor caricatures or pictures of a masked Iraqi hostage-taker slashing the throat of a victim live on camera, or a suicide bomber blowing himself up during a wedding ceremony, acts carried out by fanatical extremists in the name of jihad.

Diplomatic action against Denmark by Saudi Arabia, Syria and Libya – none of them famous for their free press, vibrant democracy or toleration – is a bit rich. It was revealing to hear Prince Nayef, the Saudi interior minister, call on the Vatican to halt publication of the cartoons, anachronistically assuming a role in European secular life for a supranational religious authority. State-controlled newspapers in these and other Arab states, including Egypt, print anti-semitic, not just anti-Israeli, cartoons and articles that would not have embarrassed the Nazis. Iran's president is a Holocaust denier. In many Arab countries reactionary clerics set a tone that is followed by governments fearful of Islamist opposition. Not all those sympathetic to the insurgency in Iraq or resistance in Palestine are comfortable with the theological justification of suicide attacks on civilians. Nor is it clear that Arab opinion-formers care about the genocidal attacks on black Muslims and Christians in Sudan or the bombing of churches in Pakistan.

The UN's Arab Human Development Reports have devastatingly exposed the shortcomings of societies that centuries ago made huge contributions to science and thought but in too many ways are now intellectually stultified, uncreative and unfree. Freedom of expression as it has developed in the democratic west is a value to be cherished, but not abused. And it is above all a universal value. Insults, in cartoons or elsewhere, are best ignored, not punished – and not incorporated into a culture of victimhood and intimidation.

# DOES THE RIGHT TO FREEDOM OF SPEECH JUSTIFY PRINTING THE DANISH CARTOONS?

## Philip Hensher and Gary Younge

**Philip Hensher: Yes**

The first thing to say about the contested cartoons published by a Danish paper last September is that some are, indeed, offensive. *Jyllands-Posten* took up the case of a Danish author who could find no one to illustrate a book about the prophet Muhammad. The paper, presenting this as a case of self-censorship, asked 12 illustrators for depictions of the prophet, and the one that has caused immense offence shows the prophet wearing a turban that conceals a fizzing bomb.

The cartoonist can't be accused of ignorance or lack of research – he has scrupulously transcribed a verse from the *Qur'an* on the turban – and there's no doubt that this is seriously offensive, and not just to Muslims but anyone who values truthful debate. It just isn't true to say that, from its founding, Islam would inevitably lead to suicide bombing, or even that its founder's teachings bear responsibility for this particular brand of atrocity.

That accusation, if made of any religion or secular school of thought that has spawned violent followers – a comparable image of Marx, say, or, quite plausibly, Darwin – would in most cases be just as offensive and wrong. In this case there is a special, deliberate offence to Muslims because the religion has an edict against such depictions.

Whether action should be taken, in a western democracy, against an argument that is just wrong, or against deliberate offence caused, however great, is another question. It's difficult to see that personal offence should be the basis of legal action in a state professing commitment to freedom of speech. The state takes a view on when personal offence is reasonable and when it threatens to infringe someone else's liberty, largely based on whether offence is caused generally, or just to a section of the community. Do the Danish cartoons cause offence only to isolated individuals? Or do they so attack anyone professing to be a Muslim that they would be caught by the UK's religious hatred law?

The cartoons almost certainly look very different to a Muslim living in a western democracy than to someone in the Muslim world. It's easy to sympathise with a Muslim living in Denmark, who would feel directly persecuted by these images. The Copenhagen Muslim interviewed in yesterday's *Guardian* certainly had a point when he compared them to the comments of a Danish MP who apparently called Muslims 'a cancer in Denmark'. Many people in his situation live difficult lives, and such images won't improve matters much.

But along with the sympathy one has to feel for people in that beleaguered situation, the uses that the Danish cartoons have been put to in the Muslim world must be challenged. Around the world, the anti-Danish campaign is being used by Islamist political groups to rally support for extreme causes. The aim of many such pressure groups is to limit free speech on religious matters in the west, and entirely suppress it at home.

It is often forgotten to what degree law-making in the west is still seen across the globe as a model of good practice and for that single reason our freedom of speech, even if exercised for the purposes of causing offence, even if simply wrong in practice, can't be eroded. To take an example: in Bangladesh in 1994, an attempt was made to introduce a law limiting what could be said on religious subjects. It failed because, it was argued, its terms could not be paralleled in the laws of any democracy. Britain's new law on religious hatred, even in its limited form, removes that defence from liberal voices outside Europe.

Debate on a great many subjects is already severely limited in the Muslim world. Reading Robert Irwin's brilliant book, *For Lust of Knowing: The Orientalists and their Enemies*, it is a shock to learn that serious scholarly work by historians on the first years of Islam has to be expressed in code, lest it cause offence to the faithful by contradicting the received account. It is unlikely that a newspaper in a Muslim country will ever want to commission a cartoon along the Danish lines. But we are really talking about groups, even in relatively liberal Muslim countries, that want to draw the lines of permitted debate much tighter than they are at present.

In practice, our freedom of speech is not seriously threatened. Cartoonists will probably be careful about exercising good taste in such an area, as they already do on parallel subjects – for instance, in drawing an Israeli or Jewish politician, a cartoonist will probably avoid the hateful conventions of anti-semitic caricature. After the boycotts and a few noble-sounding words, we will probably go on much as before.

And that's probably the best thing to do. If anti-democratic forces in the Muslim world can make such effective use of a cartoon in a small European country, they would be much more encouraged by any signs of restriction on our part. Anyone in the Muslim world arguing for freedom of speech, on religious or other matters, has only one place to look to – the west. We ought to take into account the sorts of factions in the Muslim world who would regard legal restrictions on our side as part of a wider victory.

**Gary Younge: No**

In January 2002 the *New Statesman* published a front page displaying a shimmering golden Star of David impaling a union flag, with the words 'A kosher conspiracy?' The cover was widely and rightly condemned as anti-semitic. It's not difficult to see why. It played into vile stereotypes of money-grabbing Jewish cabals out to undermine the country they live in. Some put it down to a lapse of editorial judgment. But many saw it not as an aberration but part of a trend – one more broadside in an attack on Jews from the liberal left.

A group calling itself Action Against Anti-Semitism marched into the *Statesman*'s offices, demanding a printed apology, which eventually followed. The then editor, Peter Wilby, later confessed that he had not appreciated 'the historic sensitivities' of Britain's Jews. I do not remember talk of a clash of civilisations in which Jewish values were inconsistent with the western traditions of freedom of speech or democracy. Nor do I recall editors across Europe rushing to reprint the cover in solidarity.

Quite why the Muslim response to 12 cartoons printed by *Jyllands-Posten* last September should be treated differently is illuminating. There seems to be almost universal agreement that these cartoons are offensive. There should also be universal agreement that the paper has a right to publish them. When it comes to freedom of speech the liberal left should not sacrifice its values one inch to those who seek censorship on religious grounds, whether US evangelists, Irish Catholics or Danish Muslims.

But the right to freedom of speech equates to neither an obligation to offend nor a duty to be insensitive. There is no contradiction between supporting someone's right to do something and condemning them for doing it. If our commitment to free speech is important, our belief in anti-racism should be no less so. These cartoons spoke not to historic sensitivities, but to modern ones. Muslims in Europe are now subjected to routine discrimination on suspicion that they are terrorists, and Denmark has some of Europe's most draconian immigration policies. These cartoons served only to compound such prejudice.

The right to offend must come with at least one consequent right and one subsequent responsibility. If newspapers have the right to offend then surely their targets have the right to be offended. Moreover, if you are bold enough to knowingly offend a community then you should be bold enough to withstand the consequences, so long as that community expresses displeasure within the law.

The *Jyllands-Posten* editor took four months to apologise. That was his decision. If he was not truly sorry then he shouldn't have done so. If he was then he should have done so sooner. Given that it took yet one more month for the situation to deteriorate to this level, these recent demonstrations can hardly be described as kneejerk.

'This is a far bigger story than just the question of 12 cartoons in a small Danish newspaper,' Flemming Rose, the culture editor of *Jyllands-Posten*, told the *New York Times*. Too right, but it is not the story Rose thinks it is. Rose says: 'This is about the question of integration and how compatible is the religion of Islam with a modern secular society.'

Rose displays his ignorance of both modern secular society and the role of religion in it. Freedom of the press has never been sacrosanct in the west. Last year Ireland banned the film *Boy Eats Girl* because of graphic suicide scenes. Madonna's book *Sex* was unbanned there only in 2004. American schoolboards routinely ban the works of Alice Walker, JK Rowling and JD Salinger. Such measures should be opposed, but not in a manner that condemns all Catholics or Protestants for being inherently intolerant or incapable of understanding satire.

Even as this debate rages, David Irving sits in jail in Austria charged with Holocaust denial for a speech he made 17 years ago, the Muslim cleric Abu Hamza is on trial in London for inciting racial hatred and a retrial has been ordered for the BNP leader, Nick Griffin, on the same charges. The question has never been whether you draw a line under what is and what is not acceptable, but where you draw it. Rose and others clearly believe Muslims, by virtue of their religion, exist on the wrong side of the line. As a result they are vilified twice: once through the cartoon, and again for exercising their democratic right to protest. The inflammatory response to their protest reminds me of the quote from Steve Biko, the South African black nationalist: 'Not only are whites kicking us, they are telling us how to react to being kicked.'

# THE BRITISH IN BASRA

## Jasem al-Aqrab

Since April 2003, the people of Basra have consistently been bemused by reports that they and their city enjoy a state of calm and stability under the command of the British forces, in contrast to the north of Iraq and the so-called Sunni triangle. As someone born and bred in Basra, I hope that the recent images of British troops beating young Basra boys to within an inch of their lives will allow such claims to be laid to rest and show a fraction of the reality that has made life throughout Iraq a living hell.

When the Abu Ghraib scandal broke a couple of years ago, I recall a commentator on the BBC World Service smugly saying that the Americans were heavy-handed and undisciplined when it came to dealing with civilians, while the British were far more restrained, touring Basra in their berets as peacekeepers rather than occupiers. My estimation of the BBC World Service dipped when the other side of the picture was not presented.

The truth is that ever since the fall of Saddam Hussein's tyrannical regime, abuses and atrocities committed against Iraqi civilians have been a regular, at times daily, occurrence throughout the country, including in Basra. These have been committed by American, British and Iraqi official forces. Hearing the British prime minister describe this latest incident as an isolated case fills me and fellow Iraqis with anger.

It adds insult to very serious injury when we are told that this humiliation, torture and violence is the work of a few 'bad apples'. From previous experience, the most we can look forward to is a whitewash inquiry and possibly a young, low-ranking soldier being made a scapegoat.

As a strong believer in the need for Iraqis to use the political process to bring about change, it is not difficult to see how innocent youngsters are radicalised and why they turn to widely available arms. Those who were beaten mercilessly while being mocked by the filmmaker for their pain and humiliation will never listen to me or my colleagues when we try to win them over to peaceful ways of venting their anger and frustration. Their families, loved ones, friends and even those who see the horrific images on TV will be ever more convinced that such degradation can only be met with fire and force.

The allegation that insurgents have flooded into Iraq from neighbouring Syria and Iran may hold some truth, but the flooding I fear is the daily recruitment of insurgents by the brutal, inhumane and tyrannical treatment that young Iraqis experience every day at the hands of occupation forces, as well as the Iraqi government forces they support.

Although I and numerous members of my family suffered personally, physically and otherwise at the hands of the Saddam Hussein regime, and dreamed for many years of the day he would be gone, I always opposed the invasion and occupation of our country. Subsequent events have made me even more convinced of the fallacy and immorality of the military campaign that Britain and the US have pursued in Iraq. The biggest indictment of the war and occupation is surely that more and more Iraqis are speaking publicly of how life was far better when Saddam was in power – an achievement most Iraqis never imagined possible.

Tony Blair's suggestion that British forces are in Iraq to educate Iraqis in democracy has only added salt to our bleeding wounds. This rhetoric harks back to imperial times when Britain was a colonial power and treated my forefathers, as well as many other peoples in the world, as backward savages. It hurts me that despite Mr Blair's first-class education, he seems to have learned so little. Until recently, Britain was admired and respected by Iraqis. The few who had the chance to visit or study in the UK were envied. The past three years have ensured the obliteration of that respect.

Iraqis have suffered immensely over recent years, first from the west's support for a despotic dictatorship, then from 13 years of sanctions that ravaged the country, and finally from a war and occupation that reduced a once-affluent country and its highly educated people to rubble and dust. It saddens me that Britain has had a significant hand in every episode that has heaped misery on Iraqis. I suggest that next time Britain hears of a fallen British soldier in Iraq, Mr Blair should be asked about his role in that tragedy.

I share with the majority of Iraqis the belief that the only way forward is the immediate departure of American and British troops from our country. The suggestion that this would make matters worse is at best laughable and at worst a scurrilous lie. Matters cannot get any worse, and they only became this bad because of the decision by American and British leaders to wage war against a people who were already suffering.

I have no doubt that I will see my country truly free and liberated from tyranny and occupation. I pray that this happens without the further spilling of blood – Iraqi, American or British.

# LIVE BLOG FROM THE BRIT AWARDS

## Dorian Lynskey

**The Preamble:** Are you sitting comfortably? Then we'll begin.

Unlike the Oscars, there is no great suspense about the Brits. Can you even remember who won, say, Best Male Solo Artist in 2003? (It was probably Robbie Williams, but you get my drift.) And do you doubt for even a minute that tonight's winners' list will be some combination of Kaiserplay and Kanye Blunt? The awards themselves are underwhelming interludes between big flamboyant showpieces designed to make pop look like a candy-coloured wonderland in which anything can happen. This year's can't attain the barmy heights of previous years, surely.

**7.25pm** OK, here we go … Kaiser Chiefs make their appearance in the traditional fashion, not fired from a cannon or abseiling from a helicopter piloted by Gwen Stefani. They predict a riot, as is their wont, but there are few places less likely to host a riot than the Brits. Nobody seems to be getting lairy, although Chris Evans is not very pretty, I tell thee.

**7:31pm** Harry Hill introduces Best Pop Act. First chance to enjoy the little-heard 'You're Beautiful'. James Blunt comes across like someone who's just been made head boy.

**7:36pm** Jamelia introduces Best Urban Act. Given the disheartening advance publicity about urban music's commercial ills, this might be retitled the Well Done For Having A Go award. Lemar wins. Did he have a record out this year? Seems so.

**7.46pm** Prince comes on and plays a song that is conspicuously not one of his hits. Come on, Prince. Play the game, son …

**7.50pm** Ah, that's better. 'Purple Rain'. He looks weirdly ageless, as if he's been preserved in ice in between public appearances. Last time he appeared here, a decade ago, he wrote SLAVE on his cheek in a somewhat hyperbolic protest against his record label. Blur's Dave Rowntree responded by writing DAVE on his own face, which is my favourite ever Brits moment not to involve Jarvis Cocker and Michael Jackson. Prince is playing 'Let's Go Crazy' now. The air is filled with metal confetti, which I suppose is kind of crazy.

**7.55pm** Good God. A drum solo.

**7.57pm** International Breakthrough Artist. Daniel Powter? Pussycat Dolls? Jack Johnson? Maybe 2005 wasn't such a great year. Go on, give it to the Arcade Fire. No, it's Jack Johnson. Presenter Beth Orton pretends to look excited. Jack Johnson looks like a baseball player. Singers shouldn't look like sportsmen. That's not right.

**8.01pm** There really is an awful lot of hanging around at these things. Chris Evans spends a lot of time waiting for instructions in his earpiece while everyone else twiddles their thumbs. You're better off watching it on telly tomorrow night, to be honest. Then you could have a beer. And watch it in your pants.

**8.03pm** Best International Male, courtesy of Boy George. Chris Evans makes a tense joke about George's drug problems. George seems displeased. I'd leave it if I were you, Chris.

**8.08pm** Boy George gives the gong to 'the first rapper to say something positive about gay people – and about fucking time'. Kanye West bounds up wearing one of Adam Ant's old jackets and a pair of sunglasses that look like 3D specs. He tells us how European his records sound. What, like Kraftwerk? Nena? Julio Iglesias? He promises a third album is on its way: 'Please don't drop any albums around that time for your own safety.' I love Kanye West. He should win everything.

**8.13pm** They're the biggest band in the world! They've been taking over the planet! They've refused to let UN weapons inspectors into their armed studio compound! They've broken off diplomatic relations with

Denmark! They're monitoring your thoughts even as you read this! Anyway, that's the gist of Chris Evans's introduction. He means Coldplay, presumably. But they're playing 'Square One', which is one of their least world-conquering songs. At a push it might subdue a small principality.

**8.16pm** Best British Rock Act, presented by Tamsin Grieg, who was in *Black Books* and therefore can do no wrong. She says she's here because someone thinks she looks like Sharleen Spiteri. She does a bit. If Hard-Fi win we might as well shut down the British record industry right now. We've had a good run, but it's all over. Oh good, it's Kaiser Chiefs. Carry on, everybody. Their speech is very poor. When it's on telly it will probably be edited down to about half a second. Some fat skinhead runs on stage and off again. Who he?

**8.24pm** Chris O'Dowd (*The IT Crowd*) announces the next award. It's never an ego boost when your name has to appear on the running order with brackets after it. It's British Breakthrough Act. Got to be Arctic Monkeys, hasn't it? They haven't turned up, preferring the evergreen, giggling-in-video-clip option.

**8.28pm** James Blunt plays … wait for it! … 'You're Beautiful'. I don't have a view on this song any more. It just is, like the weather. Or flu.

**8.32pm** Thandie Newton gives Best Live Act to Kaiser Chiefs, who have prepared a speech this time. Afterwards, drummer Nick Hodgson tells Chris Evans that he's against the second runway at Stansted airport, which is politics of a sort I suppose but it's not exactly 'George Bush doesn't care about black people', is it?

**8.42pm** Kelly Clarkson sings 'Since U Been Gone'. Do you understand the fuss about this song? It's the kind of arena rock Americans have been banging out for years, only with a Strokes bassline stapled to it. Still, she works the crowd like a pro. I admire her gleaming efficiency, in the same way I might admire a sports car I had no intention of ever driving.

**8.45pm** Wayne Coyne, avuncular ringleader of the peerless Flaming Lips, should become Dr Who one of these days – he has the look. He's presenting Best Male Solo Artist, but first: 'I'm an American so I feel obligated to say remember that George Bush is an idiot.' Still not exactly 'George Bush doesn't care about black people', but getting there. Nice to let a bit of politics into this glittering bubble of self-congratulation. Who wins? James Blunt, who promises to retire and become a mercenary in South America. I would pay good money to see that. I bet he'd be very gifted. He probably knows how to kill a man with a length of bamboo.

**8.53pm** Another James Blunt nomination, another bit of 'You're Beautiful'. Can you imagine the kind of bastard who would vote for Shayne Ward's 'That's My Goal' for Best Single? Let's hope there aren't enough of them.

**9.00pm** KT Tunstall is hard to dislike, and believe me I've tried. And she plays 'Suddenly I See', which is one of her good 'uns.

**9.08pm** Green Day accept Best International Group via videolink. They all look very, very tired. What a white-knuckle thrillride this is turning out to be.

**9.10pm** A tipsy-seeming Debbie Harry gives Best British Group to a tipsy-seeming Kaiser Chiefs. Vic Reeves joins them, unfunnily. Nick Hodgson is still banging on about stansted Airport.

**9.30pm** The most remarkable thing about Kanye West is that he really is as good as he thinks he is. His three-song set has everything the rest of the night has lacked: wit, drama, flamboyance, an orchestra, a harp (a harp!), and a parade of bikini-clad women spray-painted gold. If you had to explain to somebody why pop music is worth getting implausibly excited about, despite ample James Blunt-shaped evidence to the contrary, then just sit them down and watch this.

**9.32pm** Best British Female. Natasha Bedingfield? Charlotte Church? Scraping the barrel a bit here, aren't we? KT Tunstall wins. Hmm, I think I'm beginning to fancy her. I'm sure she'll be thrilled to hear that.

**9.40pm** God, Jack Johnson is dull isn't he? He's like a busker who won a competition.

**9.43pm** It's distinguished Pet Shop Boy Neil Tennant in a dinner jacket. Maybe Madonna personally requested the most English Englishman available to present her with Best International Female? Having given Guy Ritchie the most cursory of pecks, she delivers a bizarre speech about how much she loves Merrie Olde England and David Bowie and Elvis Costello and Graham Greene and Elgar and Noel Coward and Dick Van Dyke in Mary Poppins and fish and chips and Oyster cards and the staff down the old Dog & Duck, Gawd bless 'em.

**9.51pm** Chris Evans introduces Paris Hilton thus: 'You've heard of the X-factor. This next woman has the Y-factor.' Surely he means the why-the-fuck factor. Green Day win Best International Album. There is something beautiful about Paris Hilton shouting the words 'American idiot'.

**9.55pm** Oh yes. Gorillaz' performance consists of giant animated figures, a string section, Bootie Brown from the Pharcyde and a vast choir of breakdancing children. Damon Albarn: he's our Kanye West.

**10.01pm** Is there a more underwhelming phrase than Mastercard British Album Of The Year? Possibly only the SmithKline Beecham British Album Of The Year. The winners are Coldplay. Chris Martin tells us to lay off James Blunt. 'Be proud of him, he's British.' Well, so's Nick Griffin. Do we have to be proud of him too? Then he says we won't see them for 'a long time'. Maybe they're going to join James Blunt wielding lethal lengths of bamboo in the jungles of South America.

**10.30pm** I bet the Brits organisers wish they'd given the Lifetime Achievement award to someone else now. Paul Weller's turned into the mod Norman Tebbit. It's sad that someone who documented British life with such fire and wit has now transformed into the kind of sociopathic Little Englander you can imagine petitioning to remove travellers from nearby wasteground. Is this what the future holds for Arctic Monkeys or the Streets? A lifetime of pissing and moaning and dour insularity? He's an inspiration in a negative way at least – don't grow up to be like him, kids. (And, yes, having pissed and moaned for the last three hours, I'm aware of the irony.)

# ON SMOKING BEING BANNED

## David Hockney

I can tell you don't seem to get it. I don't think the MPs know what they are actually doing. I do not have a high opinion of them. The case against the medical evidence about smoking is this. They have their statistics. I have read them. I have read what they shout on the uglified cigarette packets, but I will make this observation.

In the Labour party – let's get a lot more human in our observations – the 80-year-old Mr Benn is a happy pipe smoker. Mr Robin Cook took up 'healthy' fell walking, it killed him; same with Mr Smith. Tony Banks, another non-smoking vegetarian health fiend, falls over with a stroke at the age of 61.

What does one deduce from this? That fate plays a part in life, that mysterious forces are at work, it is not all 'material'. The medical statistician cannot grasp this, but almost everyone else does. This is why people will always ignore the prude and prig.

Gordon Brown is a prig P.R.I.G., a dreary atheistic Calvinistic prig, who I'm sure will never be elected in England. He goes along with a 'health lobby' whose view of life itself I detest. I have utter contempt for it. I don't mind prigs but when they want to take my little corner as well, I have a right to argue against their dreary view of life contaminating mine.

I am spending time in provincial England. There is an anger here that the press don't seem to know about. This utterly over the top legislation is spreading a dreadful intolerance.

You ask me: 'What didn't we report?' You didn't report that you could smoke in hospitals and prisons but not pubs. It's barmy and just where bossiness leads. I repeat you should be ashamed of yourselves for what you are supporting. There are plenty of no-smoking places, leave things to their natural path.

It's not just your job to give us an opinion but actually to report on things. You missed the ridiculous side of this. Wake up.

# THE CENTRE-LEFT NEEDS TO BE MORE HONEST ABOUT WEALTH

## Martin Kettle

I was due to have lunch with Tessa Jowell on Thursday, and in an Italian restaurant too (her choice, my treat). Still it was no surprise when her office rang that morning to say she was cancelling. It was too good to last – a date that had been long in the diary morphing into an exclusive one-on-one with the politician at the heart of the day's biggest story. But, to be honest, it was also a bit of a relief. It would not have been one of those easy gossip-filled political lunches. Sometimes you just have to be brutal over the bresaola.

Here's what I would have had to say to Jowell (assuming she had asked). I'd have said that ignorance of the law is no defence. And though the ministerial code of ethics is a code not a law, the same principle is heavily written into it. The code is clearly expressed. It says ministers are 'expected to behave according to the the highest standards of constitutional and personal conduct'. They are 'personally responsible' for conducting themselves according to the code. They must ensure that 'no conflict arises or appears to arise' between their public duties and their private interests. They (and their spouses, since the code covers immediate family too) should 'avoid accepting any gift' that might or 'might reasonably appear to' compromise them. And the code concludes: 'Ultimately it is the responsibility of ministers individually to order their own private lives in such a way as to avoid criticism.'

Those words seem pretty clear to me. And so does the spirit behind them. In some ways the code goes further than the law. Not only is ignorance no defence, but it is also a minister's responsibility to ensure that he or she is code-compliant. The onus, in other words, is on ministers. Their responsibility explicitly extends to the financial and other interests of their spouses too. On that basis I think Jowell's failure

154

to report that in 2000 her husband, David Mills, had received a £350,000 gift was a breach of the code, albeit inadvertent. Indeed Jowell more or less admitted that point in the statement that she put out on Thursday, around the time when the two of us might otherwise have been enjoying a nice glass of prosecco.

Some reports this week said that the cabinet secretary, Sir Gus O'Donnell, cleared Jowell. But he didn't. At no point in his letter to Theresa May did he say that Jowell did not breach the code. He said that Jowell stated that she did not breach it, and that Tony Blair agreed – which is a significantly different thing. O'Donnell pointedly added that it is ministers' responsibility to disclose their own and their partners' interests. But it is not his role to police the code – or to make rulings about compliance – but to gather facts. The verdict, he said, must rest with the prime minister.

It was Blair who cleared Jowell this week, not O'Donnell. In his Thursday statement, he said: 'I accept Tessa's assurance. In these circumstances, she is not in breach of her obligations under the ministerial code.' In the end, these are political decisions. You and I (and Gus O'Donnell) may conclude that Jowell failed to observe the code as she should have done. But a prime minister is judge and jury in the case. Blair made the decision he did because he judged that the damage involved in retaining Jowell was less than the damage involved in losing her. She is, if you want to see it this way, the beneficiary of Blair's own current weakness.

It does not necessarily follow that Blair was wrong to do this. Jowell is considered a good minister and a popular one. She is also, to an extent, the victim of a sometimes hypocritical puritanism from people who have more in common with her than they care to admit: people who themselves own more than one property, who remortgage their homes to pay for their outgoings or to get a better repayment rate, and who themselves employ accountants and investment advisers to ensure that their tax liabilities are minimised. If Jowell lives some parts of her life in a moral maze, then she is not the only one.

I am more interested in a larger issue, which is whether left and liberal politics in this country can learn to be more honest, more modern and more consistent about the balance between individual and collective wealth in the kind of society we are all likely to live in for the foreseeable future. The elephant in the room in the Jowell affair is not really Silvio Berlusconi. It is the fact that a Labour minister is married to someone who moves with assurance, and makes a very large amount of money, in a world that is alien (though not necessarily unacceptable) to most Labour voters.

With his network of directorships, off-shore investments, tax avoidance schemes and hedge funds, Mills (and thus Jowell) appear to many to inhabit a world in which it can sometimes seem that taxes are for the little people, greed is good, and there are no proper limits to how much an individual can earn or possess. Many in the Labour party take the traditional roundhead view of such cavaliers, expressing outrage that any Labour person should have anything to do with them. For them, Jowell is literally sleeping with the enemy.

This is, though, a world to which very many people aspire in some way, including Labour voters. Was Adam Smith not right, after all, when he said that 'every man, so long as he does not violate the laws of justice, is left perfectly free to pursue his own interests in his own way'? With the exception of Gordon Brown, who at least tries, few modern post-socialist politicians know how to discuss the relationship between morality and economics. Jowell's case shows how important it is to supply the compass that she lacked.

# A BIAS AGAINST BABIES

## Madeleine Bunting

Pregnancy has become the occasion not for congratulations, but for anxious questions about childcare, leave and work. Watch how the announcement of a pregnancy among women is followed within minutes by the 'What are you going to do?' question. We've replaced the age-old anxiety around life-threatening childbirth with a new – and sometimes it appears just as vast – cargo of anxiety around who is going to care.

This anxiety is the backdrop to the 90,000 baby gap – the number of additional babies that women would like to have had – identified by a recent Institute of Public Policy Research report on how the birth rate is falling below replenishment levels. A bias against having babies has permeated our culture. This phenomenon needs a new word – anti-natalism – and it is this that prompts a good part of that pregnancy trepidation. The only consolation to my mind is the spectacular everyday acts of rebellion by which thousands of babies still manage to get born in this country.

The anti-natalist bias is implicit in many of the influences that shape our sense of self and purpose, our identity, our aspirations and our understanding of success and the good life. That bias is evident in our consumer culture and our work culture. The problem about motherhood (and, to a lesser extent, fatherhood) is that it comes at the cost of failure – or at least compromise – as consumer or worker, or both.

Hence you are a good mother in direct proportion to how useless a consumer you are. You can always tell the mum in the office because she's wearing last season's coat. The increasing impatience of consumer cycles means that anyone who is not devoting inordinate amounts of their weekend to shopping and browsing magazines is just not cutting it.

Not cutting it – that's pretty much the gist at work too. The entire debate on women's work is about mothers failing in the labour market: they don't earn much, they're in dead-end jobs, they don't make it to the top, they take the easy option and duck responsibility, they're less productive than men. This was the refrain of the Women and Work Commission last week. It reminded me of a summit on women's productivity at No 11 just over a year ago. Women had to get into better jobs and work harder, a selection of highly productive women and Gordon Brown declared. You could hear the lashing of whips from these well-meaning slave drivers.

The whole debate about women's place in work is lopsided. They are not failures but astonishing successes. What gets missed out of the equation is that mothers' productivity is staggeringly high: the Office for National Statistics did a valuation of women's homemaking and care, and came up with a figure of £929bn, or 104% of GDP. Combine that with the value of women's paid work, and they are easily outperforming the shockingly low productivity of men.

The point is that parenthood is against the grain of all the aspirations of our culture. Go back to the pregnancy anxiety around care. That anxiety is provoked by more than just the logistics of childcare availability, despite what the nursery campaigners argue. It's there because pregnancy sabotages three characteristics highly valued by our culture.

First, independence: pregnancy heralds at least one relationship of dependence, and there is often greater dependence on partners, mothers and, eventually, childminders and the like. But you've spent much of the previous 10 years attempting to eradicate any hint of dependence, either of your own or of others on you. Secondly, pregnancy is about a long-term commitment, and having avoided all such (including probably to your partner), you are, at the very least, uneasy about it. Finally, the big bump in your stomach spells out one thing for sure – a huge constraint on many choices, and choice has been integral to your sense of a life worth living.

In other words, the self we are encouraged to develop through much of our education system and early adulthood is of no use whatsoever to a new parent. What use is that sassy, independent, self-assertive, knowing-what-you-want-and-how-to-get-it type when you fast forward five years to the emotional labour of helping a child develop self-confidence? Once there's a baby in the cot, you need steadiness, loyalty, endurance, patience, sensitivity and even self-denial – all the characteristics that you've spent the previous decade trashing as dull or, even worse, for losers. Forget trying to work out your own feelings – you'll be too busy trying to work out those of your children. Ditto self-confidence and self-expression.

Motherhood hits most women like a car crash: they have absolutely no idea of what is coming. Nothing in our culture recognises, let alone encourages, the characteristics you will need once a bawling infant has been tenderly placed in your arms. So the debate about the baby gap is about far more than tweaking parental leave. It's about what a culture values and promotes. And it matters not just because of that falling birthrate, but because of how women stumble towards their own private insights into the importance of mothering – to which they cling in the face of not just zero endorsement from wider society but active contempt.

The painful paradox is that while women have liberated themselves from being defined by their biology – the fate of the girl in many African and Asian societies who is not truly a woman until she has given birth – mothers have ended up relegated to the status of constant abject failure in a culture driven by consumerism and workaholism. There is no kudos in being a mum, only in being other things – such as thin, or the boss – despite being a mum. Motherhood is a form of handicap.

The fact that we still have as many births in the UK as we do is extraordinary. Some cynics would say it's the triumph of biology over culture – we are programmed to reproduce regardless. I prefer a more romantic notion: that it's a form of popular rebellion by which the prevailing anti-natalist mores of a manipulative consumer capitalism are trumped by the innate understanding of millions of women (and men) of what really constitutes love and fulfilment – dependence, commitment, the pleasure of guiding enthusiasm and, above all, the privilege of nurturing innocence.

March 14 2006

# THE SCRAMBLE FOR SCHOOLS

## Matt Seaton

She sounded completely beside herself. She was calling me because her child had not been offered a place at secondary school next September. Not one of her five choices had come up. Not her first, her second, her third, fourth or fifth. She had got my phone number because my daughter is in the same Year-6 class as her child, so she wanted to know what our situation was. I confessed that our daughter had, in fact, got her first choice. As soon as this mother heard that, the conversation was over, and she was on to the next call. I couldn't work out whether she was conducting some kind of poll, or simply looking for another embittered, desperate person to commiserate with. But I recognised the state of hysteria she had been driven to.

Because, for the past six months, so many of us have been there. If you are a parent with a child around the age of 10, especially if you live in a city, then there is probably one subject that has occupied your waking hours, and a good many of what ought to have been your sleeping ones: secondary school transfer. With your child now nearing the end of primary school, this is the crunch year for deciding which secondary school your child should go to next autumn.

The whole process starts the previous September with a seemingly endless round of open days, where hundreds of parents at a time are herded around to inspect the art school, the gym and the library. Encounters with headteachers vary from slick PowerPoint presentations to informal meet-and-greets. You get tea and biscuits if you're lucky.

After a while, one IT room looks much like another. It is a deeply bewildering, anxiety-provoking experience. In practice, there is not a great deal you can learn from traipsing up and down the corridors, or from listening to the head's marketing patter. Instead, you try to pick up a school's 'atmosphere' osmotically and bludgeon the hapless kid assigned as your tour guide with questions. But mostly you listen to the grapevine: hungry for any clues about which school will be right for their child, Year-6 parents spend the entire autumn term forming neurotic information-sharing huddles.

Never mind the compendious guide to secondary schools you've been poring over every night, trying to divine something meaningful from its bland digest of Ofsted reports: it is here that you learn which schools are 'in' and which are 'out'. Here, too, if you have the money, you can get the phone number of a private tutor who will coach your child in the art of passing verbal and non-verbal reasoning tests. And it is here that you discover the occult art of giving your child a shot at one of the 'good' schools' selective places – how to wangle a place on their special music, languages or drama programme.

The easiest way to wangle a place at a 'good' school is to get God. For every atheist parent fulminating against the injustice of public money funding faith schools, there must be a dozen un-lapsed Christians and former agnostics finding fresh religious conviction if it will get a priest's signature on their church school admission form. Others of us, willing to sacrifice long-held principles, remortgage the house so that we can apply to private schools as an insurance policy. A few will muster whatever financial clout they can in a different way: moving house – or renting one – to ensure an address within the secure catchment area of the school *de choix*. Others have their eyes on an academically selective grammar school in a distant borough, and resign themselves to the fact that their child will spend three hours a day commuting for the next seven years.

But somehow, by the end of October, you have to have figured out which schools to apply for and what order to rank them in. There is a blizzard of forms to be filled in, then an endless succession of exams and auditions to put your child through. By the end of November, entire families are at risk of nervous breakdown. And then there's the agonising wait until early March, when all your choices are, by some unimaginable computerised alchemy, matched with the schools' offers.

Although the broad outline of this temporary insanity may be familiar wherever you live, this phenomenon reaches a particular pitch of mania in the capital. In London, the chasm between the successful schools and the failing ones yawns more broadly than in most cities. Thus the premium on obtaining your first or second choice is higher. The difficulties of inner-city schools are all too apparent when you learn that London parents buy secondary school education at nearly double the national rate of 7%. And those who can't pay vote with their feet: some deprived inner boroughs, such as Southwark and Lambeth, inadvertently export vast numbers of students because their undernourished secondary schools have such poor results and reputations.

The clearing system run by the Pan London Admissions Board is only in its second year, and claims success in reducing the number of students not allocated places: from over 8,000 in 2004 to about 3,000 this year. Nearly 93% (of approximately 77,000) have been offered a place at a school of their choice, and almost all of the remainder will, it claims, be offered places within weeks (as some parents move away or reject a state school offer in favour of a private school).

The word 'choice' here is misleading. After last year, when some parents thought they could railroad the system by nominating only one preference (only to be allocated a place at their nearest failing school instead), people were warned to list realistic choices as well as aspirational ones. My son got his third choice at a Westminster comprehensive, and we feel fortunate with that. Many others will get their fourth, fifth or sixth choices. No figures are available on what percentage of parents got which choice. Nor, for some time, will we know how many will be appealing against their school offer. The stakes are so high that 'appeals consultants' have built up a tidy little business advising parents on how to present their child's case.

What is to be done? Under the banner of a 'choice' that is largely illusory, parents and children are well and truly put through the wringer. The simple answer is that people would be much happier with a better local school and less 'choice'. Yet the government's education bill – at least until it ran into trouble – seemed designed to promote successful schools' freedom to cherry-pick the best students, boosting the already substantial degree of under-the-counter selection that goes on in the comprehensive sector. If there is a system that can be played, middle-class parents will always play it – and usually win. But to coerce everyone into a game where many are virtually preordained to come out losers … that's just cruel.

March 14 2006

# NEW MARMITE: A WARNING

## Laura Barton

There are only certain things that should come in squeezy tubes, and broadly speaking we can refer to these as toothpaste and antiseptic cream. Where foodstuffs are concerned I pretty much draw the line at tomato ketchup, and that vivid yellow American mustard. It should not include cheese spread, and absolutely on no occasion should it ever mean Marmite.

But the powers that be have announced that, as of this week, Marmite will indeed be available in squeezy bottles. 'It's all about versatility and the end of crumbs in the jar,' says a spokesperson. 'And the beauty of it is, it can be stored either way up. It's perfect.'

Would you landscape the Hanging Gardens of Babylon? Inject collagen into Mona Lisa's smile? How, in other words, can you improve upon perfection? For generations, the Marmite jar and its delectable contents have together represented the pinnacle of human achievement, the weighty glass of the jar mirroring the gleaming viscosity of its contents.

And now they give us squeezy plastic. The new Marmite bottle has been five years in development, apparently at the behest of Marmite lovers who wrote to specifically request the invention. Who are these 'Marmite lovers'? Curiously, every Marmite lover I spoke to yesterday found the notion of a squeezy bottle utterly detestable. Can we be certain that these letter-writing 'lovers' aren't actually from the Peanut Butter Liberation Front, hellbent on promoting the cause of their favourite spread? I demand an investigation.

Anyway, the main concerns are of course whether the new squeezy container will affect the actual Marmite we know and love. 'It tastes exactly the same,' the spokesperson says, before adding worryingly: 'It is slightly thinner than the Marmite you get in a jar. Naturally yeast extract can be made in different textures, and this is brewed to a medium rather than the thicker scale.' Already the alarm bells are ringing. I saw what happened to Hellmann's mayonnaise when they put it in a squeezy bottle: a poor watery glug of an excuse for a mayonnaise.

And with Marmite the consistency is arguably even more vital. You can't have it squelching all over the place in a great splurge of yeast as you spread it finely across your toast, it should display the same dark stickiness as walking on hot tarmac. How can I be certain the new bottle won't squelch Marmite left right and centre? 'It's got a really controlled nozzle, you get a tiny line when you drizzle it,' says the spokesperson jovially. Drizzle? 'Yes! You can even draw with it on your toast. It's really funny.'

Oh really. That's the kind of gag you would expect to be pulled by Vegemite. Maybe even Bovril. But Marmite? People, I'm not laughing.

# BAD SCIENCE: BRAIN GYM

## Ben Goldacre

While all the proper grown-up public intellectuals such as Rod Liddle are getting a bee in their bonnet about creationism being taught in a handful of British schools, I've accidentally stumbled upon a vast empire of pseudoscience being peddled in hundreds of state schools up and down the country.

I'll lower you in gently. It's called Brain Gym, and it's a string of very complicated exercises for kids to do which 'enhance the experience of whole brain learning'. Firstly, they're very keen on water. 'Drink a glass of water before Brain Gym activities. As it is a major component of blood, water is vital for transporting oxygen to the brain.' Heaven forbid that your blood should dry out.

Is there anything else I can do to make blood and oxygen get to my brain better? Yes, an exercise called 'Brain Buttons': 'Make a "C" shape with your thumb and forefinger and place on either side of the breast bone just below the collar bone. Gently rub for 20 or 30 seconds whilst placing your other hand over your navel. Change hands and repeat. This exercise stimulates the flow of oxygen-carrying blood through the carotid arteries to the brain to awaken it and increase concentration and relaxation.' Why? 'Brain buttons lie directly over and stimulate the carotid arteries.'

Now, I'm waiting to be very impressed by any kid who can stimulate his carotid arteries inside his ribcage, but it's going to involve dissection with the sharp scissors that only mummy can use.

Someone mischievous and anonymous has kindly sent in the *Teacher's Notes* on Brain Gym to keep me entertained. This seems to be the master document behind the operation.

'Processed foods do not contain water,' they announce, in what has to be the most readily falsifiable statement I've seen all week. How about soup? 'All other liquids are processed in the body as food, and do not serve the body's water needs.' It goes on. 'Water is best absorbed by the body, when provided in frequent small amounts.' And if I drink too much in one go, will it leak out of my anus instead?

But this nonsense must all be some teeny, peripheral act of madness by a few schools, surely? No. Many hundreds of UK state schools, at least. So many I couldn't name them all in a month of columns. So many, I've posted a list on www.badscience.net, so you can check your child is safe.

Because telling stories about fairies and monsters is fine, but lying to children about science is wrong. Children are predisposed to learn about the world from adults, and especially from teachers. Children listen to what you tell them: that's the point of being a child, that's the reason why you don't come out fully-formed, speaking English, with a favourite album.

With Brain Gym, the same teacher who tells children that blood is pumped around the lungs and then the body by the heart, is also telling them that when they do 'The Energizer' exercise (far too complicated to describe) then 'this back and forward movement of the head increases the circulation to the frontal lobe for greater comprehension and rational thinking.'

I've just kicked the Brain Gym *Teacher's Edition* around the room for two minutes and I'm feeling minty fresh. Taking a break and doing some exercise is obviously great for improving performance. Is that all you get with Brain Gym in schools, or does it really come parcelled up with the nonsense?

# TONY BLAIR: NINE YEARS IS LONG ENOUGH

## Leading article

To Tony Blair's immense credit he can still control the circumstances of his departure from office. By fighting for a third term but not a fourth and by accepting the consensus that Gordon Brown must be his successor, the prime minister has prepared the way for what should be an elegant passing of the baton, testimony to his character and political command. But this orderly transition places a responsibility on Mr Blair. The departure must be timely. There is no excuse for foot-dragging, no excuse for trading on the patience of his party, the country or his successor. Carrying on simply because he can will begin to look self-indulgent. Better reasons are needed if the transition is to be postponed.

It is increasingly hard to think what these might be. Adrift in Iraq, opposed by much of his own party on education reform at home, caught in a net of soft loans that looks worse by the hour (and yesterday led even John Prescott to admit he was unhappy), Mr Blair risks becoming a leader without purpose beyond power: accident-prone and asking for trouble. The longer he waits, the greater his troubles will be and the greater the damage to his party, the country and his reputation. The fact is clear: Mr Brown (barring the unexpected) will replace Mr Blair as prime minister and Labour leader either this year or next, or the one after, though there must be a contest.

Having created the expectation, the onus is on Mr Blair to explain his strategy and his plan. His successor is ready for office and will come to it with much to do. Mr Blair made the case for re-election last year jointly with the man who should take over from him – and who will not only continue much of what he has already started, but who shared in its creation. But if the promise is continuity as well as renewal, where is the case for delay? What is it that Mr Blair thinks would be lost under

Mr Brown? If he has doubts, he has (mostly) hidden them. If he has wands left to wave, he should know that his friends are less sure.

This is a truth about political magic. It fades. In most spheres where Mr Blair might claim he needs to finish the job, the job is either done, or beyond his capacity to complete. Abroad, Britain's EU and G8 presidencies are over and the 2012 Olympics has been won for London. Peace between Israel and Palestine is far enough off to be a task for his successor, as is African renewal, EU reform and the accession of Turkey. Iraq's elections are over and yet the situation in the country gets more ghastly by the day. At home, education reform has reached a point where Mr Blair's involvement has become a hindrance not an advantage. The NHS is struggling to keep pace with the scale of what has been done to it, and regressing in parts, while new political challenges – on climate change, the replacement of Trident, energy supplies, terror and the constitution, as well as confronting a newly vigorous Conservative party – will outlast the handover whenever it comes. Mr Blair needs to ask himself: why drag things on for another 12 or 24 awkward and empty months just because he can?

That he can, if he wants, should not be in doubt. For now, the timing of the transfer is still of his own choosing. He is ahead in the polls (further ahead than Mr Brown might be, according to this month's *Guardian*/ICM study), he faces no immediate call to quit from most Labour MPs and his successor is apparently content to wait. The jeers of a rancorous minority on the Labour left hold no fears for him. But though the foundations remain in place, the facade is taking many hits. The fact that he can survive as prime minister does not mean it is in his interests to cling on until he cannot remain. Choosing is a bolder thing when there is still a choice.

At heart, the question is how much longer Mr Blair can convince the nation, his party or himself that Britain would be better governed – or he more kindly remembered – if he stayed in office than if he left it. Even his friends have reason to raise that question after the struggle to secure the education bill, and there is a sense that a prime minister who promised in 1998 to be purer than pure can no longer claim to be so. That may be unavoidable: office degrades all its holders. But from now on the calls for renewal will only grow stronger. There is no better time ahead. He has already decided to leave. In the end it comes down to announcing he will stand down this summer, or next year, or forcing himself on his party until 2008 or 2009. He should go this year. Mr Brown's last budget speech as chancellor this week should be followed this autumn by his first conference speech as prime minister.

# HERCEPTIN: THE SELLING
# OF A WONDER DRUG

## Sarah Boseley

Lisa Jardine was at home recovering from chemotherapy one evening last May when the phone rang. She was not feeling all that well, and the conversation that followed made her feel worse. Then, as now, there was only one breast cancer story around: Herceptin. It was a wonder drug – it halved some women's chances of having a recurrence of their cancer. But women who would die without it were being denied access, apparently for financial reasons – or so the story went. Women with aggressive, early-stage breast cancers had taken to the streets and the courts for their right to get it. So when – a week before the phone call – Jardine, who had had breast cancer, was asked in a newspaper interview what she thought about Herceptin, she responded that although she was confident she was receiving the best of care, 'if Herceptin really is as effective as we are being told, I do feel I ought to be given the choice.'

Then came the phone call. 'Halfway through the following week, the phone goes at home,' says Jardine, professor of Renaissance studies at Queen Mary, University of London, writer and well-known television presenter. 'It's a really nice woman. She says to me, "I read about you in the paper and I gather you'd like access to Herceptin and you can't get it."' But Jardine had decided that she did not want the drug.

'I said, "No – that's not the case with me. I have decided not to have Herceptin."

'She said, "Even if you don't want it yourself, would you come and talk to some of our seminars because we're running a big promotion campaign? Either we could find funding for Herceptin or, if you really don't want it or decide against it, there would be fees for appearances."

'I said, "Could you tell me where you are from?" She said, "We work for Roche."

'I wasn't feeling well. I said, "Would you please get off the phone?" Then I hung up.

'There was no mistaking the directness of the approach – she said she would make it worth my while.'

Jardine was shocked, but the fact is that this sort of approach is exactly what pharmaceutical marketing is all about in an era when the stakes for drug companies seeking to make profits are climbing steadily higher. Jardine's experience only highlights the increasingly sophisticated way in which new drugs are sold to us, generally without us realising that a marketing operation is even under way. It helps to explain how a drug such as Herceptin, despite being as yet unlicensed for use on women with early-stage cancer, and despite there being only a few years of test data from its manufacturers, Roche, to support claims being made by some for the benefits for this group of women, came to be a household name and a *cause célèbre*. At the time that Jardine received the phone call from Roche, the health secretary, Patricia Hewitt, had already appeared to cave in to demands and publicly declared that cost alone should not prevent women from being given it. It was a green light to doctors to prescribe and to primary care trusts to pay up, even though the National Institute for Clinical Excellence (Nice) had not yet approved the drug for use on women with early-stage cancer.

Herceptin is a new type of drug, suitable only for 20% of breast cancer patients. Roche, naturally, having spent many millions of pounds on developing the drug, badly wants as big a slice of this restricted market as it can get. It cannot buy television advertising, as drug companies, unlike any other industry, are forbidden to promote their goods directly to us. So instead, Roche has found itself some powerful allies. It cannot sing the praises of its latest drug from the rooftops and demand that doctors hand it out – but patients can, and will, too, if they become convinced that this is the pill they need.

Just a few years ago, nobody had heard of Herceptin, although stories about a new generation of 'targeted drugs' had begun to circulate, raising hopes of medicines with better cancer-killing powers. In 2002, Nice licensed Herceptin for use on women with advanced breast cancer. It undoubtedly saved lives. But then Roche did trials on women who had just finished chemotherapy for early-stage cancer. The company had not yet applied for a licence for this change of use in this country, but it decided to announce interim results showing that the drug halved the risk of the cancer recurring. The clamour for Herceptin began, and amid all the noise, any chance of a reasoned debate about the drug was lost.

Unlike many in the UK, Jardine knew that the drug was not problem-free. Some women in the US had suffered from heart problems after taking it. That was why Jardine and her consultant had decided the drug was not for her.

Roche argues that the cardiotoxicity – which led to 18.6% of the women in one US trial stopping the drug within a year – was down to the other chemotherapy drugs not used here that are taken routinely by women in the US. It says the damage is reversible and that doctors will monitor patients closely for it. Only 0.5% in British trials had heart problems on the drug, they say. That translates as nine patients developing severe congestive heart failure out of a group of 1,694 women who had been carefully scrutinised and monitored for potential heart problems before they were enrolled on to the trial. A larger 1.7% developed warning symptoms of heart failure during the trial, and a total of 8.5% stopped taking the drug before the year was up either because of side effects or other reasons.

Critics also argue that, due to Roche's Herceptin trials ending early – on the grounds that results were so good that it had become unethical not to give the drug to women on the trial receiving a placebo – and with only a year of data in existence for Herceptin used alone (although one of the trials is following up patients to two years), the best that can yet be said is that the drug lengthens the interval before cancer recurs.

The statistic that keeps being repeated is that Herceptin halves a woman's chances of getting a cancer again. But the bottom line is that 9.4% of the women in the British trial on Herceptin found their cancer returned, compared to 17.2% among those who did not have the drug. It is a good result, but it does not have quite the simplistic punch of 'halving the rate of recurrence'. And we do not know if the benefit lasts. We cannot possibly know yet, from the data available, whether the drug stops people dying, so why are women talking of selling their homes for a 'life-saving drug' and going to court for a 'lifeline'? Dot Griffiths has some of the answers. This is the formidable woman behind the successful struggle in Staffordshire to get Herceptin funded on the NHS for eight women with early breast cancer that turned into a nationwide campaign for 'all women who need it'. But Griffiths has advanced breast cancer – not early breast cancer. More than four years ago, Herceptin was only available privately even for advanced cancers, and she successfully fought her own campaign to get it. Her clinicians thought she would be dead by now, she says.

'I have always believed in fair play and justice. I was a magistrate for 16 years – I hate injustice of any kind,' she says. 'All that I say to everyone is that I'm living proof that it is as good as I think it is. I'm still here four and a half to five years after having it, with a very good quality of life.'

When, in March 2002, Nice approved Herceptin for general NHS use for advanced breast cancer like Griffiths', that meant all primary care trusts should pay the £30,000-a-year cost if a doctor wanted to give it to his or her patient. Roche hoped that there would be a big take-up. The following year, the drug company carried out a survey to see how many of the women who were suitable were being given Herceptin. Its figures suggested only a third. Roche gave the survey to the patient group CancerBacup, which publicised the results widely. Its chief executive, Joanne Rule, went on the BBC's *Breakfast Time* programme. Naturally, the show wanted a patient, too. Roche's PR company contacted Griffiths.

'There was a PR agency called Ketchum that worked for Roche,' she says. 'They put me in touch with CancerBacup. I'm very grateful to Roche, but I wasn't campaigning for Roche. I was campaigning for women like myself who need the drug.'

Griffiths' campaign moved on from the women with advanced breast cancer like herself, to the women with early breast cancer who might equally benefit from Herceptin. She is insistent that the drug company did not support her in all this. 'They didn't help me at all. I have had contact with Roche, naturally, because I wanted facts and figures, and I have done a presentation for breast cancer awareness month at Roche, but [I didn't] mention the campaign at all, because they want to keep well away from [it].'

But the PR agencies that bid for lucrative contracts from the drug companies did. Rebecca Hunt, formerly a Roche employee but now with the agency Porter Novelli, offered the services of her team for free. Griffiths was working so hard that she had put herself in hospital for several weeks. She gladly accepted Hunt's offer. 'We gave our time for free,' says Hunt. 'It was pro bono. It was really inspiring to the team here to get involved in something that makes so much difference to people.'

Griffiths' campaign is a one-off. Pharmaceuticals do not usually get that lucky. It is far more normal for the companies to offer support to large, established patient support groups.

It is not just the patient groups that drug companies hope to get support from. They also want 'opinion leaders' – people with credibility who can be quoted in the papers and on TV – people such as Jardine. And they want journalists. A fortnight ago, Roche held a thinktank for journalists from national newspapers, magazines and television. The journalists were asked for their opinions on how best the company could get stories into the media about its drug for breast cancers that have spread into the bones. They were promised £200 each for their time and given dinner at an expensive restaurant.

But patient groups are the most rewarding target, and there is an obvious risk that they could be influenced by companies with turnovers as large as the GDP of small nations. The industry journal *Pharmaceutical Marketing* ran a recent piece describing how 'motivated patients can move mountains and boost your drug's fortunes'. The Labour MP Paul Flynn has done a survey to find out which patient groups accept drug-company money. Out of 24 major organisations, only five did not. They were Alcohol Concern, Action for ME, Young Minds, Mind and the National Autistic Society.

From April, under new industry rules, the drug companies will have to declare on their websites what money they give to patient groups. It should make interesting reading.

# SPRING

April 11 2006

# THE RETURN OF SNOBBERY

## John Harris

The headline inside was 'Future Bling of England', the strapline screamed, 'Wills Wears Chav Gear in Army Snap'. Over two pages built around a snap of 30 trainee officers at Sandhurst, yesterday's *Sun* gleefully recounted how the heir to the throne 'joined in the fun as his platoon donned chav-themed fancy dress to mark the completion of their first term'. Wills, we were told, 'went to a lot of trouble thinking up what to wear' (white baseball cap, sweatshirt, two gold chains), and was challenged to 'put on a chavvy accent and stop speaking like a royal'. Apparently, he struggled to sound quite as proletarian as required, though he was said to be 'making hand gestures and swaggering from side to side as he walked across the parade square'.

If the *Sun*'s coverage of the wheeze suggested nothing more worrying than innocuous high jinks, one might wonder how a fair share of their readership responded not only to the news, but the way it was delivered. Within four paragraphs, Wills's 'working-class accent' had mutated into a 'silly accent' by way of hammering home the Sandhurst chaps' close resemblance to what the *Sun* called 'any bunch of lads from your neighbourhood street corner'. They printed a shot of Michael Carroll, a man from Norfolk who won the lottery but is now serving nine months for affray. The snobby tone of the coverage, in fact, was much like the underlying spirit of the episode itself. Simply put, the Eton-educated heir to the throne – along with some aristocratic mates – has a right old laugh dressing up as a member of the white working class, and thereby providing conclusive proof of the blatant, shameless return of snobbery.

There is a lot of this kind of stuff about, as proved by a conversation with Matthew Holehouse, an 18-year-old A-level student from Harrogate and occasional *Times Education Supplement* columnist. Last year, he found himself dispatched by his state school to a debating seminar organised by the English Speaking Union. It was staged at Oakham, a private school in Rutland, whose website lays claim to 'forward-looking educational thinking'. The fact that he was from a comprehensive put him in a noticeable minority, he tells me, a sense of disorientation compounded by a set of pictures he found hanging on one of the school's walls.

'There were various things on display,' he says. 'Pictures of rugby teams, of parties and discos. But the one that really jumped out was of a chav-themed school disco: all these rosy-cheeked, foppish-looking public schoolkids dressed in baseball caps and Adidas tracksuits. It looked a bit pathetic. At first I suppose I felt slight pity for them. But then I thought about it another way: here were the most privileged kids in Britain pretending to be poor people.'

Holehouse is preparing to take up a place at Oxford University, where he will study history. His perusal of the entertainment currently offered to undergraduates has only confirmed that the so-called 'chav bop' is an immovable fixture not only at public schools, but also throughout Oxford's colleges. Google the phrase and you receive instant pictorial proof that such events have taken place at Lady Margaret Hall, Trinity and St Peter's.

The chav phenomenon – the mass mockery of a certain kind of young, Burberry-check wearing, borderline criminal, proletarian youth – has been with us for more than three years. Its collision with public schools, military academies and high-end universities, however, surely serves to confirm what some people suspected all along: that the C-word actually denotes the mind-boggling revival of privileged people revelling in looking down their noses at the white working class, that social entity whose mere mention in certain company can cause either a palpable frisson of unease or loud ridicule.

In retrospect, the germ of the idea was evident in the mid-1990s, in the press's gleeful response to Wayne and Waynetta Slob, the degenerate, perma-smoking welfare claimants who became a fixture of Harry Enfield's BBC1 show. You could also detect its beginnings in some of the supposed social comment associated with Britpop – not least the snide songs about forlorn proletarian lives that were briefly the calling card of Blur's Damon Albarn, who affected a mewling 'Essex' accent, but was in fact raised in one of that county's more upscale corners. 'The strange thing about Damon's songs,' said the critic Jim Shelley, 'is that, unlike a writer such as Morrissey or Ian Dury, he has no sympathy for his characters … Albarn's attitude is totally uncharitable, a kind of snide contempt.'

From there, it was a short hop to the repopularisation of the kind of archetypes that, in the 80s, were the preserve of boneheaded Tory MPs – not least that of the 'Pram Face', defined on the website Urban Dictionary as 'a girl who is a little rough round the edges and wouldn't look at all out of place at 14 years of age pushing a newborn through a council estate'. In turn, the duty to combine haughtiness with supposed humour duly fell away, and the acceptable voice of snobbery started to sound uncomfortably sharp: in *Tourism*, the much-hyped novel by Nirpal Singh Dhaliwal, a rather clumsy attempt to come up with a voice that might shine light on modern Britain with the same odorous scorn you find in Michel Houllebecq, presents a principal character nicknamed Puppy. 'I hate poor white people,' runs one of his more unpleasant lines. 'No one is more stupid or useless.'

That said, comedy remains Nu Snobbery's most influential vehicle – and in 2003, its decisive arrival was proved by the most successful British comedy programme since *The Office*. *Little Britain* was emblematic of that post-PC nihilism whereby a little misogyny or homophobia was all part of the fun, but its fondness for laughing at the people now fashionably termed 'the disadvantaged' was surely its most insidious aspect. It is hard to cry foul at these things without sounding hopelessly po-faced, but still: somewhere in the characterisation of Lou and Andy, the hapless carer and his wheelchair-using charge, there surely lurks the whiff not only of welfare fraud, but the idea that people so obviously at society's bottom end are so stupid that they probably deserve their fate.

And what of Vicky Pollard? Her portrayal might shine light on Matt Lucas's comedic talent, but her transformation into a signifier for a pretty hideous archetype speaks volumes about the people we now consider to be fair game. On one *Little Britain* web forum, cited last year by the columnist Johann Hari, the link between prime-time tomfoolery and social attitudes became crystal clear: 'Down here in Bristol,' wrote one subscriber, 'we have an area called Southmead, which is absolutely packed with Vickys wearing fluorescent tracksuits. I was coming home on the bus today, and as always, there were millions sat at the back all holding their babies that they had when they were 12, and every other word was "Fuck this" and "Fuck that", and that's just the babies! They all have council flats and not a GCSE to their name. Do the Vickys out there not watch television, because if they do they surely would have seen Vicky on TV and thought, "That's me!" Do they not realise we are taking the piss out of them?'

Naturally enough, the New Snobbery is not restricted to the more frivolous end of our pop culture. In the eyes of an increasing number of people, those who define our politics – led, of course, by two more public schoolboys – have pulled off a remarkable trick: scything the working class out of mainstream politics, and using them as an embodiment of all the fear and failure that our politicians claim to hold at bay. To back up the stereotypes, they need look no further than the nearest TV: as the dissident Labour MP and former Blair adviser Jon Cruddas put it in a recent issue of the centre-left journal *Renewal*, 'in popular culture, the working class is everywhere, albeit successively demonised in comedy or in debate around fear, crime and antisocial behaviour – seen through caricature while patronised by reality TV. Arguably, the cumulative effect of this is that the working class itself has been dehumanised – now to be feared and simultaneously served up as entertainment.' Stranger still, despite five decades of the supposed decline of deference, the rise of David Cameron suggests that simple poshness might still be a very potent political asset.

A 20-minute chat with Cruddas – who finds *Little Britain* 'wretched' – proves to be very enlightening indeed. As he sees it, the three main parties now build their tactics around the 'very precise calibration' of crucial voters who live in a mythical middle England, and thereby leave the kind of people who live in his Dagenham constituency out of their calculations.

Worse still, when things get sticky, they reach for the ghoulish stereotypes that spread fear through *Daily Mail*-land: benefit scroungers, feral youths, problem families. Throw in Cameron and Blair's celebration of 'meritocracy' and both parties' pursuit of a social mobility that the economy stubbornly refuses to deliver, and you end up with two very important questions. If, as Alan Milburn put it just before the last election, it's one of the government's main objectives to 'give more people the opportunity to join the middle class', doesn't that imply a very negative judgment on those they might leave behind? And if no leading politician wants to depart, just occasionally, from the dreamy rhetoric of aspiration and opportunity, might that not leave a gap for some very unpleasant people indeed?

Cruddas's stomping ground, he explains with no little urgency, is currently the focus for an ongoing battle with the BNP. I'm reminded of a passage from Michael Collins' memoir-cum-biography of the white working class, *The Likes of Us*, published in 2004. In his account, the early New Labour period saw the final confirmation that as far as what used to be called the proletariat was concerned, 'middle-class progressives who had traditionally come out fighting these underdogs' corner, or reporting their condition as missionaries or journalists, were keen to silence them, or bury them without an obituary. They loved Gucci, loathed the Euro. More important, to their pall-bearers in the press, they were racist, xenophobic, thick, illiterate, parochial. All they represent and hold dear was reportedly redundant in modern, multicultural Britain. It was dead.'

The strange thing is, society is perhaps not quite in the same shape as most of the political elite – or for that matter, the siren voices who would have you believe that 'everyone's middle class nowadays' – suggest. As Cruddas points out, people in manual occupations still account for a relatively stable 10.5 million of the population. Throw in clerical and secretarial work, and what he calls the 'traditional labour force' stands at around 15 million, and represents just over half of all jobs. Small wonder that, according to a Mori survey published four years ago, two-thirds of Britons said they were 'working class and proud of it'.

There is, of course, a conversation to be had about whether an increasingly diverse Britain has made the old notion of working-class identity redundant, but the numbers still point up an absurd aspect of the new snobbery. If, as evidenced by politicians, comedians and our future king, mocking and demonising supposed white trash is our new national pastime, we're victimising an awful lot of people.

In Rawa, Iraq, some of the men arrested at the border town in Anbar province (the heartland of Sunni insurgency) are herded by US marines towards a helicopter. (SEAN SMITH/GUARDIAN)

Iranian President Mahmoud Ahmadinejad sits with commanders from the Basij Militia in Tehran. (STRINGER – IRAN/REUTERS)

*Overleaf:* A Key West resident walks in the flooded coast boulevard after hurricane Wilma hit Florida's southern west coast. (REUTERS/CARLOS BARRIA, COURTESY OF DAKINI BOOKS FROM *GLOBAL WARNING: THE LAST CHANCE FOR CHANGE*)

A giant mechanical puppet of a little girl walks through central London. She is part of a four-day performance of the *The Sultan's Elephant*, a Jules Verne fairytale performed by the French street theatre company Royal de Luxe. (GRAEME ROBERTSON)

In Trafalgar Square, pigeons fly past *Alison Lapper Pregnant*, the marble statue by the artist Marc Quinn. (DAN CHUNG/GUARDIAN)

April 13 2006

# WHY RESURGENT RELIGION HAS DONE AWAY WITH THE COUNTRY VICAR

## Giles Fraser

There was a time when the country vicar was a staple of the English dramatis personæ. This gentle, tea-drinking eccentric, with his polished shoes and kindly manners, represented a type of religion that didn't make nonreligious people uncomfortable. He wouldn't break into an existential sweat or press you against a wall to ask if you were saved, still less launch crusades from the pulpit or plant roadside bombs in the name of some higher power.

In exchange for a walk-on part during major family occasions and the opportunity to be custodian of the country's most impressive collection of buildings, the vicar promised discretion in all things pertaining to faith: he agreed to treat God as a private matter. In a country exhausted by wars about religion, the creation of the nonreligious priest was a masterstroke of English inventiveness. And once the priest had been cut off from the source of his fire and reassigned to judge marrows at the village fete, his transformation from figure of fear to figure of fun was complete.

The same genius at containing the power of religion was at work in the establishment of the Church of England. Secularists think this arrangement gives the church too much influence over the state, but it's the other way round: it secularises the church. When Puritan settlers in America set up a firewall between church and state, it wasn't to protect the state from the church, but to protect their church from the state. And comparing England and the US, it would seem – however counter-intuitive – that it's precisely this separation that allows the American churches more influence over their government. Establishment domesticates the potentially dangerous enthusiasm of religion so that we might be 'quietly governed'.

It's not simply that the English sought to quarantine God so as to eliminate Him. Take choral evensong. Safe in the knowledge that proceedings will be ordered, beautiful and modest, the English are happy enough to creep in at the back of the church and allow their spirits to take flight on the back of an anthem by Stanford or Howells. In England, even God succumbs to principles of good housekeeping: 'a place for everything and everything in its place'.

The country vicar, the established church, choral evensong – they represented threads of a complex settlement that developed over centuries between Christianity and the English. No one has yet worked out the consequences of this settlement having come to an end. But come to an end it most certainly has. The country vicar is a dying breed, his natural habitat slowly eroded as villages become pretty dormitories for people who work in towns. Economics did for the village shop and the pub – and may well do for the traditional country church too. The only reason disestablishment doesn't stand a chance is that no government will ever assign it the vast amount of parliamentary time that would be required. And only tourists go to choral evensong these days.

Many people confuse these changes with the declining influence of religion. In fact religion has returned to top of the agenda. Belief is now back, often red in tooth and claw. In the minds of many, God is about terrorism, hatred and gay-bashing. And the ghost of the country vicar looks on with puzzled anguish. As Yeats put it: 'The best lack all conviction, while the worst are full of passionate intensity.' The challenge for today's church is to prove Yeats wrong. Liberals need to rediscover their fight and evangelicals need to learn that there is much in religious belief that is right and proper to fear.

On Good Friday Christians remember the crucifixion. Those who welcomed Christ into Jerusalem on Palm Sunday now bay for his blood. Even the hard-nosed career soldier Pontius Pilate fears the passionate intensity of the mob. As day falls, God is butchered on a cross. There's no way of doing theological justice to any of this without breaking into a serious existential sweat. And that's why the central-casting country vicar just didn't add up. But the intense energy of Good Friday is easily purloined for hysterical and destructive purposes. One only has to think of the ways the story of the cross has been used to fuel centuries of anti-semitism. The life of faith has to come with a public health warning: religion can kill.

We are currently witnessing the slow break-up of the last great nationalised industry: the Church of England. And these changing circumstances require a new settlement. As a public body, the English church became mired in procedure, pomp and bureaucracy. It failed to live up to the daring energy and enthusiasm of its founding message.

Even the Archbishop of Canterbury is now calling for a new order: 'A lot of the training of clergy has tended to prepare for maintenance rather than expansion, or even sometimes for managing decline. We've got to find new ways of encouraging the sort of ministry that will be prepared to be entrepreneurial, that will take risks, that will step outside the conventional patterns, the conventional boundaries of the way church is done.'

The new buzz in the C of E is towards a free market in religious expression. Still frustratingly cautious, none the less these fresh expressions of church suggest a religion without the checks and balances provided by the traditional English settlement. What's being imagined is a more energetic and vigorous church. And if the transformation to an entrepreneurial model is followed through, it will undoubtedly see many more people coming to church. But it will also see religion conducted beyond the hesitancy for which the old Church of England has always been known. And that will make it unstable and unpredictable. As the old order breaks apart, the worry is that we may release the genie of English religious fanaticism from the establishment box in which it has been dormant for centuries.

April 21 2006

# THROW OPEN THE BOOKS
# SO THAT WE CAN SEE
# WHAT EVERYONE EARNS

## Polly Toynbee

What is anyone worth? As people trust GPs above all others, it may reflect popular will to super-pay some of them £250,000, with their average £100,000 doubling since 2000. But if you want proof for the counterintuitive truth that more money doesn't make people happier, then the miserable doctors are a good example. Their union, the BMA, pumps out ever angrier anti-government press releases complaining of 'vindictive treatment' in this year's 'shocking' pay offer as they demand another 4.5%.

If higher pay does not lead to happiness or gratitude, how people feel about their pay is complicated and exceedingly important. Research finds the absolute sum matters less than the way people perceive fairness and transparency in pay. So when a dazzle of daylight was shone on the pay of BBC radio stars, it sent out a frisson of shock. Bloggers and letter-writers fulminated about the BBC licence fee – one grumbling that his 30 years of fee-paying barely covers one hour of Jonathan Ross. And that was before the news that a bidding war for Ross has just risen to £15m.

News like that makes people stop and think about pay, reward and merit. The first rule should always be transparency. The BBC should reveal all fees to ensure there really is a genuine market in talent out there. And that should be a general rule, not just in public bodies but everywhere. People do know more or less what everyone else earns in the public sector, so why not make it compulsory for all?

In Norway and Finland, anyone can summon up anyone else's tax return on the internet – and why not? The shock at first would be seismic, with eruptions of rage and embarrassment all round. But it would put a stop to secretive employers who divide and rule by spreading uncertainty and insecurity about what the person at the next desk might be getting. It would help to stamp out fraud and tax evasion, risking exposure of any undeclared income. After the initial shock, people would soon get used to the idea. As it is, money is the great taboo. People are more likely to reveal intimate secrets of their sex lives than ask someone what they earn.

Shocking facts emerge from time to time: chief executives who in 1979 paid themselves 10 times more than their workers now pay themselves 54 times more. Such revelations cause intermittent indignation, but it soon subsides into a 'nothing can be done' gloom. Margaret Thatcher's deadly legacy has been to spread her TINA economic fatalism. 'There is no alternative' has entered the British soul, leaving a helpless, sour sense that iron economic laws shape our destiny: we ignore them at our peril. But there is only political choice. The Nordic countries, with far more successful economies, refuse to suffer our unjustifiable pay gap. Nations can and do choose differently how they share rewards: that's politics, not economics.

For example, the Work Foundation proved that the globalised market for CEOs is a myth. Most top CEOs are not only British, but bred within their own companies. They pay each other these stonking great sums by mutually agreed cartel, all racing to prove they are top dog for no extra productivity or risk.

Their pay distorts the public sector with odious comparisons, especially now that the division between the public and the contracted-out is blurred. Envy and discontent spill over through failing to nurture a distinct public ethos in the public sector, with its own honourable rewards. Even with pay briefly having risen faster than in the private sector, public employees are still paid less than the private workforce. The old compensations of secure pension, stability, security are exchanged for constant turbulence and badly managed 'reform' at risk of Gershon downsizing. So what's the upside?

The Work Foundation finds that the happiest employees are not the best paid but the best respected. People who work collaboratively, who profit-share. Teams deciding their own work practices and rewards are the most content and stay the longest, even if pay is higher elsewhere. Mammon is not king.

Performance-related pay is another Thatcherite hangover. Her spirit of cut-throat competition, 'reward the good and punish the bad', remains the prevailing management dogma, though there is no research evidence that it increases productivity one iota. On the contrary, research finds performance-related pay detested by the managers administering appraisals with half-hearted embarrassment, and by the workforce on the receiving end of arbitrary judgment. Most extra sums earned are piffling, for the affront they cause. Equally, they can become automatic – fat City bonuses now so predictable that mortgage companies accept them as part of regular pay. This evidence-free management mantra persists, despite proof that it is collaboration, not pay competition, that best retains the best people.

Unchallenged by Labour, the greed-is-good culture corrodes trust and social solidarity, spreading dismay and unease. Am I getting enough? What is enough? What am I worth? The myth of a rational market in pay is mainly a cloak for rewards that make little sense. A transparent, functioning market does exist for a few scarce skills: plumbers are hard to find, there is only one David Beckham and probably only one Jonathan Ross. Admired entrepreneurs such as Richard Branson are reckoned to deserve whatever they have created.

But the great majority of people work in markets that are artificial, dominated by tradition, where no one can explain quite why X job is worth more than Y. Women's jobs are marked down because women traditionally do them. Unspoken cartels operate: employers need not illegally conspire to keep cleaning, checkout and care jobs at rock-bottom wages even when there is a shortage, preferring to go short-staffed rather than up the local pay rate for all.

Because the highly paid command the citadels of public debate, they grossly distort the true picture of the way most people live now. Knowing only people like themselves, they refuse to believe that fewer than 4% earn over £52,000 – or that two-thirds earn less than the average £28,000. There are questions that need asking. Is there any good reason why any public servant (including the head of the BBC) should earn more than the prime minister?

Making sense of reward is difficult – but the debate has to begin by throwing open the books. It wouldn't hurt much if everyone had to do it together. Let's see how the culture changes when we can all read each other's tax returns. Why not? What's to hide? The most equal countries do it.

# IS NEW TECHNOLOGY CHANGING OUR BRAINS?

## Jackie Ashley

Sometimes the House of Lords throws out speeches so interesting and radical that you simply cannot imagine them being made in the Commons. One such came this week from the neurobiologist Susan Greenfield. She asked a question that affects all of us, yet which I have never heard discussed by mainstream politicians: is technology changing our brains?

The context is the clicking, bleeping, flashing world of screens. There has been a change in our environment that is so all-embracing and in a way so banal that we barely notice it. In just a couple of decades, we have slipped away from a culture based essentially on words to one based essentially on images, or pictures. This is probably one of the great shifts in modern human history, but we take it almost for granted.

It is most striking when you watch children and young adults. This is not just the obvious ageing person's whinge because my kids can sort out computer or digital camera problems that baffle me. It is more about the way they absorb information and entertainment.

There are the 'icons' (a word to dwell on) of the iPod or Windows, those cute and reassuring little pictures that perform the role of Chinese ideograms rather than western culture's words. Then there are the winking corporate mini-logos, which are more familiar to children than national flags or famous authors. Just watch a teenager navigate, with thumbs or fingertips, through a world of instructions, suggestions, offers and threats, scrolling through songs, adverts, film clips and software.

This, of course, is only the start. What is actually on these enticing little cubes of plastic? My children communicate by text and computer messaging, using the concertinaed, post-grammar, post-spelling shorthand that everyone under 30 finds normal and everyone over 40 finds menacing. There can be little doubt that the structures, never mind the surface form, of the English language are changing fast.

But the main change is that even these shorthand sentences are surrounded by pictures. With mobile phone cameras, digital sticks and emailing, people no longer need to describe where they are but can just point, click and show a view, a friend's face or 'happy slapping'. Children carry portfolios of images on their mobiles and send each other more. The latest iPods and similar gadgets are used as much for watching TV shows, film clips or music videos as for listening.

Most of us are probably ambivalent about all this. We know the world is changing and don't want to seem fuddy-duddy or to be left behind. We are instinctively nervous about the new culture of icons and pictures but shrink from saying it is worse than the old culture of long bored afternoons with the rain drumming on the windows, struggling to concentrate on a book. Pictures are easier on the eye, why hesitate?

But with her speech, Baroness Greenfield hit straight at the dangers posed by this culture. A recent survey of 8- to 18-year-olds, she says, suggests they are spending six and a half hours a day using electronic media, and multi-tasking (using different devices in parallel) is rocketing. Could this be having an impact on thinking and learning?

She began by analysing the process of traditional book-reading, which involves following an author through a series of interconnected steps in a logical fashion. We read other narratives and compare them, and so 'build up a conceptual framework that enables us to evaluate further journeys ... One might argue that this is the basis of education ... It is the building up of a personalised conceptual framework, where we can relate incoming information to what we know already. We can place an isolated fact in a context that gives it significance.' Traditional education, she says, enables us to 'turn information into knowledge'.

Put like that, it is obvious where her worries lie. The flickering up and flashing away again of multimedia images do not allow those connections, and therefore the context, to build up. Instant 'yuk' or 'wow' factors take over. Memory, which was once built up in a verbal and reading culture, matters less when everything can be summoned at the touch of a button (or, soon, with voice recognition, by merely speaking). In a world of short attention-spans, fed on pictures, the habit of contemplation and the patient acquisition of knowledge are in retreat. Is this, perhaps, the source of the hyperactivity and attention-deficit malaise now being treated with industrial quantities of Ritalin, Prozac and other drugs to help sustain attention in the classroom? If so, what will these drugs do in turn to the brain? Greenfield points out, in some of the most chilling words ever heard in the Lords, that 'the human brain is exquisitely sensitive to any and every event: we cannot complacently take it as an article of faith that it will remain inviolate, and that consequently human nature and ways of learning and thinking will remain consistent.'

While not suggesting a revolt by mere democracies against the corporate power of the IT industries, Greenfield suggests this is an idea that should at least be investigated further. She wants more government funding for the scientists and educators trying to understand the impact of the digital-picture world on how children learn to think – surely a more important area for state-backed research than endless lifestyle or obesity surveys.

Politicians should be seriously concerned. Parliamentary democracy has depended on a citizenry prepared to think logically about policies, to remember promises and to follow arguments. Greenfield's feared world without context is therefore also a world more prone to political illogic and fad.

Perhaps, instead of boasting about the tunes they download on to their iPods, or courting publicity for their website inanities, our politicians could all take a valuable 10 minutes to read and reflect on Baroness Greenfield's fine speech. It's available in a hard copy of Hansard, or on the internet at: www.publications.parliament.uk/pa/ld199900/ldhansrd/pdvn/lds06/text/60420-18.htm#60420-18_spopq0. Yes, really.

April 25 2006

# ME AND MY G-WIZ

## Alan Rusbridger

My guess is that all London cyclists occasionally prefigure the moment of their death. I used to predict the most likely place for my premature end would be in Kentish Town high street. Half a mile of swinging car doors, unpredictably weaving buses, sleepwalking pedestrians and impatient fellow cyclists. If ever I were to come a cropper it would be here.

I was wrong. My death nearly came just before Christmas on a straight and empty stretch of road before I even made it to the high street. The sun was out, the city was deserted and I was looking forward to a carefree ride to work.

In an instant I was lying on my side. Instinctively I shot a hand in the air in case there was a car behind me. I opened my eyes and craned my head round. There – towering over me – was a double-decker bus. Another six feet and the *Guardian* would have been looking for a new editor.

As I leaned against a nearby wall I felt both shaken and stupid. I hadn't hit anything and nothing had hit me. The wheels had just disappeared from underneath me – and there was a sharp dent in my crash helmet to prove it. I must have slipped on a solid metal drain cover, still slightly dew-coated, though the road itself was dry.

My wrist was really hurting, so I took myself off to hospital. It was badly sprained and bruised, not broken. But my nerve was. Talking through the incident with Matt Seaton, the cycling guru of Farringdon Road, was not reassuring. 'Yes, slippery drain covers … a bit of a menace,' he conceded. 'Not much you can do about them – except avoid them.'

Ah, no one had told me about the mortal threat of drain covers when I'd bought my little silver fold-up bike in a warm surge of wanting to get a tiny bit fitter while making a nanoscopic contribution to reducing north London's total carbon emissions.

I tried to imagine a journey down the Kentish Town obstacle course while simultaneously keeping half an eye out for killer drains. And it was this that decided it for me. Any form of transport that can involve an unprovoked near-death experience on a deserted stretch of open road in broad daylight was not for me.

But nor could I quite face a return to lumbering in as the solitary occupant of a Volvo estate. There are, of course, buses and tubes – but time is short in the morning: both would take a good 45 minutes with changes and walks each end, and my morning schedule was now constructed around a door-to-door journey of 18 minutes.

It was my eldest daughter who told me about the G-Wiz – a tiny electric car made in Bangalore that looks as though it was designed with a crayon set by a committee of six-year-olds. I'd always hankered for a tiny electric car ever since test-driving a prototype Danish-made Perspex banana a dozen or more years ago. For some reason it never caught on, but from that moment I was sold on the idea of whizzing around London in a tiny little silent bubble.

My daughter directed me to www.goingreen.co.uk, the car's British website, and I was soon gazing longingly at an up-to-date version of what Noddy and Big Ears might use to nip around the inner congestion charge zone of Toytown. It boasts that this is the greenest car available – emission free, carbon neutral and capable of doing the equivalent of 600mpg. It also claims to be the cheapest: no road tax, no congestion charge, free parking in central London, etc. The savings on the congestion charge alone (£173 a month) would – it was promised – outweigh the cost of monthly repayments on £9,000. I could be greener than even David Cameron could dream of – and all for nothing! I booked a test drive. Within a few days I was perched inside a G-Wiz, feeling ever so slightly self-conscious and just possibly a teeny bit smug.

It's a tall car, which is just as well, given my height (6ft 2in), and ridiculously short – stubby enough to park lengthways to the kerb in the average London parking bay. The plastic body reinforces the impression that it could well be a toy rather than a fully functioning car and you half expect to find pedalo-style foot pedals.

Those of you who have driven a golf buggy, milk float or dodgem car will have some idea of what to expect as you plunge the accelerator to the ground for the first time. The total silence is, at first, unnerving, but the idea is to hold your nerve and press on.

Well, I was hooked within minutes. The G-Wiz is both nippy and a bit cumbersome (no power steering, rotten over speed bumps). It's happiest whistling along at a steady 25mph – which is not totally silly in a city like London, with an average traffic speed of 12mph. Uphill it may strain to nudge 22mph. Downhill you can feel something of the thrill that George Stephenson must have felt when he coaxed 29mph out of the Rocket.

Reader, I bought one. Which was not quite as simple as it sounds: there's a waiting list of at least three months.

Mine came with alloy wheels and climate-controlled seats, which are supposed to eat up less power than conventional heating. Ah yes, the power. Well, they do warn you about that. Officially, you can travel 30 miles before having to charge up the car by plugging it into any normal socket – but the car arrives with a tariff of non-green behaviour for which you must expect to be penalised. Knock off a mile if you insist on listening to the radio, three miles if you must use windscreen wipers at the same time. The heater could cost you 10 miles and a combination of steep hills and cold weather is not recommended.

And then there's the question of where to plug it in. The options at home are not good. I could either sling a cable from the house, through the trees and down to the roadside (they say it has been done) or I would have to dig up part of the hedge and rearrange the front garden for off-street parking. Unless I can persuade nice Camden council (which does actually have a Green Transport Strategy) to install a roadside charging point.

My car arrived last week and, for the time being, I'm squatting in the back yard of the *Guardian*, where there's a handy all-weather 13-amp power socket. The car came with a large bottle of distilled water (the batteries need watering every fortnight), a long blue flex and a certificate saying that GoinGreen had offset 3.0 tonnes of emissions on my behalf.

I feared moments of road rage from white vans trapped behind me on an unavoidable uphill incline near King's Cross – but, so far, the car has attracted nothing worse than craned necks, a few smiles and the odd belly laugh. A taciturn subeditor gazed at it in the back yard and commented: 'You'd have to be very confident in your sexuality to drive such a thing.' It is, perhaps, not a car for Jeremy Clarkson. And, yes, that is a non sequitur.

A friend came round to play music last night and, just to prove a point, we did, indeed, manage to fit his cello in the back. Early days and all, but so far I'm a very happy customer.

Or I was until the deputy editor just poked his head round the door and smirkingly flourished a picture of David Cameron, taken yesterday, posing beside a G-Wiz. Of course, he actually drives a £38,000 Lexus GS 450, which spews out 186g of pollutants per kilometre. But I'm prepared to take the picture as a sincere attempt at flattery.

April 26 2006

# TESCO...EVERY LITTLE FROG HELPS

## Jonathan Watts

Supermarket food does not come any fresher or friskier than at the Happy Shopper store in Tianjin, where the frogs and fish literally leap out at the customers. Customers are enticed to net live carp and rainbow trout from brightly illuminated blue-and-green tanks. For 9.8 yuan (66p), they can pick out whichever soft-shelled turtle they think will make the best soup. And for the health conscious, there are trays full of wriggling silkworm grubs on offer for 31 yuan a kilo. 'Each grub has the same nutritional value as three chicken eggs,' enthused one consumer.

This is the frontline of Tesco's expansion into China – potentially the world's biggest retail market with 1.3 billion customers. Happy Shopper – a 17,000 square-metre mix of traditional eastern wet market and modern western hypermarket in Tianjin's industrial zone – is one of 39 Chinese stores that Tesco operates in conjunction with its local partner and Taiwanese food supplier, Ting Hsing.

Since the signing of the joint venture, Hymall, in 2004, the firm has expanded its workforce by 20% to 14,500 staff. By the end of the coming financial year, it plans to have opened 12 more hypermarkets, including a first in Beijing.

In any other country, it would be an impressive expansion, but by Chinese standards it is cautious. WalMart recently announced plans to create 150,000 jobs in China over the next five years. Carrefour – the biggest international operator in the market – has 70 hypermarkets, eight supermarkets and more than 100 discount shops. All the companies are lagging behind the domestic leader, Hualian, which runs nearly 2,000 stores.

Unlike its foreign rivals, Tesco appears unconcerned about building on its established brand. While Carrefour and WalMart sell under their own names, there is nothing in Hymall's Happy Shopper that even remotely suggests a British link. The colour scheme is orange, all of the managers and shop floor staff are Chinese and – with the exception of a few cans of Boddington's – there are few brands on the shelves that would be familiar to a UK shopper.

'We are going into local markets in a local fashion,' said Lucy Neville-Rolfe, group corporate affairs director. 'It doesn't seem to be essential to use the Tesco name.' She said the UK side provides expertise in information technology, food safety and retail management, but the shops are distinctly Chinese with lots of live fish tanks inside and huge bicycle parking areas outside. Ms Neville-Rolfe said Tesco predicted continued growth. 'China is very important. The population of 1.3 billion people has a huge potential.'

With less than one expatriate for every 1,000 Hymall staff, Tesco appears to have a hands-off approach to its Chinese investment. This has gone down well with the local staff.

'When we heard that a British firm had bought a stake in the company, everyone was a bit worried that it would mean big changes, but so far there hasn't been anything that noticeable,' said one staff member. 'The middle managers are all Chinese. Only the most senior executives are British.'

Huge layoffs and costcutting were never likely. This is partly because wages are low (supermarket salaries in China are usually less than £70 for a 160-hour month), but also because high staff numbers are necessary to provide service to customers who shop more frequently, but spend less than their counterparts in Britain. Hymall stores – which are concentrated in Shanghai – get about 2.3 million customers a week, but each spends less than £1 a visit.

Given the early stage of development of the Chinese market, foreign entrants are also more concerned about building their presence than their efficiency. 'The retail cycle is more about growth than profitability at the moment,' said Atiff Gill, senior manager of the consultancy Kurt Salmon Associates.

The market is already worth $240bn (£135bn), and like everything in China these days, it is growing at double-digit pace. But it is a long way from the company's dominance in Britain, where Tesco takes one in every eight pounds spent at supermarket checkouts. Even if business increases, the company looks unlikely to be a household name in China.

Shoppers in Tianjin yesterday seemed oblivious to the fact that their local store was partly owned by a British firm. Liu Honghua, who spends about 100 yuan on her daily trips to Happy Shopper, said the only change she had noticed in the past year was an increased variety of products.

'I guess that is because the competition is increasing,' she said. 'Does Happy Shopper have a British owner? I didn't know.'

April 27 2006

# IS IT EVER OK TO BOO?

## Charlotte Higgins

I went to the first night of Wagner's *Götterdämmerung* at the Royal Opera House. It's an event that invites big reactions: this opera is absolutely immense, in length (four hours and 15 minutes), in scale (vast orchestra, massed ranks of harps, enormous choruses) and in scope (you've got the Fates, hordes of vassals being called to war, poison, murders and the dwelling of the gods being burned to the ground). In other words, it's a big deal.

At the Opera House, the curtain calls covered all bases. There was middling applause for the guy who sang Siegfried, while for John Tomlinson, a compelling Hagen and a national treasure, the audience practically took the roof off, cheering and stamping.

Then the director, lighting designer, costume designer et al came on. Wow – they were booed hard. People hadn't liked the production at all, and indeed the last hour or so was crashingly awful.

Is it fair to boo, though? No one actually tries to mess something up. Imagine it: your big night comes, and you are greeted by a wall of booing. Maybe it's better than total indifference, but I doubt it.

May 2 2006

# IT'S HARD TO FIND SOMEONE TO START A FAMILY WITH

## Libby Brooks

It's hard to legislate for hearts, and impossible to schedule attraction. That's what's so liberating about love. But it would appear that fate is no longer working in couples' favour. One of the most striking findings of our ICM poll on attitudes to having children is that of the people interviewed, one in two believes that it is becoming more difficult to meet someone to start a family with. One of the top reasons cited for this country's low birthrate is that couples do not stay together in the same way as in the past.

Of course, the increase in single-person households and divorce is well documented. But it is interesting that, amid the incessant chatter about our national fertility anxiety (Not enough babies to pay for pensions! Women climb career ladder while eggs shrivel! Men put PlayStation before relationships!), the fact that people are finding it harder than ever to hook up is seldom discussed as a cause rather than a symptom.

So why are many people finding it increasingly difficult to start and sustain intimate relationships? Perhaps it's about which end of the telescope you're looking down: making the first move feels impossible before you've done it, and the easiest part once you're navigating the challenges of a long-term relationship. Does modern life really make it harder to fall in love? Or are we making it harder for ourselves?

It is certainly the case that contemporary couples benefit differently from relationships than in the past. Women no longer rely upon partners for economic security or status, and a man doesn't expect his spouse to be in sole charge of running his household and raising his children. But perhaps the knowledge that we can live perfectly well without a partnership means that it takes much more to persuade people to abandon those modern absolutes of autonomy and independence.

In theory, finding a partner should be much simpler these days. Only a few generations ago, one's choice of soulmate was constrained by geography, social convention and family tradition. Although it was never explicit, many liaisons were essentially arranged. An elderly friend of mine married his wife at the age of 20, after marking her card twice at a dance.

Now those barriers have been broken down, and one can approach a builder or a brain surgeon in any bar in any city on any given evening. When the world is your oyster, you surely have a better chance of finding a pearl. But it would seem that the old conventions have been replaced by an even tighter constraint: the tyranny of choice. There has been some debate on these pages about the marketisation of sexuality, and the manner in which the expectation of sexual availability leads both men and women to outsource the role of seducer to media culture. Is the commodification of love a logical extension of this?

The because-you're-worth-it rubric has inflated expectations of partners to an unmanageable degree: good looks, GSOH, impressive career, even more impressive salary, kind to Gran, the right socks, knows all the words to the Proclaimers' greatest hits. In his book *Blink*, the *New Yorker* writer Malcolm Gladwell lauds the veracity of the instant impression. There is no room for error, or anything so unglamorous as compromise.

We are encouraged to think of relationships as perfectible and, when they prove not to be, disposable. The premium on self-determination insists that we inoculate ourselves against future heartache, rather than tolerate uncertainty and the hard emotional labour intimacy can demand.

Of course, this is compounded by structural realities. Twelve-hour stretches at the office do not lend themselves to relaxed after-hours flirtation. The cost of housing and child-rearing creates pressure to have a stable income and career before a life partnership. And there will always be an uneven fit biologically between the fertility spans of men and women.

It's ironic that, at a time when we are allegedly more emotionally literate than ever, the *Oprah*fication of our public discourse has not made us better at forming relationships. Our witness culture dictates that no experience is valid unless it's shared, whether with a million reality-TV viewers or a textable friend (perhaps with the new specially designed jacket that allows the wearer to hug loved ones via the internet). But it seems to me that the faux-connections we use to shore ourselves up against solitude serve only to erode genuine intimacy.

As the growing pains of 21st-century living encroach on our emotional lives, we need to be watchful – but also hopeful. While it seems harder to meet someone to start a family with, as the ICM poll and our own experiences show, it doesn't mean people have stopped trying.

May 2 2006

# ANIMAL PAIN COUNTS, ANIMAL LIFE DOESN'T

## Julian Baggini

Is it right to slaughter 35,000 bootiful Norfolk chickens just because some of them have been irresponsible enough to get the flu? Killing animals for their meat is one thing, but knocking off healthy ones to control disease seems particularly harsh. Yet the latest bird flu cull is mere chicken feed compared to the 6 million animals culled during the 2001 foot and mouth outbreak, and the 1 million cattle slaughtered to halt the spread of BSE in 1996 alone.

You would expect vegetarians to be troubled by these statistics, but many meat-eaters should be disturbed by the death toll too. For every vegetarian there are a dozen flesh-eaters who none the less take animal welfare seriously. By avoiding factory-farmed produce and buying free range, organic or RSPCA Freedom Food, we feel we can have our happy animals and eat them too.

Well, maybe we can, but the culls to eliminate infections are a discomforting reminder that even these 'ethical' foods are part of a meat industry with a tough-minded attitude to livestock. Animals are replaceable units of protein, and shame though it is to waste any resource, scrapping a million such products because of a manufacturing glitch is like recalling a million Star Wars figurines because of a light sabre fracture.

It sounds callous but to be consistent, a carnivore who professes a concern for animal welfare must maintain that while causing unnecessary pain and distress to an animal is wrong, ending its life prematurely is not. Animal pain counts for much, but animal life counts for almost nothing. Given that meat eating is not essential – at least not in modern western countries – you can quantify its relative worth by saying that there is more value in our enjoyment of a carcass's worth of juicy steak than there is in the life of the cow that involuntarily donated it.

If that sounds brutal, live with it or pass the tofu. So-called ethical consumers have a tendency to tinker with their purchasing decisions in order to feel virtuous, rather than grasp head-on the fundamental issues that require hard choices. In the case of meat, good though it is to try to avoid needless suffering, the fundamental issue is whether animals are replaceable things that can be killed by the million to secure their meat for us. If you can't swallow that, perhaps you need to reconsider what you're prepared to chew.

# THE SECRET DIARY OF TRACEY TEMPLE, AGED 43 ¾

## Emily Wilson

'I never travel without my diary,' says Gwendolen Fairfax, in *The Importance of Being Earnest*. 'One should always have something sensational to read in the train.' This Sunday all of us, diary writers and non-diary writers alike, had something sensational to read on the train. The *Mail on Sunday* published extracts from the secret diary of Tracey Temple, age 43¾, and by golly, was it zippy.

Temple is no great scribe. Not even her best friends would describe her as writerly. She sprinkles her prose with words such as 'bizi' (busy) and 'coz' – more in the manner of a carefree 12-year-old than a 43-year-old civil servant with a government department to help run. She appears uninterested in much beyond the minutiae of office life and nights out at work-related 'do's'. As a diarist, she combines the giddiness of Bridget Jones with the naivety of Adrian Mole.

But like the great Samuel Pepys, Temple is ruthlessly honest in the recording of her sexual adventures, however badly they might reflect upon her, and it's here that her diaries really shine. Pepys, of course, had other strings to his bow – but then he didn't have an affair with the deputy prime minister, did he?

At first, glancing at Temple's diaries, you are struck by the grinding ordinariness of it all. These are meant to be the best bits, you think – what else would the *Mail on Sunday* splash out (a rumoured) £250,000 on? Temple is like some extra from *The Office* ... it's all what train she managed to get to work and her boring job, and whether she'll leave her boring job to take a different boring job at Downing Street – or not.

Prescott says that much of what appeared in the *Mail on Sunday* this week is 'simply untrue', but it's a safe bet that he doesn't mean these bits.

Then, on Wednesday December 18 2002, pretty much with no warning, the diary morphs from *The Office* into some kind of 70s soft porn film, and it's rather easier to see what Prescott might take issue with. Temple dresses up for an office party in a black dress ('low, button up the back') and … 'as soon as the boss arrived he lifted my dress jokingly to see my stockings'.

Yes, the boss is the big man, John Prescott himself, and, you know, he lifted up his secretary's dress, but in a 'joking' way – because of course if he hadn't done it jokingly, it would be a gross abuse of his position as her boss. But it gets worse.

Temple finds herself dancing away the night with the DPM, as she calls him – this is presumably the night on which those now-famous pictures of them dancing together were taken – and she 'ended up with him all night. He was really coming on to me – I didn't mind – paying me compliments + telling me what he wld like to do to me'.

It would be utterly unworldly of me to be staggered by the DPM behaving like that in front of all those people – after all, office affairs are two a penny and if Bill Clinton has taught us anything, it's that top politicians can be morons in the trouser department too. But if I was an unworldly sort, I would at this point say something like (to quote Janice from *Friends*): OH MY GOD.

This, however, is Temple's take on all that dancing and 'what he wld like to do to me' business: 'I am rather surprised, + flattered I suppose, that the DPM was like he was. He did say he was embarrassed when he made a pass at me a while back + apologised. I told him no problem. In fact all night I really did play it cool.'

If Temple really had been playing it cool, what she would have done at this point would have been to think, hmm, employment law has moved on a bit since the 70s, think I might take my boss to an industrial tribunal. But I digress.

The next day, according to the diary, the DPM starts stroking Temple's back while she is trying to go through some 'diary issues' with him at the office. Like you do. She ends up back at his flat – where else? Sensitive readers should – seriously now – look away: 'He carried me into his bedroom + did everything to try to plse me,' she writes.

But then – things get exponentially worse! This is her the next day: 'I did pop out today just for peace of mind + got the morning-after Pill. It wld be disastrous if anything were to happen but I am confident everything is fine.'

She had unprotected sex with him! This is when you realise that Bridget Jones at her flightiest is eight billion times as streetwise as Temple, that Adrian Mole at his least self-knowing is still a star system more savvy than Temple. And as for Prescott ... a man in *The Times* was going on yesterday about how 'odious' it was that the DPM's private life had been splashed all over the media, but for anyone unsure about whether Prescott should survive this, surely the morning-after pill incident must be the clincher. Prescott is Clinton. Um, without the looks, of course, and the sex appeal, and oh, the megawatt charisma, and the politics, and there's no argument here about what was or wasn't sex – but you get the point: they're both men prepared to take moronic risks.

After the DPM had done everything he could to please the woman he had employed to look after his diary, well – there's not a lot else really. Their much trumpeted two-year affair turns out to be two years of nothing, with a tiny bit of wham, bam and my driver will drive you home, ma'am. Most of it was apparently a bit disappointing (shock). We get him groping her at the office, some phone sex, him barging into her room at party conference (which his wife was attending) and asking for sex ... that kind of thing.

It's all vaguely comic and for good measure there's the odd highly surreal moment, apropos of nothing. For example: 'Got stopped for speeding on way home from Farnham but eventually let off. I don't know how fast I was going cos the speedo was not working.'

But lighthearted as it all mostly is, with no analysis of what might happen should 'B', Temple's shadowy boyfriend, ever stumble upon her diaries (as apparently did eventually happen ... hence last week's exclusive about the affair in the *Daily Mirror*), or how Mrs P would feel if she knew – we do get hints of how badly screwed-up the whole thing is. This is a line from July 10 2003, written after the DPM and Temple had had sex at his flat: 'One thing I was pleased about was that he did kiss me. Can you believe this – I called him sweetheart.'

Er… did he normally not kiss her? A bit like when prostitutes don't kiss their clients because they are saving it for their boyfriends – but in reverse?

Then on October 10 2003, she writes: 'Had to go to the flat with the boss. He can be a randy old sod at times coz he wanted sex again … but I didn't let it go any further. He was so up for it though.'

It's got to be telling, hasn't it, that 'randy old sod'? Isn't that normally how you would describe someone when you really don't want to have sex with them? How on earth did Temple get herself into all this?

I, for one, hope that Temple is not too dented by her adventures with the DPM, and now in Fleet Street, and that she is allowed to keep her job, and also that, like Gwendolen Fairfax, she continues to write sensational diaries. Perhaps though, in future, she'll find somewhere better to hide them.

# THE SULTAN'S ELEPHANT

## Emma Brockes

Ken Livingstone himself couldn't have choreographed a better advertisement for the capital at play: under a baking sun, hundreds gathered in central London yesterday to watch a story loosely based on the work of Jules Verne being enacted by 12m puppets and a giant wooden elephant. 'It's The Sultan's Elephant,' a worker for Westminster city council said to a tourist, and looked instantly stunned that those words were his own.

If the phrase 'street theatre' summons unhappy images of mime artists in Covent Garden, then the events that took place in the capital yesterday, and will continue until Sunday, showed what could be done with a large enough scale of ambition. The Sultan's Elephant, a theatrical event by the French theatre company Royal de Luxe, is to street art what a glacier is to ice cubes.

This wasn't theatre, said the director, Jean-Luc Courcoult, but 'meteorology', and he backed up the grandness of his claims with a spectacle that has been five years in the making. His intended theme was 'intimacy', but he said it was up to the crowds to make what they would of his work. And they did. For two days the sight of the elephant had been provoking small acts of self-revelation and actual smiles in the traditionally suicidal-looking London pedestrians.

Things began to happen on Thursday morning when commuters rounding the corner at Waterloo Place encountered what looked like a huge wooden torpedo embedded in the asphalt, smoke pouring from it. 'Is it advertising?' asked a passerby. 'It's a bomb,' said an American tourist, while a South African teenager said doubtfully, 'If this was real there'd be Swat teams all round it.'

There was no branding and no merchandising. There were no signposts and no tickets, either, and thus there was no revenue. The project has been almost entirely funded by the Arts Council. In an age when even the Notting Hill carnival is plastered with sponsors' logos, The Sultan's Elephant offered a rare thing in modern life: a bit of mystery. By Thursday lunchtime, the shifting crowds were still unsure of what it was.

'Has it come down from the sky?' said a Japanese tourist to Dawn Adams, who works around the corner in St James' Square.

'No,' she said. 'I don't think so. But there's a big elephant down the road.'

'I don't understand, what's the point?' said a young man who, if the weather had been cooler, would almost certainly have been wearing a hoodie.

'Media attraction, innit,' said his friend, who turned to a well-to-do woman and asked politely what the score was. 'It's moveable art,' she said, and the boy frowned. 'I thought it was a rocket.'

'I'm a gecko,' said the woman's child. 'Can we go to McDonald's?'

'No darling. We're doing something cultural.'

In the way of all fairy tales it was left to a small boy to interpret Mr Courcoult's idea most succinctly and, with pitch-perfect surrealism, to run around the base of the rocket shrieking, 'Somebody pinch my nose!' His mother said, 'Honey, don't put your hand in the hole,' and a yellow-vested council officer muttered about health and safety. 'I argued for a barrier,' she said. But there were no rules here.

By Friday lunchtime a crane had appeared alongside the time machine, to lift off the lid, and a large crowd gathered. People in Carlton House Terrace pressed against the upper windows and office workers massed on the roofs of Pall Mall. Builders from a nearby construction site looked on and assumed instant authority on the subject of giant wooden time machines. 'That's been dug up, mate,' said one, 'no question. There's seven tonnes of material there,' while in front of him two men in suits discussed the price of polyurethane. At 2pm a live band played soft French rock and men in footmen's livery climbed the gantry and lifted the lid on the rocket.

Speculation about what was inside had ranged from a giraffe to 'a Frenchman' to the sultan himself, but it was a 12m wooden girl in a green dress who was eventually hoisted out of the barrel. She wore old-fashioned aviator goggles.

The crowd stared, open-mouthed, while the footmen swarmed over her like Lilliputians and, working the wires, got her to take off her helmet. Then she set off down Regent Street, taking the back route to Horse Guards Parade. No one had the faintest idea what any of it meant, but it didn't much matter: as the puppet and the elephant met up on the concourse, imaginative musings broke out all over the crowd.

'Do you think it'll spray water?' a girl asked a policewoman.

'It might do,' she said. 'I would.'

'If there's a serious point,' said Nicky Webb, one of the British organisers with partner company Artichoke, 'it's that with the Olympics coming this shows that London can be a joined-up city, that all agencies can work together.'

The event took so long to organise because shutting down the Mall and parts of Regent Street takes, as Ms Webb put it with pained understatement, 'some doing'. But the council had been marvellous, she said.

When the elephant sprayed water and made trumpeting sounds, the crowd cheered. Julian, a young hedge-fund manager who wouldn't give his surname because he had bunked off work, said: 'If this is coming out of my council tax, I don't mind. Exactly the kind of thing we should be spending it on.'

And – is there any higher compliment to be paid to an artist? – he looked thoroughly surprised at himself.

May 9 2006

# TONY BLAIR SHOULD SACK GORDON BROWN

## Robert Harris

Tony Blair ought to sack Gordon Brown. In fact, he ought to have done it years ago. I cannot think of any prime minister who has put up with such chronic disloyalty from a senior colleague over such a long period. But a combination of factors – fear of consigning this brooding, remorseless enemy to the backbenches, genuine regard for his abilities and possibly even a kind of rueful, brotherly affection after so many years in politics together – has always stayed his hand. Now, in a denouement worthy of Shakespearean tragedy, it appears that Blair's fatal weakness is about to be punished, and that his relentless opponent will soon drive him from the stage.

This curious weakness of Blair's has a long history. It dates all the way back to that notorious pact, agreed in 1994 in the Granita restaurant, under which Brown was granted unprecedented powers within any future Labour government and an assurance that he would be next in line of succession, in return for his grudging withdrawal from the leadership contest. This has always been presented by the chancellor's supporters as a brutal stab in the back by his ruthless young colleague. But a moment's reflection on the nature of Brown, and of politics at that level, tells one that this must be nonsense.

A poll of Labour party members, on the weekend before the Granita agreement, showed Blair with 47%, John Prescott with 15%, and Brown trailing a poor third, with 11%. Brown could not command an absolute majority even in his main powerbase of Scottish MPs. He knew he was going to lose, and probably lose badly, and having bitterly resigned himself to the fact, then proceeded to play a poor hand with consummate skill, extracting the enormous concessions that have hobbled Blair's leadership ever since.

This is not just ancient history. Think how much stronger Blair's position would have been if only he had invited Brown to continue his candidacy in 1994. The true low level of Brown's support within the party at that time would have been revealed once and for all. He and his acolytes would never have been able to cast doubt on the legitimacy of Blair's position. And, most importantly, he would never have been able to portray himself as virtually the prime minister's co-equal: unsackable, with a permanent lien on the Treasury, a colleague for whom any hint of a transfer in a reshuffle, even to the Foreign Office, was regarded as an act of *lèse-majesté*.

I suppose, given the inherent instability of this arrangement, politically and psychologically, the miracle is that the whole edifice of their partnership has not collapsed long before now. But at last it seems that the moment has arrived. Every television viewer in the country can see that these two men really cannot abide one another, and for the government to go on pretending otherwise will only invite contempt and ridicule. Someone must very soon take charge and give the government a fresh sense of direction (or 'renewal', to use the current buzzword), and the universal assumption – it's certainly his assumption – is that it must be Brown.

But why is this such a certainty? It is, after all, only a year since Blair led his party to an unprecedented third successive election victory, pledging that he would 'serve a full term' before standing down – widely accepted at the time to mean a transfer of power in 2008. This may be regarded by the 50 or so Labour MPs clamouring for Blair's immediate resignation – who, incidentally, only account for one-seventh of the parliamentary party – as a mere technicality. I am not sure that the electorate will agree, at least not once the Tory party and press start repeatedly reminding them of this broken promise, which at the moment they are intriguingly failing to do. I am also not sure that the prime minister would agree, either. It was, after all, his personal promise to the British people: will Blair really want history to hang around his neck that he went out on such a blatant lie?

The most plausible scenario for what will happen next is that Brown will soon demand, either overtly or covertly, an end to this period of instability, and that the pressure on Blair to go by the autumn, or next spring at the latest, will become overwhelming. That is what almost every lobby journalist assures us. But what about an alternative scenario: that Blair agrees with Brown that the succession crisis is out of control, and invites him publicly to stick by Labour's election pledge, and support his continued occupancy of No 10 until 2008?

That seems to me an entirely legitimate demand for Blair to make, not least because, if Brown acceded to it, it would release much of the steam from the present crisis, which is largely generated from No 11, and the government could then get back to doing its job. Ah, you will reply, but of course Brown would refuse. Well then, in my view, Blair would be perfectly within his rights to draw the obvious inference of his continuing disloyalty, announce that the chancellor has forfeited his confidence, and sack him.

This is not, I guess, a course with which most *Guardian* readers would agree, not least because there seems to be a peculiar – one might almost say touching – view prevalent on these pages that Brown, once he becomes prime minister, is suddenly going to provide an entirely different kind of Labour government. Once again, one has to pay tribute to Brown's skill as a political operator: to have convinced some sections of the party and the media that he has actually been radicalised by nine years at the Treasury is a considerable achievement.

But he has never, as far as one knows, as a passionate Atlanticist, emitted a grunt of opposition to the Iraq war. Rather, he has declared that he would have done exactly the same as Blair. On pensions, his enthusiasm for means testing is more Gradgrindish than the prime minister's. He has been globalisation's most proselytising friend. And if you think Blair's No 10 has been overfond of soundbites, over-centralising and anti-democratic – well, brothers and sisters, judging by the Treasury's record, you ain't seen nothin' yet.

Above all, why have Brown and his friends waited until now to launch their internal coup d'etat – three or possibly even four years before the people will get a chance to give their approval in a general election? If Brown wanted Blair out of the leadership, he should have had the courage to strike when he had the chance, in 2004, and not hidden behind the formula deployed at the subsequent general election that the prime minister would serve a 'full term'. Abandoning that pledge now shows the machine politician's typical contempt for democracy.

I am no uncritical admirer of Blair. I share the exasperation with many aspects of his premiership, especially the war in Iraq. But I still find myself hoping he stands up to his rival, and that if Brown does ever pluck up the nerve to tell him he is banished, Blair will retort like Coriolanus: 'No, no: I banish you.'

May 9 2006

# MAYBE MARK OATEN'S JUST GAY

## Marina Hyde

Loath as one should always be to get involved in other couples' domestic finances, I do hope Mark and Belinda Oaten aren't lavishing too much of the housekeeping on this psychiatrist he is seeing.

Writing in the *Sunday Times*, the Lib Dem MP took £20,000 for what is known in the often facile parlance of Fleet Street as 'telling his side of the story'. He revealed that as he drove to a safe house on the morning that the story of his liaison with a male prostitute broke, he phoned his psychiatrist, a man he had been seeing 'for several years'.

'But, as I now realised,' wrote Mark, 'we had never really worked out why a 40-year-old married man with two children goes to a male prostitute. It certainly made no sense on that drive from my home.'

Yes, it is most baffling. What on earth could be behind his behaviour? A small fluctuation in the Japanese futures markets, perhaps, precipitating some sort of butterfly effect? A shift of tectonic plates, imperceptible to Britons, but causing a seismograph needle to jump somewhere in the South Pacific? Or even – but no, it's too stratospherically outlandish – the possibility that Mark likes sex with men?

Not that there's anything wrong with that, to give the old *Seinfeld* line an airing.

When it comes to the calibre of its personnel, the mental health profession is a famously mixed bag. No one likes to lose a customer, of course, and there are those cynics who believe that some practitioners have an almost pathological aversion to simple answers, and that this might be rooted in the desire to make the relationship with their clients as long and financially fruitful as possible.

Yet even considering all this, it does seem a genuine achievement that there was apparently never a moment in all these years when the psychiatrist steepled his fingertips together, and after a long, exceptionally ruminative pause, said: 'Do bear with me, Mark, because I'm thinking right outside the box here … but do you reckon you might be gay?'

This failure to assume anything puts me in mind of an episode of *Doctor Who*, in which the Doctor, Rose and Queen Victoria are en route to Balmoral, and use the house of a highland lord as a staging post. Little do they realise that the owner's wife has been taken prisoner and his staff replaced by psychotic, shaven-headed men, who force him to act as if nothing is amiss. Towards the end of the episode, when the day has been saved, his lordship asks the Doctor why he didn't realise sooner that something was up.

'Well,' comes the cheeky reply, 'your wife was away, you were surrounded by bald, athletic men … I just thought you were enjoying yourself.'

Ah, beware the simple answer, Doctor! As the Time Lord eventually discovered, the wife and servants were in fact being held hostage by a werewolf-worshipping cult. If only Mr Oaten had cared to name the psychiatrist he has been seeing for all these years, I would call him and moot the possibility that the MP and his family were in the thrall of some terrible evil – probably lupine – and advise him to flag down the Tardis without delay.

Not that Mark hasn't done his best to impose a narrative on it all, complete with references to 'demons', and that headline-grabbing suggestion that it was because he couldn't handle going bald. Oh, and this old chestnut: 'It's as if I was daring the world to bring [my career] crashing down.'

It's rather difficult not to recall Ron Davies's explanation of that business on Clapham Common, which he described as 'a moment of madness'. Again, I put it to you that far from the incident being some sudden porphyric episode, Davies simply likes sexual encounters with men.

By opening up in this manner, Mark Oaten has invited an amateur psychology free-for-all. So let us posit some alternative theories. Given the lack of progress he had evidently made with his shrink, one could view his seeing a psychiatrist at all as a kind of displacement activity. It provides the illusion of taking a problem in hand, while at the same time resolutely resisting the temptation to get to the bottom of it when the answer, you might suggest, should be bleeding obvious.

I do hope that Mark who, understandably, is devoted to his young family, is not in the process of being 'ungayed' – I believe the official term is 'cured' – by himself or his shrink, in the manner of those poor benighted souls persuaded that the Christian communion is much too exclusive to include them in their current state. The longest journey starts with a single step, and we can only hope that by next year Mark will have 'moved on' from blaming all this on male-pattern baldness. Failing that, he could put off the inevitable by devising a whole new syndrome: male-prostitute baldness.

May 11 2006

# HOW MUCH IS A 2P WORTH? ACTUALLY, 3P

## Richard Adams and Patrick Collinson

For the ultra-rich, it involves investing millions in an original Warhol or Picasso. For others, it will be gold, silver or rare stamps. Economists are puzzling over how almost every type of asset – commodities, property, precious metals, shares, bonds and even art – are testing dizzying new price levels.

This parallel rise in all asset prices is unheard of in economic history. Traditionally, when commodities go up, stock markets go down. Stock markets don't like soaring commodity prices, which have in the past translated rapidly into higher inflation and higher interest rates.

But the link appears – for now – to have broken. This week global stock markets hit a new high, finally surpassing the 'new economy' peak during the dotcom boom of 1999 – 2000. The Dow Jones average in New York rose again yesterday, and is just a few points short of its all-time high of 11,722 on January 19 2000.

So, now a way has emerged for the more humble investor to make a killing on the international markets. Yesterday the price of copper hit an all-time record of $8,000 a tonne, driven by frantic buying and selling by commodity brokers and futures traders. But a little-noticed fact is that every 2p piece made before 1992 is 97% copper – meaning that each coin contains 6.9g of the metal. Collect together 145 of them, and you've got a kilo's worth of copper. Now, just find another 999kg, a total of 145,000 coins, and you've got a tonne.

On their face value, those coins are worth just £2,900. But taking them to a scrap merchant and selling them on the open market for their metal content will make you a cool £1,500 profit, especially if you throw in the 25kg of zinc that are also sitting in your goldmine of loose change. The same trick can be pulled off with pennies, so long as they were circulated before September 1992, when the Royal Mint introduced new 1p and 2p coins made from steel with only a thin copper plating. For a 50% return on an original investment, that's very good even for the likes of George Soros.

It's not just copper that is booming in price: gold this week broke through the $700-an-ounce level for the first time in 25 years, representing a 250% gain since 2001 alone.

In New York, auction houses are achieving breathtaking new prices for modern art, with the buyers believed to be Russian billionaires on an oil and commodity-fuelled spending spree.

At Christie's in New York on Tuesday night, a world record was set for one of Andy Warhol's Campbell's soup cans. The £6.3m paid for *Small Torn Campbell's Soup Can* (1962) was the highest ever for one of the images that heralded the birth of pop art. Works by Damien Hirst and David Hockney also achieved record prices, although nowhere near the £51.5m paid for Picasso's *Dora Maar au Chat* last week.

Just as puzzling is the behaviour of gold. Market folklore has it that gold goes up in price when investors are looking for a safe haven during choppy economic times, yet all the major global indicators – economic growth, inflation and unemployment – are relatively benign.

Meanwhile, the much-heralded UK property crash failed to materialise. Instead the boom moved to the United States, where house prices have surged dramatically.

In the late 1990s market traders talked of the 'goldilocks economy' of surging productivity and growth, to justify eye-watering valuations of some companies. Today the buzzword is the 'super-cycle', an expansion in demand for commodities that could last for decades and which has at its core one factor: China. In the first quarter of 2006 China posted breakneck economic growth of 10.2%, sucking in commodities and guzzling petroleum on a phenomenal scale.

Low interest rates are the underpinning for the super-cycle, providing the cheap money for traders to speculate in assets. But yesterday Legal & General, one of the biggest investors on the London stock market, joined the growing chorus of voices predicting a soggy end to the boom. It warned that global bottlenecks will stoke up inflation and force central banks, led by the US Federal Reserve, to raise interest rates and choke off the boom. Even in China, wages (which are still only 3% of US labour rates) are beginning to rise strongly: in the Shenzhen region, at the core of Chinese manufacturing, workers will receive a 23% rise in minimum wages in July.

Meanwhile, the message from art history is that when sudden wealth on a vast scale is poured into buying art, a slump won't be far away. In 1990 the buyers were Japanese billionaires and the target was Van Goghs. The Japanese industrialist Ryoei Saito stunned the art world by bidding $82.5m for *Portrait of Dr Gachet*. Just weeks later, when the Japanese central bank raised interest rates, the art market collapsed as the loans used to buy the art works went sour.

*Portrait of Dr Gachet* remains the art world's most enduring mystery. Saito died in 1996, and the whereabouts of the Van Gogh masterpiece is today unknown.

May 13 2006

# THE DEAD SOCIALITE LOOK

## Jess Cartner-Morley

Even by the standards of the fashion industry, where political correctness is largely dismissed as the whingeing of those too poor for minks and too fat for minis, this summer's newest 'look' is not for sensitive types. This season, according to *Tatler* magazine, those in the know are aiming for the 'dead socialite' look. For day, this charming moniker translates as an understated-but-expensive get-up of gym-honed legs and salon-blown hair, cashmere sweater, crocodile handbag – a little bit Jackie Onassis, a touch Nan Kempner. Imagine the film *Heathers*, but updated and set in the world of Park Avenue baby showers. For evening, it means something extravagant and opulent, with lots of Pucci: note, for reference, the line of fashion genealogy that runs directly from Talitha Getty in Morocco to Tamara Mellon in Ibiza. The 'mission statement' of the 'dead socialite' look is, according to *Tatler*, to let the world know that you are chic and married but still sexy. (If you can relate to this as a description of your self-image, then the fact that you are also an insufferably smug cow is, I would imagine, so self-evident as to have no need of sartorial signposting.)

What is striking about the look is that it is not confined to the tiny social set of Upper East Side 30-year-olds who dress like their mothers-in-law in the hope of getting their hands on the best of the family earrings. In LA, a west coast version – more theatrical, less uptight – has grown up around the celebrity stylist Rachel Zoe and her 'girls', who include Lindsay Lohan and Nicole Richie. Zoe's girls, like Zoe herself, dress like the coke-snorting trophy wives of 70s Hollywood producers – in other words, like dead socialites. So think, before you buy those bug-eyed Richie-esque sunglasses: what, exactly, are you trying to say?

May 18 2006

# IS THE BNP SECRETLY SMIRKING?

## Joseph Harker

Is it just me, or is anyone else slightly worried about the number of St George's flags flying from road vehicles right now? Of course, these displays of patriotism are to be expected in the build-up to next month's World Cup – which England enters with more confidence than at any time since 1970. This time, though, the flags seem to be on show earlier than ever. The domestic season ended only on Saturday, and until just over a week ago most fans were focused on their own club's desperate struggle for the last few precious league points. Yet in London I've been seeing these flags for two weeks now – since well before the national squad was even announced.

In fact, they started appearing the day after the local elections on May 4. Apart from the Labour meltdown and the Tories getting their first respectable vote for 14 years, the big story of the election was the rise of the British National Party, which gained 28 seats, nearly 20 in London alone. Could it be that many of the England flag-wavers are in fact supporters of this racist party, glorying in their 'victory' and celebrating their racial pride?

Until the 'Three Lions' Euro 96 football tournament hosted in this country, the only place the cross of St George was normally seen was at far-right political rallies. The flag has a long association with racism, intolerance and bigotry. In the past decade, though, the symbol has gone mainstream – you can't pass a petrol station without seeing piles of them on sale – and its old link has largely been forgotten. And though many racial minorities in this country are still instinctively repulsed by the cross, some among them have begun to embrace it.

But are extremists now trying to take advantage of its availability? I've been looking at the drivers of these flag-waving vehicles, and – OK, I admit this isn't exactly scientific – half of them are in white vans, and the rest are white, male, tattooed, pot-bellied 35- to 55-year-olds: exactly the type I've been seeing on TV for the past month complaining about 'our houses going to the asylum seekers', or that 'we're losing control of our country'. I can't tell if these drivers come from Barking and Dagenham, where the BNP gained 11 seats, but that borough is just a short drive from where I live, so who knows?

Since May 4 we have no longer been able to assume that the racist extremists will simply fade away. The biggest fillip they received was when the MP Margaret Hodge told the *Sunday Telegraph* that 8 out of 10 voters in her area were considering voting BNP. This was hugely irresponsible. First, because it was a wild exaggeration – no party has ever had anything like that kind of support. Second, why say it to the Telegraph group, whose views on saving the nation are often not so dissimilar to the BNP's? Third, and most serious, in claiming that such a huge number had BNP sympathies, she helped the local bigots lose their shame. No longer did they feel they should hide their illogical and ignorant prejudices now they'd been told that their neighbours all thought the same. This is the start of a potentially very dangerous path. Once people feel free to espouse these views publicly, talk to TV reporters, call up radio phone-ins, we risk reinforcing and spreading the bigotry.

Now, I wouldn't want to malign all east Londoners (though every time I saw shots of the West Ham fans at last Saturday's FA Cup final I couldn't help thinking: are you from Dagenham, did you vote BNP?), or all overweight male van drivers. And I certainly wouldn't want to deny football fans the right to these fluttering displays of national support come the big kick-off against Paraguay next month. But right now I can't help thinking that the BNP's leaders are secretly smirking every time they see the flag. And, even more, I wouldn't want to do anything that emboldens their hateful doctrine. So, is it just me?

May 19 2006

# THE DA VINCI CODE
# AND THE NEXT POPE

Peter Bradshaw

Millions of readers have devoured Dan Brown's Vatican conspiracy thriller about the handsome American scholar Robert Langdon and his gamine French sidekick Sophie Neveu, who uncover shocking secrets about the 900-year-old cult the Priory of Sion, formed to guard the terrifying truth about Jesus Christ and his relationship with Mary Madgalene – a secret encoded in the paintings of top Priory of Sion member Leonardo da Vinci. Now a movie, starring Tom Hanks and Audrey 'Amelie' Tautou, has faithfully brought the distinctive qualities of Brown's prose to the silver screen.

I was approached to join the Priory of Sion as an undergraduate at Cambridge. I was a naive, beardless youth reading for the Church, and an eminent literary scholar had invited me to tea in his rooms in Magdalene College. Pushing a subtly recessed mahogany panel, he opened a secret door and I was led, wonderingly, into the gigantic underground vault beneath that college, rarely, if ever, shown to outsiders. An inner chamber, lit by flickering candlelight, was thronged with sinister chanting figures in monkish robes, gathered round an enormous silver pentangle. I recognised the former Cabinet minister Norman St John Stevas under one cowl. A female figure, the Prioress of Sion, sat enthroned above them. Suddenly, the chanting stopped, and there was a loud animal squealing as one monk dragged a terrified billy goat into the centre of the pentangle, its hooves skittering frantically on the marble floor. The Prioress drew back her hood and the face of Princess Margaret was revealed, contorted with livid emotion. She stood up, and produced a jewel-encrusted dagger. The floor was soon awash with blood as the Prioress slaughtered Norman St John Stevas in front of the poor animal – and the organisation arranged for a double to take his place.

Priapic dancing followed and then over coffee and petit-fours my host explained to me that in about 20 years' time, with their connivance, a novel describing the Priory's activities would appear, a novel of such deliberate and ineffable clunkiness that no one would believe it. Billions would be mesmerised. The plan was that a film would follow, which would be the same only more so, imitating the jaunty plonking rhythm of the book. It was to be sublimely implausible: the Priory's secret would be safe for another generation.

And so it has come to pass. It has to be the only explanation for this film: a bizarre succession of baffling travelogue escapades taking Hanks and Tautou, as two cardboard cutout characters on the trail of the terrible secret, scampering from the Louvre to Westminster Abbey and a remote place of worship north of the border – decoding away like billy-o with a gun-toting albino monk on their tail. If it's Wednesday, it must be Scotland. Ian McKellen plays the twinkly-eyed British scholar Sir Leigh Teabing who opens their eyes to the truth, Jean Reno is the grizzled Paris cop who suspects them of wrongdoing, and Paul Bettany is the creepo assassin-monk from Opus Dei who mortifies his flesh with a cat-o'-nine-tails and a barbed 'cilice' belt round his thigh. He could have put himself through a lot more agony just by nipping out to Borders for a copy of the book.

Hanks has trendy long hair, an open-necked shirt and modish suit, though he has not attempted the resemblance to Harrison Ford specified in the novel. Tautou models a discreetly professional outfit and a shoulder-length hairstyle, maintained in a state of glossily reflective perfection without the aid of a stylist. Their relationship is tepidly platonic; anything raunchier would be in poor taste for reasons unveiled in the final reel. Chased for days and days, they do not need to eat or sleep or use sentences that ordinary human beings would use. At one stage, our un-dynamic duo find themselves on a red London double-decker bus, jabbering about getting to 'Chelsea library'. I would love to read one of Dan Brown's deadpan descriptions of that remarkable building.

Well, every decoding is another encoding, as the structuralists used to say, and here is a paragraph by Leonardo about cryptography I have discovered in the British Library:

'We none of us are entirely sure that you, the reader, are not just ignoring our elegant devices it is really dangerous to be over-confident about this, or over-analytical, as we can never simply assume that exquisitely crafted codes work – yes, they are often wily and very often I have discovered a lurid symbol which is likely to be a buried message, secret or even a completely and totally clandestine image which has within it an eccentrically ordered and complex nucleus of visual clues, even including some weird xylophones, bizarre yes, but these could be the paintings which will disclose or unveil the most perilous truths to have existed.'

The preceding sentence, I can now reveal, has been written in the Priory of Sion code. You take the first letter from every fourth word, starting with the first: so the first word, then the 5th, then the 9th, the 13th, and so on. It spells out a message about the future of western civilisation that is too terrifying to be stated openly.

May 20 2006

# INSIDE IRAQ'S HIDDEN WAR

## Ghaith Abdul-Ahad

Some men hold paper tissues under their noses, others wrap their kuffiya ends around their mouths. It is a hot and humid day at the city's main morgue, where 20 men stand in a yard, their faces pressed with silent urgency against the bars of a window, next to a white plastic sign that baldly announces the location of 'The Refrigerator'.

Inside sits the clerk of the morgue, his computer monitor turned towards them. Faces flash on the screen: a man with his face blackened and bruised, another man, older, maybe in his 50s, with a white beard and an orange-sized hole in his forehead, and another on a green stretcher, his arms twisted unnaturally behind him.

Occasionally the silence of Baghdad's daily slideshow of death is broken by an appalled act of recognition, as one of the men mumbles, 'No god but the one God.' Or 'God is great.'

So many bodies arrive at the morgue each day – 40 is not unusual on a 'quiet' day – that it is impossible to let relatives in to identify them. Hence the slideshow in the yard outside. The bodies are dumped in sewage plants or irrigation canals, or just in the middle of the street. Many show signs of torture. Every morning a procession of pickup trucks, minibuses and cars line up with their coffins outside the concrete blast walls of the ministry of health to pick up their cargo. One death often courts another. Many Sunnis say the mourners are attacked en route. When they go to retrieve the body of a relative, family members often wait in the car clutching their weapons in anticipation.

The ministry is under the control of the Shia cleric Moqtada al-Sadr, and a large mural of his dead ayatollah father decorates the entrance to the compound. Most of the security guards in the morgue and the ministry are affiliated to his militia, the Mahdi army, one of the militias thought to be behind the sectarian killing going on in their neighbourhoods.

'Why do you want to go inside? Those inside are all terrorists, Sunni terrorists,' said Captain Abu Ahmad, in charge of security at the morgue, when the *Guardian* presented a document granting permission from the ministry of health to visit. 'If you want to see innocent victims, go to the hospitals and see the victims of Sunni terrorism on Shia civilians.'

After months of argument over whether Iraq is teetering on the verge of civil war, a 'national unity' government is due to be inaugurated today. Legislators plan to swear in a prime minister and cabinet, and much will be made in London and Washington of the fact that this completes a democratic transition which began in December with the election of its parliament. But the reality encountered during three weeks behind the barricades of Baghdad's increasingly bloody sectarian conflict has more in common with the 'ethnic cleansing' of the Balkans than the optimistic rhetoric to be heard on the manicured lawns of the embassy compounds and in western capitals.

**The Patriot**
Adel is 26. He is tall and well built, with long, thick, dark hair styled with gel and a thin goatee beard. With his basketball shirt and knee-length shorts, he looks more like a rapper than a vigilante commander. Three years ago, when most of his friends were still reeling from the shock and awe of America's occupation, Ali stepped out of his life as a wealthy playboy from the leafy neighbourhood of Yarmouk in the west of Baghdad, and into the life of a Sunni insurgent.

'When I saw the first American patrol in my street, I went to my room and cried for three days,' he said as we sat in his family's huge living room. He emerged from his bedroom, crossed the street to a school that was used during the war as a Ba'ath party office, collected some RPG (rocket propelled grenade) rounds, a launcher and ammunition, and drove around the neighbourhood looking for American troops. He soon found them.

'You think you are brave and you want to fight for your country and defend your home, but when I stood in front of them with the RPG on my shoulder, my legs were shaking from fear and my body went stiff. I just remember a huge bang and a cloud of dust, and my friend grabbed and pushed me to the car and we drove away. 'Now it's much easier. I am more focused and I know it's a split-second decision: either I kill or get killed.'

For months Adel fought the Americans almost every day, firing RPGs and laying IEDs (improvised explosive devices). His friends mocked his enthusiasm and his talk about the need to defend his country, and started calling him 'The Patriot'.

But it has been a few months since he has taken part in any attacks against the hated occupiers. Adel The Patriot has a new mission. He commands a Sunni vigilante group, a dozen or so men armed with Kalashnikovs and a heavy-calibre machine gun, attempting, they say, to defend their area against raids and 'arrests' made by Shia interior ministry commandos.

It was early afternoon when we met and he had just woken up. He doesn't get much sleep these days. At midnight, as the streets fall silent, Shia death squads roam the streets looking for prey. Adel and his group sit outside and wait. Most of the streets in Yarmouk are barricaded by bits of metal, palm tree trunks, boxes, bricks and cinder blocks. Streets are cut off to make a maze only local people know how to negotiate.

One of Adel's friends was snatched from his shop by men wearing Iraqi police force uniforms, he says. 'They knew the area where his house is was well protected, so they went to his shop.' The friend's body surfaced three days later. His nose had been mutilated, he was handcuffed and left to die in a garbage dump. 'I knew he was dead from the moment he was taken. We feel very angry. Even the people who didn't want to kill the Shia have joined the fight now.'

Adel says 10 Sunnis have been killed in his neighbourhood in the past month. In retaliation 20 Shia were kidnapped and killed by Sunni insurgents. During one week the *Guardian* spent in Yarmouk in May, a grocer, his two brothers and a cousin, a school guard, a generator operator, and four ministry of education employees, all Shia, were killed. Two Sunnis were killed in the same week.

'Look, a full-scale civil war will break out in the next few months. The Kurds only care about their independence. We, the Sunnis, will be crushed – the Shia have more fighters and are better organised, and have more than one leadership. They are supported by the Iranians. We are lost. We don't have leadership and no one is more responsible for our disarray than [Abu Musab al-] Zarqawi, may God curse him,' he said.

The logic of Adel The Patriot's sectarian struggle against the Shia is driving him and his fellow Sunnis into radical new directions. Asked what will save the Sunnis, he replies almost instinctively.

'Our only hope is if the Americans hit the Iranians, and by God's will this day will come very soon, then the Americans will give a medal to anyone who kills a Shia militiaman. When we feel that an American attack on Iran is imminent, I myself will shoot anyone who attacks the Americans, and all the mujahideen will join the US army against the Iranians.

'Most of my fellow mujahideen are not fighting the Americans at the moment, they are too busy killing the Shia, and this is only going to create hatred. If someone kills one of my family, I will do nothing else but kill to avenge their deaths.'

Most of the Shia in Yarmouk and other Sunni areas have left and their young people have joined the Shia militias. So what would Adel do to stop the cycle of violence? 'If I have some money I will pay regular salaries to my men, buy three black Opel cars [the preferred assassination car in Baghdad]. We will kidnap members of Badr brigade [the main Shia militia], we will kill some and get ransom on the other and the ransom money will finance more operations, and I can have my own mujahideen faction.'

Later he and two friends explain how to distinguish a Sunni from a Shia. One of says: 'The Shia are darker. Sunnis have coloured eyes. Shia foreheads are smaller. Sunnis walk with arms away from the body. It's so easy: look at that man, the way he is walking he is obviously a Sunni.'

### The Shia
No one tries to move the body of a man in grimy tracksuit bottoms, lying in Mu'alemeen Street, in Dora. A grocery store continues to sell vegetables across the street, and two women carrying plastic bags pass

by the body, a pool of dried blood around his head, without looking.

'He is a Shia, no one can move him. If anyone tries to touch the body, they will be killed. The mujahideen want him to rot in the street in front of his family and friends,' a local man says.

Dora used to be one of Baghdad's most mixed neighbourhoods. Shia, Sunnis and Christians all lived together. The Christians were the first to leave after attacks on their churches. They were followed by the Shia, killed and intimidated by Sunni insurgents. Then came the Shia retaliation, raids by interior ministry commandos, Mahdi army death squads scores of Sunni men detained only for their mutilated bodies to reappear later.

Today gun battles erupt every week, between Sunnis defending their patch against the Shia militias or Shia defending their homes against the Sunni insurgents.

Abu Muhammad's family is one of two Shia families left in his street. The other 18 have all left. To survive, he has to pretend he is a Sunni. He stood in front of his house and shouted insults at the Shia government. He stopped calling two of his sons by their real Shia names. He bought a Kalashnikov and gave it to the local mujahideen. Even the screen on his mobile announces 'the one of Fallujah', a reference to the battle between insurgents and US forces that is iconic to many Sunnis.

'What can I do? I have to make sure that they don't think that I am Shia. Every time I leave the house I say my prayers and kiss my children as if I am not going to see them again.'

In Karrada, another Shia neighbourhood, a man speaks with detachment about the Shia death squads. 'It's really bad what the Shia forces are doing now, but truth has to be said: most of the Sunnis who get killed deserve it. The terrorists come from the Sunni community. They are not insurgents themselves, they have cousins who are insurgents. For three years now the Shia have been patient, and now Sunnis have to see what the Shia can do.'

Sheikh Omar – director of the human rights office of the Iraqi Islamic party, one of the leading Sunni political groups – is explaining how it was all the Americans' fault for empowering Shia militia to fight the insurgency, when a man opens the door and rushs in.

'Sheikh, the ministry commandos are attacking the Mahdiya area in Dora and people are in the mosque fighting back.'

Phone calls followed. One report spoke of a force of 20 interior ministry vehicles. Sheikh Omar bashes out a number on his mobile phone.

'We are receiving reports that a force of 20 ministry of interior commandos are attacking this Sunni area and people are fighting back from the mosque. Can you ask Colonel Paul to send his troops? If our people see the Americans, we will stop fighting.'

A couple of streets from Abu Muhammad's house, in an empty house deserted by its Shia occupants, five Sunni gunmen sit on the roof, one crouched behind the roof parapet, his rifles stuck through a breeze bloc. They are the local neighbourhood watch. An old woman with a white headscarf brings them a tray of glasses of tea. 'May God protect you, my sons,' she says.

One of the gunmen explains: 'We never fire in the morning – we don't want to expose where we are.'

Back in Yarmouk, not far from Adel The Patriot's house, a group of eight-year-olds gather by a makeshift barricade, armed with plastic pistols and sunglasses. Their 'commander', a 12-year-old, orders them to pull a log of wood away from their make-believe checkpoint, to let a car through.

But then a police pickup truck appears, its Shia occupants wearing balaclavas. The children instinctively take up firing positions with their plastic Kalashnikovs.

The police pickup takes a right and disappears up a sidestreet. The kids cheer and shout.

*Some people's names have been changed to protect their identity.*

# OFF-PEAK

## Jenni Russell

In a scathing report published last Friday, the transport select committee attacked the chaotic, impenetrable and costly system of train fares in Britain. Its call for government action was welcome and overdue. For the uninitiated, buying a rail ticket has become a surreal exercise in confusion and misinformation. It's more akin to buying a lottery ticket than paying for a service.

In the week before Easter, I tried to book an off-peak day-return ticket for a teenager from Swindon to London. The one message I have understood from the railways is that it's cheaper to book in advance. So while leaving Paddington on Monday night, I queued to get a ticket for Wednesday. The helpful assistant checked his computer, and said all the cheap tickets had gone. The journey would cost more than £30 in each direction for a trip of little more than an hour each way.

I couldn't believe that could be right, so I rang the national rail inquiry line the next morning. I was quoted £41 for the outward journey, and £37 for the return. Almost £80 for a teenager to spend a day in London? We could have bought a railcard to cut the cost by a third, but that would only have been worthwhile if we expected to take other journeys. At those prices, we didn't.

Stunned, we researched coaches. It was true that they took twice as long, but the fare was £15, and paying for it could not have been simpler. A text message confirming the booking was sent to the teenager's phone.

It was only while researching this piece that I discovered that both the assistants I had talked to were giving the wrong advice. An off-peak saver return is always available on certain, restricted trains on the day for £37 – expensive, but not outrageously so. But if the staff didn't know that, how was a passenger expected to guess?

Since privatisation, the train-pricing system has become so astonishingly complex that almost no one understands it. Twenty years ago, there were just five types of tickets on sale – season, cheap day return, standard day return, ordinary and saver. Their conditions were easily understood. Now the National Fares Manual lists more than 70 fares, governed by 776 validity conditions, on 111 A4-sized pages. The national fares themselves take up 5,000 pages in eight A4-sized manuals.

The consequence is that it's impossible to guarantee to passengers that they are getting the cheapest fare available. Anomalies abound. Travel from Leicester to Carlisle and you will be charged £23. Go from Melton Mowbray to Carlisle, via Leicester, and the fare is £63.40. Yet a ticket from Melton Mowbray to Leicester can be just £5, so anyone in the know would buy two separate tickets and more than halve their costs. But you would need local knowledge to know that it is not an option the computer would offer.

Even regular passengers are utterly bemused by the prices. An architect currently travelling from London to Leicester twice a week books his tickets in advance online and finds they cost anything from £20 to £42, for no reason that he can determine. The sites, he says, are becoming like EasyJet's, with prices changing every day. A peak-time journey is £82, making it far cheaper to drive. It is playing havoc with his budget, and his time. He contrasts the system with France's unitary, subsidised, state-owned railway, where all tickets are charged per kilometre, making travel transparent and inexpensive.

A pensioner using a railcard for a day return from Brighton to Evesham can find himself paying any of 11 different fares, from £24.30 to £92.80, depending on which trains he happens to book. Some trains may have 150 cheap seats allocated on one day, on another day – or on another service – there may be only 50. Passengers wanting inexpensive seats are often told to ring every day, to catch the moment when the cheap ones are released. In the words of the chief executive of GNER, it would 'drive you spare slogging through every train' in order to identify the bargains.

There is widespread unhappiness about the cost and complexity of the system. This year, the national passenger survey showed that only 45% of travellers felt that their tickets offered value for money.

Yet if passengers are worried now, the situation may be about to get even worse. Ever since privatisation, the government has regulated certain railway fares – season tickets, cheap day returns and savers – limiting the increases allowed. But now the rail industry is lobbying hard to be allowed to scrap savers, which are available off-peak on the day, and the government is seriously considering their proposal. Yet if savers go, the cost of unplanned travel will rocket. Currently, a saver return to Manchester is £57.10. An ordinary return is £202.

The rail companies' argument for change is that they must be allowed to price tickets in line with what the market will bear. In many areas they are running at capacity and beyond, with hugely overcrowded trains. Train journeys have risen by 40% in 10 years, with no significant increase in the railways' capacity. As some of the companies told the select committee, one of their strategies is to price people off the trains by raising peak fares. Conversely, they argue, they want greater freedom to entice people on to little-used trains by replacing savers with more advance-purchase tickets.

As businesses, the companies' position is logical, and the government may find their argument appealing, because the Treasury is desperate to cut the railways' rising costs. Since privatisation, the costs involved in running a railway of different fiefdoms, and in giving profits to shareholders, have meant that public subsidy to the industry has tripled in real terms, to £4.7bn a year.

But railways will never be simply a business. No railway in the world can make a genuine profit on its costs. The question is only ever how a government splits the expense between passengers and taxpayers, how it manages costs, and what social, political and environmental purpose it expects a railway to serve.

Here the select committee is categorical: the government has failed. The railways are being run inefficiently in the short-term interests of the companies, not the public interest. They swallow vast amounts of public money, and must now be regulated to make fares simple and affordable for all.

Ten years ago, John Prescott promised an integrated transport policy, with rail at its heart. It hasn't happened. Yet with oil prices soaring and global warming taking off, there has never been a more important time to encourage people to take to rail rather than road. Our transport policy doesn't do that. Government subsidies to roads mean that the real cost of motoring has been falling, while the cost of rail rises. Inter-city trains are running on a capacity of 40% to 45%, while passengers who can't afford it drive instead.

But public-policy needs cannot be properly met, capacity increased, or costs substantially cut until privatisation is reversed. It's time for the government to recognise that Tony Blair was absolutely right when he condemned the illogicality and expense of privatisation more than a decade ago. As the current franchises for the different operating companies come to an end, each of them should be taken back into public ownership, just as the private company Railtrack has been replaced by the not-for-profit Network Rail. If we do none of those things, and leave rail fares to the pressures of the market, then trains will increasingly become the preserve of the rich.

May 29 2006

# ROBUST DEBATE ON COMMENT IS FREE

## Georgina Henry

When we launched Comment Is Free, I saw it mainly as a good way to extend the range of opinion carried by the *Guardian*. The comment pages in print are crowded and lots of people with interesting views were denied a platform. The web was the obvious place to go.

Establishing a collective, group blog was, to my un-web-educated eye, more a practical solution than a philosophical one. We wanted to recruit hundreds of people – academics, politicians, scientists, environmentalists, writers, etc – and encourage them to blog as and when they wanted. We wanted to foster all shades of opinion. We had a tiny budget – a fraction of that spent on the paper comment pages – so we needed to offer freedom and space to write instead of big fees.

We also wanted to get our professional columnists to engage with readers by allowing people to comment instantly on their articles, but I admit I thought only in passing about reader reaction and the kinds of conversation the site might provoke online. What I did not foresee was that two months on I would find myself in the middle of a raging argument about professionalism versus amateurism – with sub-headings covering language, anonymity, accountability, democracy, censorship and the art of conversation.

For those who have dwelt in the world of bloggers for years, none of this will come as a surprise. But for journalists who have spent a lifetime in print it has been a rude shock. On good days I think this is the most exciting new frontier for journalism – the immediacy of the debate, the excitement at watching readers engage with the big (and occasionally trivial) issues of the day with wit, verve and insight make print seem sluggish, out of date, even a bit dull.

Other days, when I have spent hours removing the anti-semitism and

Islamophobia that dances round any piece about Israel/Palestine, and the incoherent abuse, the swearing, the false statements, the ill-disguised misogyny, the intimidation and the downright nastiness that fuels so many comments, I wonder whether *Guardian* values – free comment, but fair comment too – are in danger of being drowned out in an anarchic, unmoderated medium populated, it seems, by weird men. I look with fondness at the rigorously edited paper, and the polite discourse on the letters page.

The answer for most media companies developing blogs (although no one is doing anything quite like Comment Is Free) is to pre-moderate comments. We have deliberately decided against that, only requiring commenters to register, because we want to keep the conversation as free-flowing as possible. So what to do?

Stung by one particularly brutal comment on a piece by a young Muslim woman we had recruited to blog, I did what Emily Bell, editor of *Guardian Unlimited*, advised and entered the fray myself. Why, I asked in an end-of-the-week post, was it necessary for commenters to personally abuse those with whom they disagreed? Why did so many resort to swearing to make their point? Would they behave like this if they weren't hiding behind the anonymity of their screen names?

Some of the response was predictable (you can read it at http://commentisfree.guardian.co.uk/georgina_henry/2006/05/post_84- .html) – but I was struck by how thoughtful others were. And funny. Commenters whose names struck fear in me when I saw them popping up on our bloggers threads turned out to be unexpectedly reasonable. While they fiercely defended their right to take on the professionals, there were many useful bits of advice about the rules of engagement.

Last week Jackie Ashley and Polly Toynbee joined in. Ashley robustly defended professional columnists – in her case, with 25 years of experience of political reporting. She wasn't claiming that she always knew more than her readers, but the least they could do was tell her so without insulting her. Toynbee attacked the anonymity of commenters and the aggression of their discourse – and revealed the contents of a particularly obnoxious email she had received that morning. (She got quite a lot of sympathy in return.) Both got plaudits from some of their fiercest critics for getting down and dirty and joining the discussion.

Is Bell right that the way to raise the standard of debate on the site is to engage properly with readers? In the long term we may look at some system that helps us to rate comments to keep out the dross, but in the meantime, I am all for engagement. It has been an education.

SUMMER

# THE BEDSER BROTHERS: SO CLOSE, YET SO FAR APART

## David McKie

Though I knew it wasn't my fault, I always, as I grew up, felt guilty about Eric Bedser. That's Eric Bedser, cricketer, twin brother of the more famous Alec, who died last week at the age of 87. They joined Surrey together – they did everything together, throughout their lives – in 1938, at the age of 19, Alec went on to become one of England's most famous cricketers: an opening bowler who took nearly 2,000 wickets in first-class cricket at an average of 20.4, and 236 in Tests at an average of 24.9, who played the game all round the world and was feted in every cricketing country, became chairman of the selectors, was awarded the Order of the British Empire and later elevated to Commander and made it into *Who's Who*.

As opposed to Eric, a decent county all-rounder – never selected for England, though he did once play in a Test trial – whose chief claim to fame thoughout his career was his twinship with Alec. You did not have to be hooked on cricket to taste the poignancy here. Romantic egalitarians, a tribe to which I belonged in those days (and still do) grieved on Eric's behalf, even if Eric himself never displayed the mildest sign of resentment, and grieved even more for the knowledge that Eric's diminished role seemed to have turned on the toss of a coin.

Both began, Eric's obituarists told us, as fast-medium bowlers with actions so nearly identical that even their coaches could not tell them apart. Faced with the problem that Surrey had room for only one new fast-medium bowler, the brothers agreed to toss for that honour, with the loser giving up fast bowling and taking up off-spin instead. Some obituaries described this account as a legend, but it's all set out in the Bedser autobiography (Alec's, of course, not Eric's), *Twin Ambitions*. 'Looking back,' Alec wrote, 'it emerges as one of the most fateful things we ever did.'

A further irony: the twins were good enough at football to play for the Surrey youth side and to dream of joining Arsenal. They both played in the same position, of course, as full-backs, and quite possibly Eric was better since he, rather than Alec, captained their school team.

When they came – on the eve of the second world war, which then cut half a decade out of their cricket careers – to choose between football and cricket, the summer game won. Nowadays, most young men making this choice would contemplate its superior rewards, its greater glamour and fame, and settle for football. Who knows: perhaps, had they made that choice, Alec might have emerged as Eric's less famous brother or perhaps, after the war, Bedser and Bedser might have supplanted Hardwick and Scott as England's full-back pairing. But it did not happen. There was always, too, as the potency of Alec's bowling began to decline, the dream of some later flowering that would somehow carry Eric into the England side. He did play on after Alec retired, but still as county journeyman, never as the star.

Such relationships have sometimes bred the most bitter envy. Abel's superior status – he was a shepherd, Cain a mere tiller of soil – led one of the first pair of siblings to slay the other. And Eric, I note, was born 10 minutes ahead of Alec. There's another irony there. Had they been not the sons of a Woking bricklayer but the progeny, let us say, of the 15th Marquis of Lucre, Eric, on the death of their father, would have inherited the great house in its acres of luscious parkland, the stablesful of fabulous horses, the Van Dycks and the minor Rembrandt, the title and the seat in the Lords, whereas Alec would never have been more than the Hon, and would probably have been ordered to make his career in the army, the fate most often reserved for a second son, living for the rest of his days with the sense of what might have been.

Yet the twins, who never married, lived together in what looked like unwavering harmony for the rest of their lives. 'Our absolute and complete affinity,' Eric wrote, 'is hard to explain, but is true and very real to us. Our lives have been so close that we are, for all purposes, one.' In that sense, Alec's huge success was Eric's too, and no one else had any right to complain on Eric's behalf. Even so, their story – two people all but identical in appearance, inherent talent and temperament, whose

At the World Cup 2006, Wayne Rooney is sent off during the England v Portugal quarter-final match by referee Horacio Rlizondo. (TOM JENKINS)

*Overleaf:* At a mass grave in Tyre, southern Lebanon, coffins of people killed in Israeli air strikes during the month-long conflict are lined up for burial by the light of ambulances and a Lebanese army lorry.
(SEAN SMITH/ GUARDIAN)

A group of boys leap in to the river Taff in Wales as the British heatwave reaches its peak. (WALES NEWS SERVICE)

In the village of Kuz Ganrshal, in Shangla province, Pakistan, young girls walk in the snow between the scattered houses. The people of Kuz Ganrshal were unprepared to move to refugee camps after last year's earthquake, preferring to live up to five families a home instead. (DAN CHUNG/GUARDIAN)

lives arrived at such different outcomes – always seemed to me a powerful example of how grossly unfair life can be. But of course you knew that already.

# UNITED 93: I NEEDED TO LIE DOWN IN A DARKENED ROOM AFTERWARDS. SO WILL YOU

## Peter Bradshaw

What other subject is there? What other event is there? Nothing is so important, so inextinguishably mind-boggling as the terrorist kamikaze flights of 9/11. Al-Qaida gave the world a situationist spectacle that dwarfed anything from the conventional workshops of politics and culture. Since then, Hollywood has indirectly registered tremors from Ground Zero, but here is the first feature film to tackle the terrible day head on, and Paul Greengrass has delivered a blazingly powerful and gripping recreation of the fourth abortive hijacking. It is conceived in a docu-style similar to *Bloody Sunday*, his movie about the 1972 civil rights march in Northern Ireland. He does not use stars or recognisable faces, and many of the characters in the air traffic control scenes are played by the actual participants themselves.

This is an anti-*Titanic* for the multiplexes – a real-life disaster movie with no Leo and Kate and no survivors: only terrorists whose emotional lives are relentlessly blank, and heroes with no backstory. Greengrass reconstructs the story of the hijacked plane that failed to reach its target (the Capitol dome in Washington DC) almost certainly owing to a desperate uprising by the passengers themselves, who were aware of the WTC crashes from mobile phonecalls home, and who finally stormed the cabin, where terrorists were flying the plane. With unbearable, claustrophobic severity, Greengrass keeps most of this final act inside the aircraft itself.

The director is able to exploit the remarkable fact that the sequence of events, from the first plane crashing into the World Trade Centre at a quarter to nine, to the fourth plane ditching into a field in Shanksville, Pennsylvania, at three minutes past 10, fits with horrible irony inside conventional feature film length, and he is able to unfold the story in real time. It is at this point that a critic might wish to say: caution, spoilers ahead. But we all know, or think we know, how the story of *United 93* comes out, and this is what makes the film such a gut-wrenching example of ordeal cinema. When the lights go down, your heartrate will inexorably start to climb. After about half an hour I was having difficulty breathing. I wasn't the only one. The whole row I was in sounded like an outing of emphysema patients.

Every last tiny detail is drenched with unbearable tension, especially at the very beginning. Every gesture, every look, every innocent greeting, every puzzled exchange of glances over the air-traffic scopes, every panicky call between the civil air authority and the military – all amplified, deafeningly, in pure meaning. And the first scenes in which the United 93 passengers enter the plane for their dull, routine early-morning flight are almost unwatchable. These passengers are quite unlike the cross-section of America much mocked in *Airplane!* – with the singing nun and the cute kid – neither are they vividly drawn individuals with ingeniously imagined present or future inter-connections, like the cast of TV's *Lost*. They are affluent professionals from pretty much the same caste, with no great interest in each other, and nothing in common except their fate. And all these people are ghosts, all of them dead men and dead women walking. When they are politely asked to pay attention to the 'safety' procedures, ordinary pre-9/11 reality all but snaps in two under the weight of historical irony.

But what does happen at the end of the story? In his memorial address, President Bush implied that the passengers committed an act of tragic self-immolation, rather than see the Capitol destroyed. Is that what happened? Greengrass evidently disagrees. In his vision, the passengers have a quixotic idea of using one passenger, a trained pilot, to wrest control and bring the plane down safely to the ground – a Hollywood ending, perhaps. But there is something very un-Hollywood in Greengrass's refusal to confirm that without the passengers' action they would have hit the Capitol. On the contrary, his script shows the terrorists making a miscalculation of their own.

*United 93* is growing, in popular legend, into the tragic and redemptive part of the 9/11 story: America's act of Sobibor defiance. It is a myth-making that is growing in parallel with jabbering conspiracy theories that the plane was shot down by US air force jets and the whole passenger-action story is a cover-up. On that latter point, Greengrass's movie shows us that it is easy to be wise after the event. It is a reminder of how unthinkable 9/11 was, of how all too likely it was that the civil and military authorities would not have mobilised in time, and that any action would indeed have to come from the passengers themselves. The film is at any rate fiercely critical of Bush and Cheney, who are shown being quite unreachable by the authorities, desperate for leadership and guidance.

*United 93* does not offer the political or analytical dimension of Antonia Bird and Ronan Bennett's 9/11 docu-drama *Hamburg Cell*. There is no analysis or explanation. The movie just lives inside that stunned, astonished 90 minutes of horror between one epoch and the next – and there is, to my mind, an overwhelming dramatic justification for simply attempting to face, directly, the terrible moment itself. The film might, I suspect, have to be viewed through an obtuse fog of punditry from those who feel that it is insufficiently anti-Bush. It shouldn't matter. Paul Greengrass and his cinematographer, Barry Ackroyd, have created an intestinally powerful and magnificent memorial to the passengers of that doomed flight. It is the film of the year. I needed to lie down in a darkened room afterwards. So will you.

June 10 2006

# INDIA AND CHINA NEED A NEW WAY OF BECOMING MODERN

## Pankaj Mishra

In the mid-19th century Karl Marx claimed that European colonisers, though corrupt and violent, were the 'unconscious tool of history' that would propel India and China into modernity. He described the backward 'Asiatic mode of production', defined by the absence of private ownership and the presence of a rigid, centralised form of government that prevents change and modernisation.

Such views prompted Edward Said to denounce Marx as an orientalist who had subsumed India and China into a narrative of human progress designed by and for Europeans. But nothing Marx said about Asia would ever be as influential or widely disseminated as the recent idea in the west that free market capitalism has finally awakened India and China from their long Asiatic slumber.

If the rise of India and China seems dramatic, it is because not so long ago India appeared in the western imagination as a poor, backward and often violent nation. With its needy millions and Luddite communist regime, China seemed sunk even deeper into darkness.

Now, abruptly, we are told that India and China are economic giants, driving world growth by converging on the European model of modernity. Francis Fukuyama first outlined this post-cold war ideology of globalisation by claiming in his 1992 book, *The End of History*, that western liberal democracy, based on private property, free markets and regular elections, was the terminus of historical development. Consecrated annually in Davos, and circulated in business-class lounges around the world, this quasi-teleological view increasingly shapes the beliefs and policies of western political, business and media elites.

The attempt to explain – and change – the world by exalting the apparently unique western virtues of free market capitalism and democracy may seem to have run into problems lately. Failed experiments with unfettered capitalism have helped install authoritarian rightwing and populist leftwing regimes in Russia and Latin America respectively. The recent irruptions of radical Islam, and the war in Iraq, have muddied further the image of a world rushing to embrace victorious western values.

Nevertheless, the abrupt rise of the two biggest countries of the orient reaffirms the faith expressed eloquently by the American columnist Thomas Friedman: that globalising free market capitalism and democracy will enable much of the world's population to reach the summit of material plenitude, political stability and social security, where western societies apparently reside.

It would be nice to imagine the spirit of altruism behind this generous desire to share the west's good fortune. But today China offers western corporations a tempting market of more than a billion customers and a seemingly endless source of cheap labour, as does India.

Indian and Chinese elites borrow no less eagerly than their western counterparts from the discourse of neo-orientalism as they attribute India and China's recent economic growth to the free markets they embraced in the 80s and 90s. But even a casual glance at their claims will reveal them to be caricatures of a complex political and economic reality.

India registered its most impressive gains from 1951 to 1980, after emerging from more than two centuries of systematic colonial exploitation, during which it was, in effect, deindustrialised. Until 1980 India achieved an average annual economic growth of 3.5% – as much as most countries achieved. In this period India's much derided socialistic economy also helped create the country's industrial capacity.

Much popular literature about China, such as Jung Chang's recent biography of Mao, makes it seem as though China did little after the communist revolution in 1949 but lurch from one disaster to another. In fact, China's national income under a planned economy grew fivefold between 1952 and 1978. Though wages were low, the welfare system – the famous 'iron rice bowl' – guaranteed lifetime employment, pensions, healthcare and other benefits that created a high degree of personal security.

Economic reforms in the 80s focused on boosting export-oriented industries on the coast. They made China a huge sweatshop for the west's cheap goods and gave it an average annual growth of 10%. It may be tempting to credit the invisible hand of the free market for this, but, as in the so-called 'Asian tiger' economies, the Chinese state has carefully regulated domestic industry and foreign trade and investment, besides maintaining control of public services.

However, economic reforms, geared to creating wealth in urban areas, have smashed the iron rice bowl and caused severe inflation. The devolution of power to provincial governments, as demanded by free-marketeers, has led to unchecked corruption. The protests in Tiananmen Square, seen by many outside China as demands for western-style freedom and democracy, were fuelled by mass rage at the dismantling of the old welfare state: inflation, for instance, reached 25% in early 1989 after remaining well below 2% for much of the Maoist era. China is now one of the most unequal countries in the world, even more so than the US.

In India, too, the pursuit of economic growth at all costs has created a gaudy elite but has also widened already alarming social and economic disparities. Facilities for healthcare and primary education have deteriorated. Economic growth, confined to urban centres, is largely jobless. Up to a third of Indians live with extreme poverty and deprivation. And militant communist movements have erupted in the poorest, most populous states.

Still, modernising India and China have become sources of existential and ideological self-affirmation for western elites, who tend to ignore anything that challenges their articles of faith – free markets and democracy – or suggests an arduous complexity.

The neo-orientalist reconceptualising of India and China ignores or suppresses large aspects of their recent history. It also fails to reckon fully with the tortured and often tragic experience of modern development. The disasters occasionally seen in the western media – the violence in Kashmir that has claimed more than 80,000 lives in the last decade and a half, the destruction of the environment and the uprooting of nearly 200 million people from their rural habitats in China – can be explained away by reference to the logic of development as manifested in Europe's history.

But the west itself has begun to feel the pain of this transition. As China's hunger for energy raises the price of oil, its cheap exports undermine the once-strong economies of Italy and Germany and it puts white-collar workers out of jobs in America. It is also true that Europe's own transition to its present state of stability and affluence was more than just painful. It involved imperial conquests, ethnic cleansing and many minor and two major wars – involving the murder and displacement of countless millions.

As India and China rise with their consumerist middle classes in a world of finite energy resources, it is easy to imagine that this century will be ravaged by the kind of economic rivalries and military conflicts that made the last century so violent. In any case, the hope that fuels the pursuit of endless economic growth – that billions of customers in India and China will one day enjoy the lifestyles of Europeans and Americans – is an absurd and dangerous fantasy. It condemns the global environment to early destruction, and looks set to create reservoirs of nihilistic rage and disappointment among hundreds of millions of have-nots.

Many intellectuals and activists in India and China grapple with this challenge of modernity every day, knowing well the disasters that lie in wait if they fail. In the meantime, we in the west will do well to dismantle the illusions of neo-orientalism – the most powerful and far-reaching yet of the many accounts of the orient shaped by western self-perceptions and self-interest. For peace in this century depends on India and China finding a less calamitous way of becoming modern.

June 16 2006

# AN ENCOUNTER WITH
# MELANIE PHILLIPS

## Jackie Ashley

Driving to my rendezvous with Melanie Phillips, scourge of the *Guardian*-reading liberal establishment, voice of rightwing moral outrage, and reflecting on her relationship with this paper, it seemed to me like the aftermath of a vicious divorce, in which both parties were obsessed with the other. Phillips, once a *Guardian* staffer, now star columnist at the *Daily Mail*, as well as being a regular on *The Moral Maze* and *Question Time*, is renowned for her scathing criticism of this country's moral and cultural malaise. Her world view, whether she is writing about the inadequacies of the education system or the sanctity of marriage, seem a world away from *Guardian* values now. She clearly sees the split in the same way.

'I worked for Guardian Newspapers for the best part of 20 years and I regard it as a bit like a family from whom one has had a terrible divorce. I look back with enormous affection at what was, and yet the relationship broke down, and that's very sad.' Acknowledging the mutual fascination, she adds: 'I think that's simply because I am an apostate and there is no one who is more hated than an apostate.' She goes on to talk of the *Guardian*'s 'rage' and 'vilification'. Within minutes she is repeatedly accusing me of misrepresenting her views and failing to understand her new book. Almost as soon as I get home, a long protest email has arrived, copied to the *Guardian*'s editor, Alan Rusbridger, claiming that I had misunderstood almost everything she stands for and warning about 'the possible inflammatory consequences of any misrepresentation of my views'.

Perhaps I should have expected that. Phillips is a renowned controversialist whose spare, lean frame seems to be sustained by argument rather than food and drink. She arrives at a French cafe in

Chiswick, west London, tense and intense, in a pink shirt, and orders only black coffee.

We are here to discuss her new book, titled *Londonistan: How Britain Is Creating a Terror State Within*. It argues that anti-semitism and liberal weakness have turned London into 'the epicentre of Islamic militancy in Europe'. Britain, she says, 'is currently locked into such a spiral of decadence, self-loathing and sentimentality that it is incapable of seeing that it is setting itself up for cultural immolation'. She concludes that 'the emergence of Londonistan should be of the greatest concern to the free world.'

This danger has been caused by decadence: 'Among Britain's governing class – the intelligentsia, its media, its politicians, its judiciary, its church and even its police – a broader and deeper pathology has allowed and even encouraged Londonistan to develop.'

Throughout the book there are shards of evidence and penetrating questions that deserve to be at the centre of political debate. Did the security services in the 80s and 90s take a naive and complacent view of the growth of extreme Islamist cells run from London by political exiles, thinking that they wouldn't bite the hand that fed them? Have we got the right balance between protecting and promoting the rights and languages of minorities on the one hand, and the safety and culture of the majority on the other? Is the left overinfluenced by the Palestinian question, and too ready to close its eyes to the brutal realities of extreme Islamist thinking and practice?

Certainly, we should discuss these matters. We are in a country with a fast-growing and increasingly assertive Muslim minority. Relations between them and the Christian or secular majority are of huge importance, as is our security from terrorist attack. And yes, some do use anti-Zionism as a cover for anti-semitism.

The problem is that Phillips's hysterical tone repels frank and thoughtful argument. She is deeply worried about the likelihood of my misrepresenting her, so I will stick to quotation and readers can make up their own minds.

Multiculturalism, she writes, 'has become the driving force of British life, ruthlessly policed by a state-financed army of local and national bureaucrats enforcing a doctrine of state-mandated virtue to promote racial, ethnic and cultural difference and stamp out majority values'. British nationhood is being disembowelled by 'mass immigration, multiculturalism and the onslaught mounted by secular nihilists against the country's Judeo-Christian values'.

It is not just Muslim terrorists: 'They are fuelled by an ideology that itself is non-negotiable and forms a continuum that links peaceful, law-abiding but nevertheless intensely ideological Muslims at one end and murderous jihadists at the other.' If you blinked at the word 'continuum', she means it: the British establishment is 'transfixed by the artificial division it has erected between those who actively espouse violence and those who do not'. Yes, artificial division.

Some columnists may be accused of wilful exaggeration, shouting to be noticed, and then having to go further simply to keep ahead of the game. Phillips is not like this. She is not cynical, or saying it for effect. She means every word and the key to her analysis is her belief in a general collapse of values or, in her words, 'the creation of a debauched and disorderly culture of instant gratification, with disintegrating families, feral children and violence, squalor and vulgarity on the streets'. This is combined, she believes, with a profound anti-semitism among people who do not realise that 'the fight against Israel is not fundamentally about land. It is about hatred of the Jews.' She hears echoes from the past today, talking of 'a climate in Britain that has alarming echoes of Weimar in the 1930s'.

At this point, armed with her book underlined and turned down, page by page, I want to say: 'Blimey, Mel' and, 'Relax, old thing' and, 'You may, just possibly, be going a little over the top.' In fact, in a cheery way, I suggest that some of this may sound a bit 'bonkers'. This really sets her off.

'If the response to the kind of things I'm saying is to pretend that it's not happening, and worse, to characterise people like me as paranoid, hysterical, mad, this is first of all nasty stuff, it's vicious, but it is aimed at shutting down discussion of this completely. It's the tactics used by Stalin to call political opponents mad. But it does have echoes of the 1930s because the Jews then tried to draw attention to what was going on in Germany, and they too were told they were hysterical and paranoid.'

Again, when I say that talking about Weimar and feral children is ruining her own case and that I really don't think things are that bad, she snaps: 'No, I'm sure you don't. That was said to people like me in the 30s, exactly the same kind of argument from the same kind of people ... it is very resonant of Weimar and the prejudice against the Jews is very resonant of Weimar.'

Phillips is quick to take offence. That she has just compared a gentle, quizzical interviewer to a complacent pre-Nazi-era German and to Stalin might – just might – have struck others as potentially offensive. That she finds a continuum between law-abiding, peaceful Muslim fellow citizens and terrorists might – just might – strike others as potentially 'inflammatory'. That her newspaper, the *Daily Mail*, pursues anyone who dares criticise it by vilifying them for years afterwards might – just might – strike her as an example of the intellectual bullying she attacks. And perhaps her emailing my editor before I have even sat down at the keyboard to write this article is, at the very least, unusually defensive behaviour.

Perhaps she simply has not the time to notice. Every question I ask she challenges, everything is a misrepresentation, everything a trap. On a personal level, I'm disposed to like her – she somehow seems vulnerable, tortured. I am genuinely interested, genuinely confused about the source of so much anger. But it's like interviewing a human cactus. Melanie, if everything is so utterly dreadful, in every way, how do you get up in the morning?

'I find your question extraordinary. I am a journalist who believes in social reform, exposing bad things that are putting vulnerable people in an appalling situation. I've never said the whole country is taken up by this. Never. This is a misrepresentation ...' Oh, keep your hair on, Mel. This is the trouble. There are plenty of things we could talk about calmly, some things we would find we agree on. But I'm too busy saying 'Ouch!' and licking the blood off my fingers.

I had been eyeing the cakes in the cafe for some time, but I decide sadly that to order one would be seen as a sign of moral weakness and that now is not the moment.

So where does it come from, this thrilling anger, this medieval self-righteousness of tone? In part, it comes from the intellectual journey she has taken, from being a woman of the left to becoming a cultural conservative. She dates this to 1987 when, as a *Guardian* columnist with two young children, she could not find a decent school and wrote about the failures of education, 'and the world literally fell on me overnight... my colleagues and readers said, "You've gone mad."' Then she started to write about the breakdown of the family and 'that's when the real damage was done, that was it, because people literally started attacking me at parties, purple in the face, waving their *Guardian*s, saying, "You personally have accused me of doing terrible things to my children."' Reacting to such anger must harden you, and she says it took a long time 'to put this together in some coherent world view'.

Perhaps the coherence is part of the problem. Though she accuses the BBC of having a default leftwing position that produces a closed belief system, Phillips's own system now seems tightly closed – immaculate, airless, finished. Everything fits too neatly together. Pressed on this, she denies it: 'I'm very aware all the time that I may be wrong. There is not a day that goes past when I don't think, "Am I wrong?"' Yet reading her book and listening to her argue, the overwhelming impression is of steely self-certainty. Any question marks in her prose are purely rhetorical.

Phillips is married to Joshua Rozenberg, the charming and self-effacing legal editor of the *Daily Telegraph*, and a former BBC employee. The couple have raised two children in west London, while Phillips has made her journey across the political spectrum. She genuinely believes that a cultural malaise now infects the country's intelligentsia, and keeps harping on about Gramsci, 'the iconic thinker of the 1960s', who laid down the blueprint for precisely what happened in Britain: 'The capture of all society's institutions, such as schools, universities, churches, the media, the legal profession, the police and voluntary groups. This intellectual elite was persuaded to sing from the same subversive hymn sheet so that the moral beliefs of the majority would be replaced by those on the margins of society, the perfect ambience in which the Muslim grievance culture could be fanned into the flames of extremism.'

After an hour and a half of tussling with Phillips, I find myself weary and dispirited. Her brow seems permanently furrowed with worry about the state of society, she exudes such pessimism – isn't all this anger immensely tiring for her? 'It's dispiriting having to make the case all the time for what seems to me just basic common sense and to find in the intelligentsia such widespread refusal to accept this.' She is heartened though, she says, by lots of ordinary people out there, willing her on.

Her belief in rising and menacing anti-semitism is striking. As someone of the generation brought up to believe that the Holocaust was the single most important fact of modern history, and anti-semitism the vilest prejudice, I find it hard to believe it so widespread. She vehemently disagrees: 'It is the oldest hatred, it's a hatred that is global and doesn't ever go away.' Did she come across it personally? 'Not often to my face ... not so long ago someone said in the middle of a very pleasant discussion, "Oh, I hate the Jews." I open my paper or listen to the radio, I find it's now an accepted view that there is an international Jewish conspiracy stretching from Jerusalem to Washington, that has subverted the foreign policy of America in the interests of Israel to put the world at risk. Sometimes the word "neocon" is substituted for Jew ... I read constantly that I am one of the many Jewish journalists who have commanded public debate.'

There is, inevitably, much about Israel and hatred of Jews in her book. The notion that it is possible for a non-Jew to deeply dislike the activities of the Israelis in Palestine, to want a free Palestinian state, and yet not be anti-semitic, seems to have been blown away by the demonology of the times. According to Phillips, the Israel-Palestine conflict is not about 'two rival peoples who have a claim' to a piece of earth but about Islam's view of the Jews as 'a cosmic evil'.

Here, I think, is the crux of the problem. She takes every extreme view seriously, follows every argument to its logical conclusion, so that words such as cosmic, immolation, obliteration and hatred litter her speech. She is personally low-voiced, polite and rather old-fashioned – apologising for a phone call that interrupts us, solicitous that my tape recorder is positioned right, keen to pay for our coffee. Yet her prose screams and rends its garments. She grabs the passing reader by the throat and shakes and shakes and doesn't let go. And yes, there are problems in our society. And yes, the government has failed in many respects. And yes, we have a tradition in Britain of tolerance and bending over backwards to understand the other point of view, which can be exploited.

But perhaps the naive, decadent, muddling-along, apologetic old British establishment knows something Phillips has not understood. Perhaps the country has held together and survived exactly by not taking overexcited youths at face value, by assuming that rational argument and debate are the best way to fight extremism. There's a lot to worry about. There always is. But London is London, not Londonistan. The Pennines are not the Khyber Pass and Chiswick, despite the wicked cakes, really isn't Weimar.

June 17 2006

# THE BATTLE OF HUDA GHALIA

## Chris McGreal

Heartrending pictures of 10-year-old Huda Ghalia running wildly along a Gaza beach crying 'Father, Father, Father' and then falling weeping beside his body turned the distraught girl into an instant icon of the Palestinian struggle even before she fully grasped that much of her family was dead.

But the images of the young girl who lost her father, stepmother and five of her siblings as picnicking families fled a barrage of Israeli shells a week ago have become their own battleground. Who and what killed the Ghalia family, and badly maimed a score of other people, has been the subject of an increasingly bitter struggle for truth all week amid accusations that a military investigation clearing the army was a cover-up, that Hamas was really responsible and even that the pictures of Huda's grief were all an act.

However, a *Guardian* investigation into the sequence of events raises new and so far unanswered questions about the Israeli military probe that cleared the army of responsibility. Evidence from hospital records, doctors' testimony and witness accounts challenges the central assertion that the shelling had stopped by the time seven members of the Ghalia family were killed.

In addition, fresh evidence from the US group Human Rights Watch, which offered the first forensic questioning of the army's account, casts doubt on another key claim – that shrapnel taken from the wounded was not from the kind of artillery used to shell Gaza.

The pictures of Huda's traumatic hunt for her father garnered instant sympathy around the world and focused unwelcome attention on Israel's tactic of firing thousands of shells into Gaza over recent weeks, killing more than 20 civilians, to deter Palestinian rocket attacks.

The Israeli prime minister, Ehud Olmert, initially apologised for the killings, but the military swiftly realised it was confronting another PR disaster to rival that of the killing of Mohammed al-Dura, the 12-year-old boy who died in his father's arms amid a barrage of gunfire six years ago and became the first iconic victim of the intifada.

The army quickly convened a committee to investigate the deaths on the beach and, almost as swiftly, absolved itself of responsibility. The committee acknowledged the army fired six shells on and around Beit Lahia beach from artillery inside Israel. But it said that by coincidence a separate explosion – probably a mine planted by Hamas, or a buried old shell – occurred in the same area at about the same time, killing the family.

The army admitted that one of the six shells was unaccounted for but said it was 'impossible', based on location and timings, for the sixth shell to have done the killing. The investigation also concluded that shrapnel taken from the wounded was not from artillery.

The military declared its version of events definitive. Others went further and saw a Palestinian conspiracy. An American pro-Israel pressure group, Camera, which seeks to influence media coverage, went so far as to suggest that the film of Huda Ghalia's trauma was faked: 'Were the bodies moved, was the girl asked to re-enact her discovery for the camera, was the video staged?'

But the army's account quickly came in for criticism, led by a former Pentagon battlefield analyst, Marc Garlasco, investigating for Human Rights Watch. 'You have the crater size, the shrapnel, the types of injuries, their location on the bodies. That all points to a shell dropping from the sky, not explosives under the sand,' he said. 'I've been to hospital and seen the injuries. The doctors say they are primarily to the head and torso. That is consistent with a shell exploding above the ground, not a mine under it.' Mr Garlasco also produced shrapnel from the site apparently marked as a 155mm shell used by the army that day.

The key part of the military's defence hinged on timings. It says it fired shells toward the beach between 4.30pm and 4.48pm, and that the artillery barrage stopped nine minutes before the explosion that killed the Ghalia family. It concluded that the deadly explosion occurred between 4.57pm and 5.10pm based on surveillance of the beach by a drone, that shows people relaxing until just before 5pm and the arrival of an ambulance at 5.15pm.

Major General Meir Kalifi, who headed the army's investigation committee, said the nine-minute gap is too wide for Israel to have been responsible for the deaths. 'I can without doubt say that no means used by the Israeli defence force during this time period caused the incident,' he said.

But hospital records, testimony from doctors and ambulance men, and eyewitness accounts, suggest that the military has the timing of the explosion wrong, and that it occurred while the army was still shelling the beach.

Palestinian officials also question the timing of video showing people relaxing on the beach just before 5pm if the army, by its own admission, was dropping shells close by. Several of those who survived the explosion say it came shortly after two or three other blasts consistent with a pattern of shells falling on the beach.

Among the survivors was Hani Asania. When the shelling began, he grabbed his two young daughters and moved towards his car on the edge of the beach. The Ghalia family was on the sand nearby awaiting a taxi.

'There was an explosion, maybe 500 metres away. Then there was a second, much closer, about two minutes later. People were running from the beach,' said Mr Asania. 'Maybe two minutes later there was a third shell. I could feel the pressure of the blast on my face it was so strong. I saw pieces of people.'

This sequence is backed by others including Huda's brother, Eyham, 20. Annan Ghalia, Huda's uncle, called an ambulance. 'We were sitting on the sand waiting for the taxis, the men on one side and the women on the other. The shell landed closer to the girls,' he said. 'I was screaming for people to help us. No one was coming. After about two minutes I called the ambulance.'

The first ambulance took children to the Kamal Odwan hospital. Its registration book records that five children wounded in the blast were admitted at 5.05pm. The book contains entries before and after the casualties from the beach, all of whom are named, and shows no sign of tampering. The hospital's computer records a blood test taken from a victim at 5.12pm. Human Rights Watch said altering the records would require re-setting the computer's clock.

The distance from the beach to the hospital is 6km. Even at speed, the drive through Beit Lahia's crowded back streets and rough roads would not take less than five minutes and would be slower with wounded patients on board.

Dr Bassam al-Masri, who treated the first wounded at Kamal Odwan, said allowing for a round trip of at least 10 minutes and time to load them, the ambulance would have left the hospital no later than 4.50pm – just two minutes after the Israelis say they stopped shelling. Factoring in additional time for emergency calls and the ambulances to be dispatched, these timings undermine the military's claim that the killer explosion occurred after the shelling stopped.

The first ambulance man to leave another Beid Lahia hospital, the Alwada, and a doctor summoned to work there say they clearly recall the time. The ambulance driver, Khaled Abu Sada, said he received a call from the emergency control room between 4.45pm and 4.50pm. 'I went to look for a nurse to come with me,' he said. 'I left the hospital at 4.50pm and was at the beach by 5pm.'

The Alwada's anaesthetist, Dr Ahmed Mouhana, was woken by a call from a fellow doctor summoning him to the hospital. 'I looked at the time. That's what you do when someone wakes you up. It was 4.55pm,' he said. He left immediately. 'It only takes 10 minutes from my house so I was there by 5.10pm or 5.15pm at the latest. I went to reception and they had already done triage on the children,' he said.

If the hospital records and medical professionals are right, then the emergency call from the beach could not have come in much later than 4.45pm, still during the Israeli shelling.

From the number of shells counted beforehand by the survivors, Mr Garlasco believes the killer shell was one the army records as fired at 4.34pm.

A military spokesman, Captain Jacob Dalal, said the army stood by its interpretation. Military investigators said shrapnel taken from Palestinians treated in Israeli hospitals was not from 155mm shells fired that day. 'We know it's not artillery,' he said. 'It could be a shell of another sort or some other device.'

The military has suggested that the explosion was rigged by Hamas against possible army landings, but Palestinian officials say that would only be an effective strategy if there were a series of mines or if Hamas knew exactly where the Israelis would land.

Mr Garlasco said the metal taken from the victims may be detritus thrown up by the explosion or shards from cars. He said shrapnel collected at the site of the explosion by Human Rights Watch and the Palestinian police was fresh and from artillery shells.

The former Pentagon analyst said that after examining a blood-encrusted piece of shrapnel given to him by the father of a 19-year-old man wounded in the beach explosion, he determined it was a piece of fuse from an artillery shell. 'The likelihood that the Ghalia family was killed by an explosive other than one of the shells fired by the Israeli army is remote.'

Captain Dalal defended the army's investigation. 'We're not trying to cover up anything. We didn't do the investigation to exonerate ourselves. If it was our fire, we'll say it,' he said.

June 20 2006

# OMEGA 3S AND A GREAT COGNITIVE LEAP BACKWARDS

## George Monbiot

The more it is tested, the more compelling the hypothesis becomes. Dyslexia, ADHD, dyspraxia and other neurological problems seem to be associated with a deficiency of Omega 3 fatty acids, especially in the womb. The evidence of a link with depression, chronic fatigue syndrome and dementia is less clear, but still suggestive. None of these conditions is caused exclusively by a lack of these chemicals, or can be entirely remedied by their application, but it's becoming pretty obvious that some of our most persistent modern diseases are, at least in part, diseases of deficiency.

Last year, for example, researchers at Oxford published a study of 117 children suffering from dyspraxia. Dyspraxia causes learning difficulties, disruptive behaviour and social problems. It affects about 5% of children. Some of the children were given supplements of Omega 3 and Omega 6 fatty acids, others were given placebos. The results were extraordinary: in three months the reading age of the experimental group rose by an average of 9.5 months, while the reading age of those given placebos rose by 3.3. Other studies have shown major improvements in attention, behaviour and IQ.

This shouldn't surprise us. During the Palaeolithic era, humans ate roughly the same amount of Omega 3 fatty acids as Omega 6s. Today we eat 17 times as much Omega 6 as Omega 3. Omega 6s are found in vegetable oils, while most of the Omega 3s we eat come from fish. John Stein, a professor of physiology at Oxford who specialises in dyslexia, believes that fish oils permitted humans to make their great cognitive leap forwards. The concentration of Omega 3s in the brain, he says, could provide more evidence that human beings were, for a while, semi-aquatic.

Stein believes that when the cells that are partly responsible for visual perception – the magnocellular neurones – are deficient in Omega 3s, they don't form as many connections with other cells, and don't pass on information as efficiently. Their impaired development explains, for example, why many dyslexic children find that letters appear to jump around on the page.

So, at first sight, the government's investigation into the idea of giving fish oil capsules to schoolchildren seems sensible. The food standards agency is conducting a review of the effects of Omega 3s on behaviour and performance in school. Alan Johnson, the secretary of state for education, is taking an interest. Given the accumulating weight of evidence, it would be surprising if he does not decide to go ahead. Already companies such as St Ivel and Marks & Spencer are selling foods laced with Omega 3s.

There is only one problem: there are not enough fish. In March, an article in the British Medical Journal observed: 'We are faced with a paradox. Health recommendations advise increased consumption of oily fish and fish oils within limits, on the grounds that intake is generally low. However ... we probably do not have a sustainable supply of long-chain Omega 3 fats.' Our brain food is disappearing.

If you want to know why, read Charles Clover's beautifully written book *The End of the Line.* Clover travelled all over the world, learning how the grotesque mismanagement of fish stocks has spread like an infectious disease. Governments help their fishermen wipe out local shoals, then pay them to build bigger and more powerful boats so they can go further afield. When they have cleaned up their own continental shelves, they are paid by taxpayers to destroy other people's stocks. The European Union, for example, has bought our pampered fishermen the right to steal protein from the malnourished people of Senegal and Angola. West African stocks are now going the same way as North Sea cod and Mediterranean tuna.

I first realised just how mad our fishing policies have become when playing a game of ultimate frisbee in my local park. Taking a long dive, I landed with my nose in the grass. It smelt of fish. To the astonishment of passersby, I crawled across the lawns, sniffing them. The whole park had been fertilised with fishmeal. Fish are used to feed cattle, pigs, poultry and other fish – in the farms now proliferating all over the world. Those rearing salmon, cod and tuna, for example, produce about half as much fish as they consume. Until 1996, when public outrage brought the practice to halt, a power station in Denmark was running on fish oil. Now I have discovered that the US department of energy is subsidising the conversion of fish oil into biodiesel, through its 'regional biomass energy programme'. It hopes that fish will be used to provide electricity and heating to homes in Alaska. It describes them as 'a sustainable energy supply'.

Three years after Ransom Myers and Boris Worm published their seminal study in *Nature*, showing that global stocks of predatory fish have declined by 90%, nothing has changed. The fish stall in my local market still sells steaks from the ocean's charismatic megafauna: swordfish, sharks and tuna, despite the fact that their conservation status is now, in many cases, similar to that of the Siberian tiger. Even the *Guardian*'s *Weekend* magazine publishes recipes for endangered species. Yesterday, the European Fisheries Council reversed the only sensible policy it has ever introduced. Having dropped them in 2002, it has decided to reinstate subsidies for new boat engines. Once again we will be paying billions to support overfishing. Franco rose to power with the help of the whalers and industrial fishermen of his native Galicia. Somehow the old fascists in Vigo – the centre of the European industry's power – still seem to exercise an extraordinary degree of control.

If fish stocks were allowed to recover and fishing policies reflected scientific advice, there might just about be enough to go round. To introduce mass medication with fish oil under current circumstances could be a recipe for the complete collapse of global stocks. Yet somehow we have to prevent many thousands of lives from being ruined by what appears to be a growing problem of malnutrition.

Some plants – such as flax and hemp – contain Omega 3 oils, but not the long-chain varieties our cell membranes need. Only some people can convert them, and even then slowly and inefficiently. But a few weeks ago, a Swiss company called Eau+ published a press release claiming that it has been farming 'a secret strain of algae called V-Pure' that produces the right kind of fatty acids. It says it's on the verge of commercialising a supplement. As the claims and the terrible names put me in mind of the slushiest kind of New Age therapy, I was, at first, suspicious. So I went to see Professor Stein to ask him whether it was likely to be true.

He could be said to have a countervailing interest: his brother is the fish chef Rick Stein. But he had met the company's founder the day before, and was impressed. The oils produced by some species of algae, he told me, are chemically identical to those found in fish: in fact this is where the fish get them from. 'I think they're fairly optimistic about the timescale. But there is no theoretical impediment. I haven't yet seen his evidence, but I formed a very strong impression that he is an honest man.'

He had better be, and his project had better work. Otherwise the human race is destined to take a great cognitive leap backwards.

June 21 2006

# PORTER'S REAL CRIME: SHE
# SLEPT WITH BLACK MEN

## Hannah Pool

Sarah Jane Porter, the 43-year-old woman who has just been jailed for 32 months for recklessly inflicting grievous bodily harm by infecting her boyfriend of two years with HIV, is a very specific kind of villain. Blonde, female, and with a sexual history, Porter has received what can only be described as the Ruth Ellis treatment.

Porter has been vilified: she is the ultimate red-top baddie, given the kind of treatment usually reserved for child killers and paedophiles. The reporting of her character is strikingly one-dimensional: she is 'Pure Evil' (the *Daily Mail*), a 'Bitter Blonde' (the *Sun*), and a 'Heartless Blonde Maneater' (the *Express*). The subtext of her depiction is that she is a promiscuous white woman who has fallen so low as to sleep with black men, the implication being that her HIV status is also a punishment.

Among the blatant misogyny and latent racism (much is made of Porter's contracting HIV from a black partner and continuing to sleep with black men 'even while she was on bail'), there is no room for understanding or compassion. 'All sympathy disappears when you consider how atrociously she has behaved,' commented Brian McCluskey, the detective in charge of the case.

Does it really?

Yes, Porter should have disclosed her HIV status to any sexual partner, and practised safe sex upon doing so; but does failure to do so automatically make her 'wicked' and 'callous'? And does the fact she has refused to help the police contact any of her other previous partners mean she is is an 'Aids Avenger'? Or might she not equally be a very troubled woman in denial about her condition and desperately looking for someone to blame.

'Denial is not uncommon, but not because you're being malicious,' says Angelina Namiba, policy manager for the charity Positively Women (www.positivelywomen.org.uk). She was diagnosed with HIV about 10 years ago. 'When someone is given an HIV diagnosis, it's a traumatic experience for anybody. You are living in fear, you're scared, you're worried.'

She feels that women who are HIV-positive face a special degree of stigma. 'If you are diagnosed with HIV today, this coverage is what you're facing. Of course, it will be difficult for you to disclose.'

Porter's portrayal heralds an unwelcome return to a view of HIV-positive people as being a threat to society. 'Those headlines hamper the work done over the last 20 years raising awareness, fighting stigma and stereotypes and supporting people to be able to come forward with their status,' says Namiba. 'People with HIV are not time bombs, we are human beings: we are mothers, sisters, taxpayers.'

Being HIV-positive is not in itself a criminal offence. Neither is promiscuity, whatever the motivation. The fact is that had any of the men Porter is reported to have had unprotected sex with insisted on taking safe-sex precautions, they would have much less to worry about. They, too, had the sex, remember.

Yes, she concealed the truth from her partner, but she's not being vilified for that. Her real crime is that she is an attractive woman who unleashed her diseased self upon helpless men. In fact, forget Ruth Ellis in the tradition of folk demons and moral panics, this is more a case of Mary Mallon – otherwise known as Typhoid Mary.

# PROUD TO BE A BRUMMIE

## Stuart Jeffries

The news that Adrian Chiles is to host a new version of *Nationwide* and thereby become the first anchor with a Brummie voice to appear on prime-time BBC1 makes me glow with civic pride. It impels me to share my love for a city (even though I live in London) that has been criminally misunderstood and misrepresented for so long. So here are 22 things about Birmingham that you didn't know – or (probably) care about – plus a guide to speaking Brummie.

1. What precisely does the Birmingham accent sound like? According to Harry Enfield, who is supposed to be a comedian, it often consists of putting the letter 'O' in front of the letter 'I' and replacing each 'U' with a 'W', with hilarious consequences. For example: 'Oi am considerably richer than yow.' Very amusing Harry. Ha, ha, ha. But in fact Enfield is so wide of the mark it isn't even funny. See point 2 for an explanation.

2. So what is Brummie, then, if you're so clever? Good question. It is not an accent, nor a dialect, nor even a kind of vernacular. It is more of a syllable. Let's see if you can say it. Repeat after me: 'Ar'. No, that's not quite right. Try again, and this time try to sound more adenoidally depressed: 'Ar.' Better. You see 'Ar' means everything in the second city: 'Yes', 'No', 'Goodbye', 'The antidisestablishment movement surely prefigures the looming schism in the Anglican church.' It's like 'Bof!' in French – you can use it everywhere and in any situation and everybody will think you're fluent. Nobody says anything else. Trust me.

3. Actually, that's not quite true. Brummies also say: 'Tara-a-bit' which means 'Au revoir, moite' – or 'Au revoir, mate,' as you non-Brummies would say.

4. Brummie offspring call their mothers 'mom', not 'mum', which makes it difficult for children to buy appropriate greeting cards in this orthographically challenged land. Unless you're a Brummie in America, in which case there's no problem, because in the US you literally can't move for 'Happy birthday, Mom' cards.

5. Birmingham has more miles of canals than Venice and more trees than Paris. But, unfortunately for the canals and trees, they are in Birmingham and not Venice or Paris. This makes them all quite sad.

6. Tony Hancock, Birmingham's most famous depressed comedian, was born in Hall Green and later committed suicide. Would a 16-hour course of cognitive therapy at a government-run so-called 'happiness centre' that 'happiness gurus' are currently recommending have helped him? Not if the centre had been in Hall Green.

7. There are more Antony Gormley statues of metal men in Birmingham's public places than there are miles of canal or trees. You can't stop him! Don't think they haven't tried!

8. The smell from the HP Sauce factory in Aston drifts over the Aston Expressway. This stretch of motorway is, as a result, the only one in the world where you are obliged by law to keep car windows up and maintain a minimum speed of 50mph. These rules are to be relaxed now that sauce production is being relocated to Holland. Do the Dutch really know what they're getting in to? I don't think so.

9. The now-demolished inner ring road was a piece of public art, just like a Gormley statue. Nobody was meant to drive on it!

10. Prince William and David Cameron support Aston Villa, no matter how much people ask them to stop.

11. There was a resin sculpture in Centenary Square called *Forward*, depicting the city's men and women marching from its smoke-stack past

into some delightful multicultural future – until some kids burned it down in 2003. Does that mean Birmingham isn't going forward, you ask? Nobody likes a smartarse, sunshine.

12. The Rotunda is the world's first rotating 20-storey restaurant, supplying balti cuisine on all floors and offering views of Birmingham – and beyond! As you know, 'balti' means 'bucket' in Urdu and, each evening, when the restaurant closes, the lid comes off the Rotunda so the restaurant can be aired. The escaped fumes usually drift over Smethwick, where they form a fetid cloud. Hence the expression 'Well, I'll go to Smethwick', which suggests that the speaker is so surprised that they would do something madly contrary to their own interests.

13. Actor Julie Walters is from Smethwick. Improbably, she's quite fragrant.

14. At the new Selfridges, you can eat sashimi and sushi. Now that's posh.

15. UB40's bestselling single did not have to be re-pressed for Birmingham record shops with the title Red Red Woine. That's just a loie. (Incidentally, there's a town near Birmingham spelled Lye but pronounced Loye. Whacked out!)

16. In a night of rioting on July 14 1791, a Birmingham mob burned down nonconformist intellectual Joseph Priestley's home in Sparkbrook and tried to lynch him. So think on.

17. Priestley was a member of the Lunar Society, a group of industrialists and scientists (also including Matthew Boulton, Erasmus Darwin and Josiah Wedgwood) who used to meet on nights when there was a full moon. They called themselves the lunaticks. Those guys! Mad or what?

18. Steel Pulse once did a great reggae album called *Handsworth Revolution*. But there wasn't one. Not really.

19. The Streets (aka Mike Skinner) is from Birmingham, but moved to that London. And yet we're supposed to believe he's somehow keeping it real!

20. Chiles supports West Bromwich Albion, which isn't really in Birmingham. It's in the Black Country, which is very different. (Stop looking at me blankly.) So maybe he isn't a true Brummie at all. Lenny Henry (Dudley), Noddy Holder (Walsall), Meera Syal (Essington, near Wolverhampton) are not Brummies either. Benjamin Zephaniah is, though.

21. George Eliot cried like a girl at a concert at Birmingham Town Hall in 1848. After that incident, nobody really believed he was a man any more.

22. They used to make Wolseleys (be still, my aching heart!) in Washwood Heath. But now hardly any cars are made in Birmingham. We will now bow our heads in two minutes' silence to pay respect to Birmingham – first city of the industrial revolution and former home to 1,000 manufacturing trades, that shall (Oh yes!) rise again. Won't we, readers? 'Ar!' Well said.

June 30 2006

# THE LATECOMER'S HANDBOOK

## Tim Dowling

Britain, you may or may not have noticed, is running behind schedule – about a day and a half late a year. On average, it's said, we now leave colleagues and friends waiting for 47.2 minutes a week, although this statistic was obtained by surveying 2,000 people in the street, people whose willingness to stop and answer questions posed by a stranger with a clipboard shows a certain lax attitude to appointment-keeping.

The main reason posited for this creeping lateness is the advent of the mobile phone. As long as we can ring up to apologise, the extra tardiness is tolerated. But with new technology comes new etiquette: just how late is it now acceptable – even advisable – to be? Below, a guide to correct arrival times.

**Two hours early or more:** Ryanair flight; Ikea sale; opening of local NHS dentist; any meeting for which you might need to plant a weapon.

**On time:** Job interview; first day of new job; day after first warning for persistent lateness; day after second warning; day after first written warning; any party with free alcohol.

**Five to 10 minutes late:** One-hour session with personal trainer; lunch with obsessively punctual friend; dinner in a restaurant; scheduled meeting with underlings; appointment with anyone who has specifically asked you to be on time.

**Fifteen to 30 minutes late:** Work, as a matter of course; lunch with habitually late friend, or obsessively punctual enemy; any Virgin train departure; rendezvous at boring museum; outdoor assignation where first person to arrive will have to stand around in the rain waiting; any party with a specific start time printed on the invitation.

**Thirty minutes to one hour late:** Day-long seminar aimed at inculcating effective work habits; any rendezvous preceded by a train journey; lunch with friend who has accepted your habitual tardiness as a regrettable part of your personality; party where there might possibly be speeches; wedding of ex-girl-/boyfriend, if invited; anything the Monday after the clocks go back.

**Two to four hours late:** Guns n' Roses gig; appointment to interview Naomi Campbell; any rendezvous preceded by a Ryanair flight; home, after a night on the lash, provided you have rung at least once to mumble incomprehensibly; wedding of ex-girl-/boyfriend, if not invited; party where you need to meet someone in order to go to another party; evening of bad theatre followed by good restaurant.

**One day late or more:** Appointment to duel; meeting certain to end with you getting the sack; anything you wish to skip, providing you can convincingly argue that you got the wrong date; start date of new fitness/dietary regime; your doomsday cult's final AGM.

# I'M TOO OLD FOR MYSPACE

## Charlie Brooker

It had to happen, and it has. Age has crept up on me. I'm becoming resistant to technological change.

It used to be so different. I've always been a geek, and proud of it. In my 20s, I lived in a chaotic mangle of keyboards and wires. I was the person people would phone up when they had a problem with their computer. I wrote for videogames magazines, making up jokes about polygon counts and cel-shading.

Then the internet roared up. I ran a website called TV Go Home, which was essentially a fortnightly pisstake of the *Radio Times* with lots of unnecessary swearing in it – just the sort of thing that's been a staple of comedy spin-off books since year dot, except because it was on the internet it was somehow seen as the shiny sharpened bleeding edge of new. My career prospects suddenly changed. Traditional media came calling – TV, newpapers. They wanted me. As far as 'they' were concerned I was someone who 'got' the 'modern' world and all that went with it. For about nine seconds, I felt vaguely cool.

Fast forward to now. I'm looking at MySpace and I'm a fumbling old colonel struggling to comprehend his nephew's digital watch.

Because I don't 'get' it. I mean, I know what MySpace is and what it's supposed to do and how influential it is. It's just that whenever I've visited a MySpace page I've thought 'is that it?' and wandered around the perimeter looking confused, like a blind man patting the walls for an exit he can't find.

So, users create a page and upload their music and photos and videoclips, they post blog entries and links to other stuff and leave witty little messages for one another. And it all meshes together to form a thriving social network. Okey dokey. On the surface it all makes sense.

Yet it's not for me. I mean, I could go and create a page myself, but somehow I'd rather scrape my retina off with a car key. At 35, I'm too ancient for MySpace – I'd look like a school-gate paedo – but that's not really the issue. No. It's simply bloody-minded 'olditude' on my part – the same sort of fusty grumbliness that made greying musos boycott CDs in favour of vinyl in the 80s because they JUST DIDN'T WANT TO KNOW about this newfangled whatchamathing.

Last week, in the US, I saw an advert for a handheld gizmo using the slogan: 'It's not a cellphone: it's MySpace on the go.' It's a terrifying first – a new gadget I know I'll never want to buy. I've never felt so lost.

Or perhaps it's MySpace's 'social' element that disturbs me. I'm a misanthrope. Everyone on MySpace seems young and happy and excited and flip and approachable, and this upsets me. Still, at least the teenage MySpacers are getting on with the business of being young and alive, unlike the fustier elements of the 'blogosphere', who just waste the world's time banging on and on about how important the 'blogosphere' is and how it spells the end of every old notion ever, when the truth is that, as with absolutely every form of media ever, 99% of the 'blogosphere' is rubbish created by idiots.

Especially the word 'blogosphere'. A word I refuse to write without sneery ironic quote marks either side of it. Because I hate it and it's crap and I JUST DON'T WANT TO KNOW.

June 22 – July 3 2006

# NANCY'S WORLD CUP DIARY

## Marina Hyde

**June 22 2006**

Aperitifs: 7 (I stop caring). Infuriating Orson Welles-based dream interpretations: 1.

I not had a chance to hear full details of Coleen's pre-match socialiser with Gary Lineker, because she cry all the way home after game. 'What's the matter darling?' Elen Rives ask her.

'She upset about late equaliser,' I cut in. 'And Wayne substitution, of course.'

When we get back to hotel she rush to room, but I too quick for her and confront her on doorstep.

'Don't you enjoy yourself?'

'I never want speak to you again,' she sob. 'You've manipulated me, you've made me ruin my happiness.'

She slam door.

And so I stuck with Sven, who pass bad night.

'I dream I like Citizen Kane at end of life,' he tell me in morning. 'We live in big house.'

'Oh yes? What it look like?' I ask.

'Like Xanadu,' he say. 'But a lot more leopardskin cushions. Nancy, I have out of body experience. I am looking at self on deathbed, and you are there, and I whisper last word to you.'

'Is it codes to Monaco bank account?' I ask, breathless.

'No,' he say. 'No, it just one word. "Jermain". Jermain … What it mean?'

'For God sake!' I scream. 'It a bit late for that. Just play the bloody child!'

## June 23 2006
Aperitifs: 4. Backfired erotic surprises: 1.

Sven he worry me. He pace room all night reading *King Lear*, muttering to self. And so, I prepare little surprise for when he return from press conference. I am paint white with big red England cross along both arm, and from face through cleavage, just like Wayne Rooney Nike advert.

I position self on bed when I hear key turn in lock. Unfortunately, thing not go to plan when he see me. 'My God! My God!' he scream. 'What new madness is this?'

'It special, transgressive surprise,' I say, grabbing his face.

'You get greasepaint all over my Umbro,' he wail, and pull angry away, so that paint smear all over his glasses.

'I can't see!' he scream.

Hotel security knock at door. 'Is everything OK?'

'My eyes, my eyes,' Sven mumble.'I can't see way out. I can't see any strikers, I can't see how fix it.'

'There, there, Mr Eriksson,' security guard say. 'I'll clean it off. Then you can see to do your teamsheet.'

Sven he push him away. 'Leave them,' he say. 'I have no way, and therefore want no eyes. I stumbled when I saw.'

He lurch wildly out into night.

'I can't take much more this!' I scream after him. 'Just play the bloody child!'

## 24 Jun 2006
Aperitifs: 9 (party). Layers of mascara: 8 (warpaint).

And so, tonight I host long awaited End of World Cup Party, by taking all wives except Victoria to dinner at castle.

'Why we having party now?' ask Elen Rives.

'Sometime,' I explain, 'if you will something hard enough, it happen.'

'You're unbelievable,' she snap.

'Thank you,' I smile. 'I call ahead make sure they got salad. I notice you put on a few pounds since we been here. Few more and you be same weight as your Frank in West Ham days.'

At end of meal, restaurant ask me where to bill dinner. 'Stick on Theo Walcott's room,' I decide. But warm glow evaporate later when newspaper contact ring to read me first editions. 'I not married to David Beckham,' Sven apparently say in press conference. 'We not even engaged.'

How many new ways he find to humiliate me? In this, however, there only be one winner. It time to open section of contacts book mark 'only for emergency', and call Martin Bashir.

I spend evening practice interview technique in mirror, and perfect image of wounded woman struggling to keep lid on fact she not quite full ticket. 'There three of us in this marriage,' I say through downcast eyelashes clot with mascara. 'So it were a bit crowded.'

**June 28 2006**
Aperitifs: 5 (excellente). Happy memories of afternoon in south London car park: 1.

Svennis he pass another bad night. 'I have strange dream. Four-man Portugal run ring round England on pitch, while Big Phil Scolari he canter up and down touchline on horseback dress as Braveheart. I make imperceptible eyebrow gesture to Beckham to get stucked in, but he turn to me and say: "Boss, I think I told you, I'm a lover not a fighter".'

'Ah, like Michael Jackson to Paul McCartney in classic 1982 duet "The Girl Is Mine",' I observe. Which remind me: I got to phone lonely gazillionaire Sir Paul Macca and ask how his despair is going.

'Thing is, Nancy,' say Sven. 'I think perhaps it just about nearing time for me to turn up volume. I can't do it self, of course, so I thought perhaps I ask John Terry if he give rousing motivational talk to players in dressing room before kick-off on Saturday. What you think?'

'Worth to try,' I muse. 'I had a few text messages from John in my time and he certainly good at forcefully set out what need to be done. If he refuse, you can cobble together motivation speech for players from ones I keep in my saved message file. I got an "I want 2CU do it like U mean it" and a couple of "try 2 look interesteds."'

'Thank you,' say Sven absent-minded. 'That the sort of thing.'

## June 30 2006

Aperitifs: 10 (understandable). Emotional rollercoaster rides: 1 (constant).

I transfix by Sven performance at press conference. I not seen anything so masterful since last erotic dream about Jose Mourinho (Wednesday). 'I could not care less if I criticised,' he tell journalists. 'Don't tell me I don't know what to do. I know exactly what to do.'

Something is stirring. What Evelyn Waugh call 'thin bat's squeak of sexuality audible only to me'. I can't be sure under table, but I don't think he even wear his shoe lifts. It take me back to first flush of love in Rome, when he famously accompany me to restaurant to tell my husband he was getting me on Bosman ruling.

It time to give him a call. 'Cara mia ...' I breathe huskily into receiver before he can answer. 'I have greatest of respect for you, really I do ...'

'Dear dear,' come sarcastic tones of Gary Neville. 'Quite the little Wearside Nancy, aren't you?'

'What the hell he doing in your room?' I screech at Sven when he come to phone.

'He make me see importance of rise up against oppression,' say Sven simply. 'And so I decide to part from you corrosive influence after we win World Cup.'

'Obviously that not going to happen,' I say as aside, before implication sinks in. 'But if you go, where do I go, what do I do?'

'Frankly my dear,' he say in heartbreakingly virile tone, 'I don't give a damn.'

## July 1 2006

Aperitifs: 8 (hot day). Potential exit strategies: 2.5 (must firm things up with Sir Macca). Vengeful thoughts: 16 (better).

And so, Svennis and I, we at war. It may be we nearing endgame. Yesterday, he say he will be leaving in Rhett Butler-style scene, forcing me to turn teary eyes to sky and remark that nevertheless, I will always have Tara. Or at the very least, £3m house in Regent's Park.

Today, unbelievable, I expected to go to game and put on display of unity by clapping from stands, much like Di and Charles at mid-80s polo match.

Situation made little better when I call my close friend Gary Lineker to tell him of my despair. 'Of course,' he muse, 'as soon as Diana realise outings to polo less agony if she start giving one to celebrated cad James Hewitt, her spirits lift. You need to find secret cad of your own.'

'What you saying, Gary?' I whisper throatily into telephone receiver.

'I think we both know what I saying,' he reply, with special snigger he normally reserve for imbecilic innuendo with John Motson about foreign player's name.

Have decided small outfit best for game. Particularly when I learn Sven have tell press that words he least like to read are 'England Out'. Ridiculous. I think he find words he actually least like to read are 'NANCY: MY STORY'.

**July 3 2006**
Aperitifs: 0. Epiphanies: 1.

When I see TV pictures of defeated Sven, it feel like great dam is breaking. Suddenly all make perfect sense. I must go to him. I run through rain, I am totally soak. Shoes come off but I don't care (actually I go back, they Ferragamo) and I not stop till I burst through Sven hotel room door.

'I can't live without you,' I gasp. 'Tell me it not over.'

Sven he push me away.

'You know,' he say, 'Richard Burton once say of Elizabeth Taylor: "She was famine, fire, destruction and plague – the only true begetter. Her breasts were apocalyptic, they would topple empires before they withered. She was lavish. She was a dark, unyielding largesse. She was, in short, too bloody much." You just too bloody much, Nancy.'

It not a bad elegy, I think. But out loud. 'Yes, but Burton also say: "I might run from her for a thousand years and she is still my baby child. Our love is so furious that we burn each other out." That is us, Svennis,' I wail through tears, on floor, clinging desperately to his legs to stop walk away. 'You know we can't rub along without each other. Tell me we always be together!'

What seem like eternity pass. Then Sven he look down at me with look of infinite resignation. 'Oh God,' he say with sigh. 'Yes, I expect we probably will be. Now let's get you out of all those wet things ...'

July 1 2006

# MINUTE BY MINUTE: ENGLAND 0-0 PORTUGAL (1-3 ON PENALTIES)

## Rob Smyth

This is it then, folks: the point at which England traditionally go out of every major tournament. But can our brave boys turn into the sunny shimmerers of the tournament? Probably not, but then they might not need to to sneak through against an under-strength Portugal.

**Our Brave Dullards (4-5-1):** 1-Paul Robinson; 2-Gary Neville, 5-Rio Ferdinand, 6-John Terry, 3-Ashley Cole; 7-David Beckham (capt), 8-Frank Lampard, 16-Owen Hargreaves, 4-Steven Gerrard, 11-Joe Cole; 9-Wayne Rooney.

**Portugal (4-2-3-1; ie 4-5-1 but with brains, and Cristiano Ronaldo is fit):** 1-Ricardo; 13-Miguel, 16-Ricardo Carvalho, 5-Fernando Meira, 14-Nuno Valente; 8-Armando Petit, 18-Maniche; 19-Tiago, 7-Luis Figo (capt), 17-Cristiano Ronaldo; 9-Pauleta

This is it. Beckham and bankrobber-mask-face Figo are having a right laugh in the tunnel, possibly at the expense of our hilariously bad cricket team. The roof is closed. The stadium is full of England's finest, who outnumber Portugal about four nuggets to one. Cheryl Tweedy's had her hair done all wavy. Posh looks sublimely beautiful as always.

**1 min** We're off. Sven is half asleep in the dugout, and Ronaldo has started on the left as predicted. By me. I rule.
**2 mins** A mistake by Carvalho gives Rooney a quarter-chance on the right corner of the box. His shot is blocked by Meira.
**3 mins** Portugal have had more of the ball so far, knocking it around as

they do so well. England have sat deep and chased shadows, as they do so well. Ronaldo looks lively thus far, invigorated by the big occasion as he so frequently is, and gets bumped over there by Neville. He is definitely the biggest threat to England today.

**5 mins** No excitement so far. 'England's Crouchless lineup spoils my new favorite pun,' emails Dan Davis. 'I was going to write that now was the time for Peter Crouch to stand tall, punning his height and his name in one very fell swoop. But now I can't.' I shudder to think what your old favourite pun was.

**7 mins** Steven Gerrard makes a bit of an idiot of the inept Nuno Valente on the right, but his left-footed cross clears everyone. It's cagey stuff, as we expected.

**9 mins** With the ball sitting up nicely 25 yards out, Rooney cuts across a stinging shot that Ricardo crouches down to hold. Thirty seconds later, also from 25 yards, the lively Ronaldo works Robinson with a low drive. It was a comfortable save, although you never know the way that big lummox has played in this tournament.

**10 mins** 'Pity Robben isn't playing,' says Geertjan Wielenga. 'And Van Persie. Then again, if they were, Holland would have won that match they lost. Damn.' This is the standard of gag so far. This is what we have to put up with.

**11 mins** Hargreaves puts in an old-fashioned reducer on Ronaldo, for which he might have been booked. He wasn't. Ronaldo has switched to the right now and is giving England lots of problems.

**13 mins** What a fiasco! Figo swung in a free kick from the right which flew right across the area, bounced off a startled Gary Neville back towards the six-yard box, and was miscontrolled by Tiago. He didn't expect it to come off Neville and so was slow to react, but he really should have done better.

**14 mins** If there was a screw, Portugal would be turning it. Joe Cole miskicks horribly on the edge of his own box and Maniche's punishing 25-yard hit is well blocked.

**16 mins** Same old England so far: absolutely nothing as an attacking force. Beckham hasn't touched the ball I don't think. But they look fairly solid defensively. Same old England.

**16 mins** Lovely one-touch move from England. Neville's long throw was flicked down by Beckham to Rooney, whose first-time pass eased Lampard in behind the defence on the right touchline. His cut-back was dying for someone to welt it into the net six yards out, but there was nobody there and Portugal cleared.

**19 mins** Ronaldo marauds in dangerously from the left but, when he should have fed Maniche, he went back outside and slashed his left-footed shot over. But he's playing very well.

**20 mins** 'When McClaren takes over as England coach, will he continue to wear hot pants?' says Dale Bruns.

**21 mins** England are getting all sorts of joy on the inept Valente's side – having Neville back certainly helps the attacking threat – and, in that attack, Gerrard coaxes in a lovely curving cross that is just too far in front of the onrushing Lampard.

**24 mins** It's been a nearly half so far – a lot of good attacking intentions and hustle and bristle, but no clear chances as yet, unless you count that Tiago miscontrol.

**28 mins** Ronaldo roasts Frank Lampard – isn't it ironic, don't ya think? – and then his shot from the edge of the box is beaten away by Robinson. Then Lampard maims Ronaldo … and the ref waves play on!

**29 mins** John Terry is out of the semi-final! (If England get there.) He clashed with Tiago, having led with the arm, went down for ages, and then got booked for his troubles.

**32 mins** Hargreaves has been excellent so far – a little robust and overzealous at times (he might get booked for repeat offending soon), but without his diligent covering and flunky-work England would have had their pants pulled down on more than one occasion. Gerrard has been good too. Lampard, Beckham and Cole have done a grand total of sod all between them. It's the best midfield in the world!

**37 mins** Ashley Cole's long pass frees Gerrard on the left, and he floats across a fairly inviting ball. As ever, though, there is only Rooney in the box. I was a big advocate of 4-5-1, but it's not working today. Get rid of Beckham and put Gerrard wide right, or take off Beckham and Lampard and put Lennon and Crouch on. Beckham, between you and me, has only kicked the ball about three times. He is painfully out of his depth in open play.

**39 mins** After Beckham loses possession, Portugal break and Figo, coming inside from the left, whips a curler wide of the far post. It was a similar position to his complete fluke for Real Madrid against United in April 2003. This time he was going for goal; this time he didn't score.

**40 mins** 'Does anyone else think Scolari kinda looks like Gene Hackman circa *A Bridge Too Far*?' says Anthony Vernal, suggesting a lookalike that has never, ever been suggested before anywhere ever.

**41 mins** Portugal win the game's first corner. It's played short to Petit, whose cross is headed gently towards goal by Tiago. It was a simple catch for Robinson, and it was going wide, but for some reason he decided to do a really dramatic one-handed paw away. 'This has got 1-0 England written all over it,' winces Scott Murray opposite me. It has too, but they have been poor so far.

**43 mins** England get their first corner, and Beckham hits the first man. But in the aftermath, Petit cleans out Joe Cole with a poor challenge 25 yards out. He's booked, so he's out of the semi as well. More to the point, this is Beckham Range™ ...

**44 mins** ... and he messes it up completely, slapping it meekly into the wall. He. Is. Useless.

**45 mins** A nice ball from Joe Cole allows Lampard to swirl one towards goal from 25 yards; Ricardo plunges to his right to save. In other news, John Terry is struggling again.

**Half time**

**46 mins** We're off again, and a rousing/soul-destroying rendition of 'God Save The Queen' is going in the stadium, and indeed GU Towers. Turner is conducting the orchestra.

**47 mins** Beckham is coming off! Go on pal, do one! He's done his ankle – Sven would never have the bottle to sub him, of course – and Aaron Lennon is getting stripped off. 'Everytime we see Beckham he seems to be rolling around waving his hands in the air like some gravitationally challenged Tony Adams,' says Neil Blakely. 'His time at Real really has expanded his game.'

**49 mins** Ronaldo nutmegs Gerrard beautifully, is brought down – and the ref waves play on again.

**50 mins** The spoilt brat Beckham wants to run his injury off, even though he can hardly run.

**51 mins** Beckham, fed by Rooney inside the box, flips a cross on to the hand of Valente, but it would have been an incredibly harsh penalty. Beckham is now hobbling off in a right sulk, which is hilarious, and Lennon is on.

**53 mins** Gerrard's corner finds Lampard unmarked, eight yards out, and he muffs his volley completely, driving it into the ground and then up and over. In the context of this toothless game, that was a big chance.

**54 mins** Beckham's in floods of tears! Brilliant stuff.

**55 mins** 'Would you **** off with Ronaldo?' says Evan Thornton. 'Just get a room, shag him and be done with it.' Yeah, I'm really sorry for liking one of the most talented players in the world. Would you prefer if I idolised John Terry?

**57 mins** Maniche dives miserably after being breathed at by Hargreaves. The ref tells him to get up, think of the children and all that. 'It's Daniel Bedingfield that's gone down injured,' chuckles Turner.

**58 mins** A thrilling run from Lennon, nailing three players on his way in from the right, leads to a great chance for Joe Cole, who stabs over from eight yards. That was wonderful stuff for Lennon, who just went straight at Valente then and roasted him effortlessly. England are bossing this at the moment.

**61 mins** Rooney sent off! He stamped on Carvalho's swingers. There was a right tussle with Carvalho for possession. He left his foot in. There has been a coiled, Gazza-91 feeling about Rooney all tournament – remember the tantrum v Sweden? – and you have to say that's been coming. I actually don't think the ref was going to send him until Portugal players came flying in – Ronaldo led the protests, and Rooney added to suspicions about them hating each other by shoving him – but ultimately he made a stamping motion, and he had to walk.

**62 mins** It's all going off! A barefooted Beckham has wondered down to the touchline to slag off the ref. Simao is on for Pauleta, which means Figo up front. In fact it's Ronaldo up front. And if England get through here, their only forwards for the rest of the World Cup are Crouch and Walcott.

**65 mins** Joe Cole off, Crouch on, so England go 4-4-1 now with, I presume, Gerrard on the left.

**67 mins** Portugal have looked so relatively punchless that England might be able to string this out for penalties, as they did so heroically in 1998.

**69 mins** The other thing about Rooney is that, had the referee done his job, Rooney would have been given a foul about five seconds before he stamped on Carvalho. Not that that excuses what followed.

**70 mins** Hargreaves goes on a wonderful, round-the-houses run before muffing his cross from the touchline wide on the left.

**73 mins** A long ball releases Gerrard on the left, but he cracks a generic cross along the face of the six-yard box even though nobody was there. England are the better team just now – Portugal can't keep the ball without an orthodox centre forward.

**76 mins** 'Replay showed Rooney didn't touch Carvalho's knackers,' says Kevin Mackenzie. 'Unjustly sent off. Yellow card at most.' It was a stamp. It was violent conduct. It was a red card.

**78 mins** Figo's swept crossshot is pawed away desperately by Robinson. In the second phase of the attack, Nuno Valente six yards out is merked by a wonderful tackle from Rio Ferdinand.

**85 mins** Maniche curls a long-range effort miles over, and my left thumb is starting to hurt where I've tucked into my fingernail.

**87 mins** Ronaldo, who's being booed all the time for his unedifying part in the Rooney red card, whips a cross just over Postiga. Then Terry cuts out another Ronaldo cross six yards out. England are rocking a bit.

**90 + 1 mins** England win a corner! Where's Sol Campbell when you need him to have a goal disallowed?

**90 + 2 mins** A wonderful run from the magnificent Hargreaves, who is redefining indefatigability, almost produces a goal. His cross leads to Terry's shot being blocked, then Lampard's follow-up is deflcted for another corner. Ricardo punches it away, Portugal break, and Postiga volleys into orbit.

**Full time: Portugal 0 England 0** So. It's extra-time, and I'm off for a really, really nervous No1.

**91 mins** Here we go again. 'If Figo is spotted in the last match with a clash of heads and gets a yellow – how come raised hands and a shove is a red?' says JP, not unreasonably. If Rooney went for the push it's a farce.

**94 mins** 'After he got Rooney sent off, Ronaldo was pictured winking and shushing his teammates rather, er, knowingly,' says Steve Hewitt. 'The French commentators are absolutely slating him: Shame on you for defending the little ★★★★.' I'm not defending his part in it at all; I'm saying that Rooney deserved to go for the stamp.

**120 mins ... It's penalties!**
Portugal 2–1 England: Carragher misses ... and if Ronaldo scores this it's all over ...

Portugal 3–1 England: Ronaldo puts England out. The pantomime villain Ronaldo wins it with an excellent penalty, to Robinson's left, and it's the same, same old story for England.

Gerrard and Lampard took awful penalties, but there was big controvery over Jamie Carragher's miss. Lampard and Gerrard are motionless, broken, it's horrible and a little poignant. Rio is crying violently; fate has merked him, and it's harsh because, quietly, he had an excellent tournament. Ultimately, however, England found their level – the quarter-finals – and all the bluster and blame and bull★★★★, particularly over Rooney's sending off, we will get over the next few days.

Can't disguise it: that dullard idiot Eriksson has trousered £4m a year to do something that you or I could have done.

July 3 2006

# ENGLAND GOT WHAT THEY DESERVED – ABSOLUTELY NICHTS

## Richard Williams

In the aftermath of a punishing defeat, no man should be called to account for his impromptu remarks. But when Frank Lampard said on Saturday night that England had 'deserved' to win the match in which defeat had just eliminated them from the World Cup, he was inadvertently exposing the problem at the heart of the team's consistent inability to scale the highest peaks.

David Beckham had used the same word earlier in the campaign. England would get to the World Cup final, the captain said, because they 'deserved' to be there. As no deeper analysis was forthcoming, his listeners were left to infer that the evidence in support of his contention might have included any or all of the following: England's historic role as the game's mother country, the vast popularity of the Premiership at home and abroad, the inflated pay and celebrity status of its players, and the attention lavished on the public appearances of their wives and girlfriends.

When Sven-Goran Eriksson also spoke about the team 'deserving' to reach the final, he tried to suggest that it was because of the quality of their football. However, strictly on the basis of their successive performances against Hungary, Jamaica, Paraguay, Trinidad & Tobago, Sweden and Ecuador, it would have taken a battalion of the world's finest legal advocates to make a case for the justice of their arrival in the final rounds of the biggest international football tournament of all.

Their attitude represents a culture of complacency at work that was evident in the climactic shoot-out against Portugal, when three of England's penalty-takers failed, with attempts in which the slackness of their body language and their shooting spoke of men who were ready to put their trust in the belief, as generations of England players before them have believed, that their reputations alone would be enough to ensure their success.

A successful apprenticeship in English football's upper echelons wraps a comfort blanket around a young player, sheltering him from the harsh realities of the outside world. He never has to confront those moments in which failure really does mean disaster. When he is called upon to summon reserves of resilience at moments of extreme pressure, he discovers those reserves either do not exist or have been depleted by the demands of domestic football.

Where, on Saturday, was the Englishman prepared to take control of the game as Zinedine Zidane would do in France's defeat of Brazil later that night? The only candidate was Owen Hargreaves, who both converted his penalty – the one Englishman to do so – and secured the man of the match award with 120 minutes of non-stop tackling, intercepting, running and passing. Alone among his colleagues, he displayed a dynamism that seemed to come from within. What also makes him unique among the squad, of course, is that he has never lived in England. The two things may not be unconnected.

Before Hargreaves was born, his parents left Britain to make a new life for their family in Canada. They succeeded, and in so doing may have laid the mental foundations for his son's career. Owen Hargreaves arrived in Munich as a 16-year-old and began a long struggle to establish himself among the superstars in the first team at Bayern, in a country where he knew no one and had to learn the language from scratch. When times were difficult, when he was dropped or suffered injuries, his parents' example of ambition and self-sufficiency can have done him no harm.

Hargreaves may also have benefited from the Bundesliga's 34-match season and its mid-winter break. Whereas he faced up to Portugal's challenge with what the English like to see as their characteristic qualities of energy and doggedness, his native-born team-mates struggled to turn their talent and desire for success into the currency of coherent football.

Individually, there was much to admire in their display – in Ashley Cole's gradual return to form, in John Terry's obduracy, in Aaron

Lennon's zigzag runs and in Peter Crouch's sheer willingness – but collectively they could only demonstrate the difficulty they experience in achieving, even sporadically, the kind of momentum that the better sides in this tournament have maintained virtually from first whistle to last.

Permutating his resources for the fifth time in five matches as he responded to the opposition's strengths and his own squad's injuries, Eriksson asked Hargreaves to provide a screen for the defence while a midfield quartet attempted to support Wayne Rooney, the lone front-runner. That it took the coach so long to reach this conclusion, after having Hargreaves in his squad for almost five years, is among the most serious indictments of his regime.

The fatal flaw in the way the formation was applied was the use of Rio Ferdinand as the launchpad for attacks. On countless occasions the ball was given to the centre-back in the expectation that he would make the first significant pass. He would take a touch to control the ball, look up, take another touch, look up again, have another think and then, after a delay often of six or seven seconds, play it – not always accurately – to a team-mate.

By the time he was ready to part with the ball, two things had invariably happened: his team-mates had in effect come to a standstill, and the Portuguese defenders had been given the time to move in to cover them. So almost every England move would start from a static position, with the opposition well prepared for countermeasures.

Although Ferdinand is a decent passer of the ball, he is not Andrea Pirlo. Neither is Hargreaves, but he should have been encouraged to become the kind of pivot that Claude Makelele represents for Chelsea and France, taking the ball from the defence and recycling it to the midfield with the minimum of fuss or wasted time, acting as the team's metronome. England might then have had a chance to develop the kind of rhythm and movement that we sometimes see from Arsenal, Chelsea and, less frequently nowadays, Manchester United, but at which English-born players in general have never been adept.

When the Football Association hired Eriksson as England's first foreign coach, it was reasonable to expect that an improvement in fluidity was among the benefits the players could expect from his long experience in Italy and Portugal. All they got, really, was a swift application of common sense to a formerly chaotic selection policy and a discovery that Eriksson's notion of an acceptable standard of living matched their own five-star expectations.

His inability to get Englishmen to play football with spontaneity and consistency means that, after its promising start, the Eriksson era must on balance be accounted a failure. Sadly, given the unerring courtesy with which he confronted an often hostile environment, he was not the man to dismantle the mental barrier that prevented his players from converting their genuine talents into real achievement at international level. In the end they, and he, deserved no more than they got.

July 5 2006

# WHAT ON EARTH ARE BRITISH SOLDIERS DOING IN AFGHANISTAN?

## Simon Jenkins

The debacle of Britain-in-Afghanistan cannot be ignored, because British troops are at risk. They were never meant to be at risk and their presence in that country has nothing to do with British security. They are sweltering and dying in Helmand not to prop up an embattled regime in Kabul, for which they are hopelessly undermanned, but to keep Nato alive in Europe, an unworthy mission. As an act of expediency, the expedition is on a par with Gladstone's fatal dispatch of Gordon to Khartoum.

The House of Commons should begin its postmortem now, in the hope of winning an early British withdrawal to Kabul. The questions it must answer are legion. How did the Americans induce Nato in 2004 to become Hamid Karzai's mercenary army? What intelligence did the cabinet receive from Washington, where officials openly spoke of dumping Afghanistan on uppity Nato to teach it a lesson after the Balkan shambles? Who created the peacekeeping convention of 36 national armies now in Kabul, most of them nothing to do with Nato and with no intention of fighting?

Did the defence secretary, Geoff Hoon, in 2004 commit Britain to the hostile south in return for the first rota of Nato command? Did his successor, John Reid, really believe that in mid-2005 the Taliban were just 'remnants' and a 'dwindling force'? This was when British officers on the ground were warning him that the south was 'not Land Rover but Warrior country ... tin hats, rifles and body armour', while the American 503rd infantry were suffering 10 killed and dozens wounded each month. Yet Reid declared that Britain could achieve success 'without a shot fired'.

By last December it was abundantly clear that Helmand and the eastern border provinces were no longer friendly territory. Aid workers were running back to Kabul. Information indicated that insurgents of every tribe and origin were reforming in Pakistan and throughout Baluchistan. With the Americans plainly tiring of the region, the tide was turning and money was pouring in, not just from opium but from oil-rich backers in the Gulf and Saudi. Did nobody tell Reid, or did he not want to listen, set on being the hammer of the Taliban?

When the Americans were allowing warlords to revert to poppy cultivation in 2002, the Commons should ask why Clare Short was charged with 'poppy eradication', resulting in the biggest crop ever in 2005. If Reid regarded eradication as 'absolutely interlinked' with the war, what did he make of a leaked American memo to Condoleezza Rice in 2005 blaming Britain as 'substantially responsible' for the poppy boom?

As this gloomy analysis has been common across the intelligence community, how far up the chain of command did it reach? Former defence chiefs emerging from briefings with John Scarlett of SIS, including Lord Guthrie, Sir Peter Inge and others, have been shocked at the gulf between his assessment and reports from the front. The impression was that cognitive dissonance (hiding what ministers do not want to hear) is still the order of the day in Blair's Whitehall.

The Commons should go on to ask who prepared the Helmand mission and its rules of engagement. These have been described as to suppress the Taliban and not suppress the Taliban, engage in hot pursuit and not engage in hot pursuit, eradicate poppies and not eradicate poppies. After blowing £1bn on aid to Afghanistan – vanished, unaudited, goodness knows where – another £1bn is being spent on a desert base in Helmand. The defence ministry is having a bad attack of *Beau Geste* syndrome at the British taxpayer's expense.

Reid declared there would be a 'fundamental difference' between his approach to peacekeeping and the Americans' aerial blitzkrieg. But who produced for him the bizarre statistic that '80% of the people in the south are floating voters' and thus potentially anti-Taliban? All of them would back anyone who could bring lasting security and protect their poppy crop. Britain can do neither, least of all with 3,300 troops.

There should be a separate Commons inquiry into that force. Who decided (Reid again?) to send so few lightly armed troops, only 900 of them front-line infantry, with flimsy vehicles and paltry air cover? Where were the generals who should have contested such an order? They knew what the Americans knew. Nothing this week has been more inexplicable than the spin from Des Browne's office that the Taliban response to the British arrival was 'unexpected'. It was widely predicted.

Finally, if 'hearts and minds' is to be the Afghan-friendly face of Nato operations, who sent British troops to join the Americans in their current farewell burst of machismo, Operation Mountain Thrust? It is reported to have slaughtered over 500 Taliban, mostly from the air and thus killing almost anyone. It was not designed to establish the secure zones advocated by Britain's Nato general, David Richards. It is merely killing young Afghans and recruiting their relatives to the Taliban cause, to Karzai's reported fury. He knows soon he must negotiate with the Taliban or die.

Every assessment I have heard suggests that the sort of campaign envisaged by the government in southern Afghanistan would require not 3,000 or even 10,000 troops, but over 100,000. Even the latter total has failed in Iraq, and Iraqis cannot hold a candle to Afghans for insurgent fanaticism. As for opium, if the west wants poor people to grow food instead of poppies, why does it refuse to curb its heroin consumption while dumping grain surpluses on the Afghan market? British policy is so contradictory and stupid as to be beyond belief. Yet intelligent diplomats, NGOs and soldiers must spout it because that is what ministers require. Those ministers should not be let off the hook.

Last week a company of the 3rd Battalion, the Parachute Regiment, visited the Helmand village of Zumbelay in an early run of 'hearts and minds'. Tailed by spies and arriving publicly in soft hats without air cover, the soldiers tried to bribe village elders with projects to reject the Taliban. They had walked into a trap. In the resulting fire-fight they were lucky to escape a massacre. Their intelligence was clearly appalling. Was it the same as is being fed to Browne and SIS? Yet if such simple operations are clearly too dangerous to attempt, what on earth are British soldiers doing in southern Afghanistan? No one can give an honest answer to this question.

July 8 2006

# THE MOODY GOOSE

## Matthew Norman

The friend who joined me on a trip to Bath and I share a love of gloriously awful movies, known to us as 'Hawks' since the 1988 shocker of that name starring Timothy Dalton. After this outing, however, the likes of *Ishtar* and *Blame It On Rio* will henceforth be called 'Geese', in tribute to the Moody Goose for providing a meal that ranks among both the worst either of us has ever had, and the most hilarious.

This restaurant moved a while ago from Bath to the Old Priory Hotel, a beautiful, ancient building with a charming walled garden. It was in the sort of sitting room in which you imagine Mr Collins oiling up to Lady Catherine de Bourgh that it started, when a very young waiter unveiled a verbal tic. 'Can I offer you two gentlemen a drink this evening?' 'Would you two gentlemen care to see a menu this evening?' 'Can I show you two gentlemen to your table this evening?' Eschewing the obvious response ('If it's all the same to you, we'll hang on here until tomorrow afternoon') placed such volcanic pressure on us that it inevitably found release in an eruption of adolescent giggling that endured for hours.

Things took an unfortunate turn in the dining room, an appealingly plain, low-ceilinged, stone-floored room largely devoid of the twee horror evident in the lavatory – or 'The Abbott's', as the sign has it – where the bog roll was adorned with a pink bow. Even the stale canapes had offered little warning of a meal that raised the question of how even those arses from Michelin could have given this place a star.

That the menu was the usual country house hotel paean to fussy pretension was no surprise. What startled was the cooking. 'What do you think?' I asked, passing my friend a forkful of smoked salmon bavarois. 'Poisonous,' he snapped back, clearly irritated by the obviousness of the question. Vile it was, a hemisphere of salmon filled with a viciously bitter

303

mousse, the ensemble garnished with halved baby tomatoes and fine beans, and surrounded by a ring of green blobs suggesting that a small mollusc, mortally wounded in the dish's creation, had voided itself as it circled the plate in its death throes.

With such friendly staff, leaving the dish almost untouched seemed too callous, so I scooped it up in a hand, covered it with my jacket and took it to the Abbott's, returning to find my friend gazing confusedly at his starter. 'Can I have a taste?' I asked of his Brixham crab tartlet with poached duck egg. 'Good luck,' was the laconic reply, and he passed over a forkful with a flavour I couldn't pin down – a faint tang of Parmesan and burned pastry, with possibly a hint of sump oil. 'I think Meredith Merridew would have preferred his doggy-woggies,' said my friend, referring to the Robert Morley character in *Theatre Of Blood* (most definitely not a Goose), force-fed poodle pie by Vincent Price in a pastiche of *Titus Andronicus*.

We surveyed the (Peter) Allissian clientele, and wondered whether this was the annual convention of the Society for People with No Tastebuds, whether they were pretending to enjoy their food in that English middle-class way, or whether somehow they actually were. Our main courses seemed to rule out the latter. 'How much paper have you got?' asked my friend of the small pile of A4 on my lap. 'I want this duck in the Abbott's as soon as possible.' His 'assiette' of Gressingham duck was most notable for a flabby confit of leg stuffed with strange, pink cubes redolent of Winston Smith's canteen stew in 1984. He made a move towards the leg. 'Not that,' I warned him. 'If they think you've eaten a long, sharp bone, they'll call an ambulance.' Eventually, he fetched a carrier bag from the car, filled it, covered it with a baseball cap and removed it, leaving me alone with some roasted squab pigeon – or slices of flaccid, fatty, acrid meat swimming in exactly the same cold, Marmitey gravy as the duck, served with a slightly burned potato cake above a slew of what struck the naked eye as hot-dog onions.

'Can I get you two gentlemen anything further this evening?' asked the waiter, as he removed the empty plates (the pigeon having made its way to the Abbott's as well). Boldly resisting the urge to request a stomach pump, we asked for coffee in the garden with the bill, and were gone.

July 12 2006

# SNUFFED OUT – ZIZOU'S LEGACY IN JUST SEVEN SECONDS

## Simon Hattenstone

Douglas Gordon recently made a film about Zinedine Zidane. The entire movie – *Zinedine Zidane: a 21st-Century Portrait* – focuses on Zizou as he prowls through a football match. There is Zidane the dancer, the casual stroller, the sprinter, the magician, and finally the transgressor, when he is sent off after a fracas. Despite receiving brilliant reviews at Cannes, and despite the fact that it has not yet been released in Britain, the movie is already past its sell-by date.

Like many football fans, I have just made my own Zidane movie. It features seven seconds of footage from Sunday's World Cup final showing the build-up to another sending off and it is currently being screened inside my head – again and again. Often against my will.

Unlike Gordon's movie, mine ignores most of the match. It doesn't even take in Zidane's audacious penalty, the leaping header that almost brought a winner, the myriad passes he sprayed round the park, the shoulder injury that should have seen him off.

It starts with a tweak of the nipples from the Italian defender Marco Materazzi – Zizou smiles enigmatically and walks off with him. They exchange words. Zidane jogs ahead, eager to get on with the match. Ten, 12, 14 steps. He stops, waits for Materazzi, pulls back his head and butts him with all his might in the chest. It is an act of ghastly, if elegant, violence. No matter how many times you see it, it continues to shock.

The footage of Zidane is only part of the film playing in my head – the film within the film, as it were. In the bigger picture I have become a character – examining the footage again and again, desperately trying, and failing, to understand. Gordon's film is arthouse, this is an action thriller. In the end it's a snuff movie, as Zidane destroys himself.

It reminds me of a real film I have seen – Michael Haneke's brilliant *Hidden*, which also happens to have a post-colonial French-Algerian protagonist at its heart and perceived racism as its subject. More important, it is also about unknowable motives.

In *Hidden*, Daniel Auteuil plays a middle-class television presenter who is being sent creepy surveillance videos of his house. The audience becomes a participant, watching and rewatching the videos alongside Auteuil, trying to work out whodunnit, and why.

With Zidane, there is no such ambiguity about the perpetrator. We saw it with the help of the camera's eye, even if the referee and his assistants didn't. The ambiguity here is motive.

Zizou, player of the tournament, was the coolest man on the pitch – think of the chipped penalty and those lovely, lazy passes. Even when he fell to the ground, his shoulder seemingly ripped from its socket, somehow he recovered and carried on, striving towards his destiny. He dominated the game and it seemed only a matter of time before his superiority would tell. And then the madness – the tweak, the walk, the jog, the stop, the butt. In *Hidden* there is one scream-aloud act of violence – it is so shocking because it comes without warning, just like Zizou's headbutt.

At least when Eric Cantona karate-kicked a Crystal Palace supporter, we could see a linear progress to madness as he moved towards his target. Going, going, gone. Here, there was nothing. Zidane even sold us a couple of dummies: the smile, the jog away. What made the attack even worse was the stage – the World Cup final – and the stage of the stage – 11 minutes to go till penalties, with Zizou as France's penalty king. He looked set to leave the game as captain of a World Cup-winning team, but left as a crazy. Even the absence of remorse seemed chilling.

What was said? Does it matter? There are numerous theories – including that he was called a 'dirty terrorist', which Materazzi has denied. What was Zizou thinking when the red mist descended? Did he think, 'I've had this shit all my life and I'm not taking it any more, and I'm going to exact retribution in front of hundreds of millions'? Did he think, 'This is for my brothers and sisters in the banlieu'? Did he think, 'Ouch! My nipples hurt, you bastard'? Did he think at all?

Perhaps we'll never know what was said or what he was thinking. Perhaps the greatest riddle of all is that in destroying his legacy as a sporting hero, he might have immortalised himself as the man who stood up to bigots, real or imagined, no matter the price.

# TOO OLD TO BE A
# MOTHER AT 62?

## Catherine Bennett

Patti Farrant, handsome, clever and rich enough to afford the £10,000 cost of her latest child, seemed, when we first encountered her, to be the most deserving candidate yet for the blessing of astonishingly late motherhood. Unlike some of her venerable predecessors – one thinks of the smallholder Liz Buttle, aged 60 when she gave birth, and of the broody Romanian, Adriana Iliescu, aged 66 – Farrant had the luck to look, with her lovely smile, tasteful clothes and nice highlights, entirely normal. In every respect, that is, except for being pregnant at the age of 62. The *Daily Mail* noted that she had a nice house.

And then – another reassuring novelty – Farrant was a child psychiatrist. A caring professional then, not some obsessed, snaggle-toothed loser. Presumably she had looked into the literature, such as it is, and concluded that the benefit of existing at all would be more than enough to console her future child for the disadvantages of acquiring, at the age of eight, a 70-year-old for a mother.

Considering her professional position, you assumed that Farrant must have her own, very good reasons for wanting to add, at this advanced age, to the grown-up children from her first marriage. And more good reasons for consulting the fertility doctor Severino Antinori, whose willingness a few years back to take orders for 'millennium babies' and habit, more recently, of making extravagant boasts about cloning, would have been enough to frighten off many other clinicians.

It only added to their deservingness when Farrant and her husband John asked to be left alone. Good for them. 'We wish to emphasise that this has not been an endeavour undertaken lightly or without courage,' they said. 'We will therefore welcome a return to an undisturbed family life, in order that the wellbeing of both mother and child may continue to be promoted.'

Within 10 days, they had courageously sold their story to the *Daily Mail*. This was in order, the paper said, to explain themselves following a 'chorus of disapproval'. But there was little, in the account that followed, to persuade doubters of the merits of 62-year-old maternity. On the contrary. For one thing, it appeared that one of the three 'grown-up' children was actually a teenager of 18, who would have been a child himself when Mrs Farrant decided to present her second husband – her children's stepfather – with a brand new baby, and set about finding an amenable medic and an egg.

'John has not been a father before,' she told the *Mail*, 'and from early on in our time together this feeling grew in me: the wish to allow John that joy of embracing a child of his own.' Moreover, John had an unhappy childhood. 'It's never too late to have a happy childhood,' the child psychiatrist explained. 'And in this baby is the opportunity for a form of reparation and healing for John.'

Her desire for this infant supplier of reparation and healing was so strong that it would overcome not only human biology, but all the obvious disadvantages of being the baby in question, and the fact that no one in this country would agree to treat her. Enter Dr Antinori. The couple flew to Rome for treatment. Following a change in Italian law, the last of five IVF procedures took place in Russia – the exact location for some reason undisclosed. Another egg was bought on the couple's behalf by the clinic, from an unknown woman whose views on the use of her gametes as a source of reparation and healing for an elderly marine historian from Lewes will never, presumably, be known. 'For us there is no moral dilemma about paying for a donor egg,' Mr Farrant told the *Mail*.

The story culminated last week in our introduction to newborn 'JJ', along with confirmation that his arrival seems to have done the trick, so far as Mr Farrant's wellbeing is concerned. 'I felt transformed, as if fatherhood had fulfilled a need in me that I hadn't acknowledged before I met Patti.' he said. Sorted!

As for Mrs Farrant, she plans to return, part-time, to her job as a child psychiatrist. An intriguing line of work for a person who designs a child as a healing opportunity for his father. But there are so many curious things about the Farrants, a pair of intelligent people who have so prioritised their own needs as to convince themselves that 'good enough' parenting – in child-psychology speak – is compatible with being 80 when your child is 18. Mrs Farrant's mother died aged 88.

Despite the Farrant's mutual proximity to retirement, Patricia Hewitt objects to the 'gender hypocrisy' of their critics. She has noticed that old men have babies all the time. But she has not noticed, it seems, that their wives – the Mrs McCartneys, Simpsons, and Douglases – are much younger, and so not at all comparable to the Farrants. Of course, if the health secretary really believes in equal birth rights for oldsters, she will presumably support the relaxation of Britain's IVF regulations in order to allow scores more sixtysomething couples to be treated by doctors with the relaxed attitude of a Dr Antinori. There would certainly be customers, if not many eggs. For at the same time as helping infertile people to have babies, new reproductive technology seems – with the help of its less scrupulous practitioners – to have legitimised baby-longing at its most perverse, or even pathological, in individuals who may need counselling more than they need eggs.

A member of the British Fertility Society's ethics committee warned against criticising Farrant because of her age, arguing, 'We do not prevent other women from getting pregnant, because there are real risks from being overweight or having diabetes, for example.' Then again, plenty of other activities would instantly be dismissed as inappropriate in the elderly. Had Farrant, the 62-year-old mother of three, proclaimed a burning desire to take up professional skateboarding, sunbathe topless in a public place or run away with a young plumber, the *Daily Mail*, a great one for dignity in middle-aged women, would not have spared her feelings. But it helped, no doubt, that she was, in every other respect, irreproachable. She was even, it noted approvingly, 'slim'. And she had Farrow & Ball paint on the nursery walls. If the first lesson of the Farrants is there is no age when longing for a child cannot drive a person mad, the second, for those who give in to the impulse, is never forget the importance of grooming.

# THINK BEFORE YOU DRINK

## Aida Edemariam

Morning rush hour on a sultry, clammy July day in King's Cross, London. It's been getting hotter for days, and though the forecast is that the weather will break soon, no one is taking chances. In the queue at WH Smith a dapper man in dark glasses clutches three one-litre bottles of Volvic, £1.49 each. A middle-aged woman stands in front of the refrigeration unit comparing waters and water prices; finally she goes for a smaller bottle, at £1.29. Much of the refrigeration unit is given over to water, but already, at 9am, it needs restocking – even though today, water has a bit of competition from the bouncy young things strategically positioned by the steps down into the Underground (which a day earlier achieved temperatures of 41C), handing out free cans. 'Pepsi Max, guys! Free Pepsi Max! Ice cold!' A hurried businesswoman grabs two as she runs for a train. A slender woman with carefully curled white hair also takes two, then secretes a third in her leather rucksack.

By platform four, a low trolley is piled high with bottled water. I ask the nearest man in uniform how much one costs, expecting the usual on-board price of £1.20 or so, but he says he doesn't know. Then – I must be looking peaky – 'Do you need one? Are you thirsty?' That wasn't the point of my question, but as he's offering, sure. He wanders down the idling train and two minutes later emerges with a bottle, and hands it over for free. Which, though I worry a little about what his bosses might say, is sweet of him. More importantly, I'm interested by the instinct he betrays – that drinking water should be freely available in public spaces. In this age of Vittel and Volvic, Malvern and Blue Water, this seems rarely to be the case.

An organisation called the Water for Health Alliance – a loose affiliation of bodies including water companies, public health charities, the Royal College of Nursing, the Men's Health Forum, local authority caterers and the Schools Health Education Unit – is hoping to change this. Think about it: when was the last time you saw fresh, free drinking water in a public space? Whereas it's possible to stumble on water fountains, for example, in all manner of places in the US, Canada, and some of continental Europe, you have to go looking for them in Britain, and if you do, you'll often be disappointed. (Though at King's Cross, to my surprise, I found two in the ladies'. One proclaimed, 'Drinking fountain out of order. Please do not use.') The borough of Westminster provides only seven drinking-water fountains.

This wasn't always the case. 'The Victorians were quite keen on providing water in public places,' says Anne Hardy, professor of the history of modern medicine at University College London and author of Health and Medicine in Britain Since 1860. Domestic water supplies in England were erratic until the 1860s and 70s, and even then water companies would provide water for only about two hours a day. Water fountains were scattered throughout cities, mainly 'in order to stop people from drinking just anything, and especially too much beer'. Thus water provision was partly related to the temperance movement, though it was noticed that men in factories, who drank beer, were far less likely to be felled by diarrhoea than women, who were restricted to water, which at that point was not filtered or chlorinated.

The Victorians were particularly concerned with providing drinking water to the underclass – not the unemployed, who were sent to poorhouses or stayed at home, but the semi-employed: the costermongers and flower-girls, the dock workers and street-sweepers who were more likely to spend their spare time in the pub. But this underclass began to disappear in the Edwardian period, and street life became tidier.

Levels of dust dropped with the disappearance of horses, licensing laws controlled drinking, and the spread of Lyons corner houses, which sold cheap tea and coffee and welcomed women, meant that alcohol was no longer the only non-water alternative.

Tap water became available in homes, and the spread of tuberculosis, for example, raised worries about the sanitariness of drinking fountains (which was good news for the paper cup). Gradually, they dropped out of sight. For years drinking water became, in a very western, privileged way, a non-issue.

The popular idea that continuous hydration is necessary for health and especially that a specific quantity is required, is, says Hardy, 'very, very recent, really appearing only in the past five or six years. Most people wouldn't have thought twice about it before. People have taught themselves to need water. I see that in myself. I never used to drink water except at mealtimes. But nowadays I'm constantly thinking, "I'm thirsty, must have a glass of water."' It is also, she notes, 'a generational thing: the bottle-clutching classes are mostly the under-30s. People who matured before this fad by and large thought they could do without it. The bottle of water is now a visible symbol of "I care about my health."'

And of course, water is integral to health. As we all learn at school, about 85% of the brain, 80% of blood and 70% of muscle is water. It removes toxins from the body, enables nutrients and oxygen to travel round it, regulates body temperature, cushions joints. But while contaminated water is no longer a big problem here, there are public health issues unrelated to cleanliness. Most are caused by not drinking enough of it.

It is next to impossible to measure the average dehydration levels of a national population, as it can vary from hour to hour in each individual, but there seems to be quite a bit of it about. It is both anecdotally observable and scientifically measurable (for example, in a study of the effect of water deprivation on cognitive-motor performance in healthy men and women published in the *American Journal of Physiology* last year) that dehydration adversely affects concentration. In older people, such dips in concentration contribute to the risk of falls, and thus bone breakage; a 2005 article in *Nutrition Reviews*, an American scientific journal, and a US Institute of Medicine panel on intakes of water and electrolytes argued that even mild dehydration could reduce the capacity for physical work by up to a quarter. It can cause headaches and depression. And a 1998 article in the *Lancet* even suggested that the low water content in cabin air might be among the reasons for the higher incidence of breast cancer in airline attendants. One 1996 study in *Cancer Epidemiology, Biomarkers and Prevention*, a publication of the American

Association of Cancer Research, has suggested that drinking four to five glasses of water a day, rather than two or fewer, can reduce the risk of colon cancer by 45% in women and 32% in men. Oh, and skin tone seems to improve.

Hence the mantra that we should all drink two litres of water a day; hence the much-observed fact that no self-respecting celebrity is ever seen these days without a bottle of Evian. But it's not that simple. Experts caution that it is actually impossible to say how much a single person should drink in a day. Two litres of water could be too much for a small woman who eats lots of vegetables, and too little for a large man. How much we should drink depends on everything from body-weight to diet – because about 20% of hydration comes from what you eat. There is more water in 100g of tomato than in 100g of cola.

Furthermore, our obsession with hydration ignores the fact that we were plainly 'designed to go quite long periods between drinking', says Ron Maughan, a professor of sport and exercise nutrition at Loughborough University, and an adviser to UK Athletics, the governing body of this field of sport in Britain. 'Throughout most of evolution we didn't have nice plastic bottles to carry water around. People still work long hours in agricultural and industrial settings with no access to fluids except at meal breaks, and there's no evidence of harm to their physiological function.' These days 'you see people who are supping water continuously, and it may be providing them with no benefit whatsoever'.

The perception now is that the more you can force down the better it is for you, but in fact too much water is dangerous because it dilutes the blood. 'There will be people in the country who die because they allow themselves to become dehydrated,' says Maughan, 'but at the same time there will be people in this country who die because they have overhydrated themselves.' Usually this happens during marathons – at least five have died in distance running events around the world in the past five years, because they have drunk up to 15 litres – but it can conceivably also happen in aggressive detox or dieting regimes.

The trouble is that blanket consciousness-raising drives, such as that for lower salt consumption, risk reaching mainly those who are health-conscious already, 'and leave untouched those who really need to change their behaviour,' says Maughan. 'That's what drives a large part of the organic market, and a large part of the supplements market – they're bought by people who already make healthy choices. Those who make poor food choices don't take them, because they're just not interested, or can't afford it. We usually don't hit the people we're aiming at. I fear the same might happen with the drink-more-water message.'

The elderly are of course particularly vulnerable; every time there is a heatwave, there is an increase in mortality among the elderly, as was seen in France in 2003. But it's hard to keep the elderly hydrated, because our ability to absorb water decreases with age, and medicines often have diuretic effects; according to a detailed fact-sheet produced by Hilary Forrester for Water UK, the water suppliers' industry body, 'a recent survey of water provision in British care homes for the elderly found that residents consumed only two to four glasses of water a day', a quarter to half of the daily amount recommended by the Food Standards Agency. This contributes, she says, to the fact that 42% of patients admitted to geriatric wards are suffering from constipation – which in turn increases the possibility of bowel cancer. Dehydration doubles the mortality of patients admitted to hospital with strokes.

It has been found that it is generally the very disabled or ill who get the most water, because staff pay more attention to them; the less ill are of a generation inclined not to want to put anyone to any trouble; they are also of a generation that would probably prefer a nice cuppa to a glass of water. Water UK has sent hydration advice kits to nearly 1,000 care homes so far, and the National Association of Care Catering and the Royal Institute of Public Health have begun training carers in how to persuade their charges to drink more $H_2O$. Coffee, tea and hot chocolate are included on most menus, but they are caffeinated, and the former two at least are mild diuretics, which exacerbates the problem. If people insist on hot drinks, carers try to persuade them to take hot water and lemon, or to grow their own mint. If all else fails, there's always the argument that an enema is much less pleasant than downing a few glasses of water.

Children, with their larger ratio of surface area to volume, and thus a greater potential for water loss, are particularly prone to dehydration.

Teachers taking part in a 40-school pilot project for Food in Schools, a joint venture between the Department of Health and the Department for Education and Skills to increase access to water, reported that 'preference for drinking water over other drinks rose by 1.6 times in primary and 1.4 times in secondary schools, while preference for carbonated drinks fell. Teachers also reported that the enhanced water provision contributed to a more settled and productive learning environment, as well as helping instil good habits.'

Dehydration can also be linked to increased levels of obesity, partly because thirst is often mistaken for hunger, leading to more frequent snacking, and partly because fat produces the most metabolic water when broken down in digestion, which in turn can mean that children prefer fatty foods because they compensate for their lack of water. Of course, water has to be part of a balanced diet, but the implications are obvious.

Schools were already concerned about obesity and nutrition – Food in Schools was in operation before Jamie Oliver's intervention – but after that the government pledged £220m to schools and local education authorities; set up a new School Food Trust, which has launched an online package of advice on healthy eating; and drew up tough new nutrition standards for school canteens. From September, these standards, which include the provision of free fresh water, preferably chilled, will be obligatory.

This has apparently been a little tricky for schools where drinking water is available only in the toilets or from vending machines. Water coolers are a useful option: and Yorkshire Water has just installed its 900th water cooler free of charge in primary schools, says Nick Ellins, health policy adviser with Water UK. 'The children like it, because it makes water special. They get to go up and get something. And they see going to a water cooler as an adult thing to do.'

Water UK is one of the main partners in the Water for Health Alliance, and it is important to note that Water UK represents Britain's private water and waste-water companies, so promoting tap water is in its interest. But it is also true that far too much of the time, if you're not at home, the only options are sweet drinks, tea or coffee, or expensively bottled water, and this is a big reason why the other partners have signed on. 'The marketing of bottled water is like the marketing of trainers,' says Angela Mawle, chief executive of the UK Public Health Association. 'There is peer-group pressure to see particular brands as more attractive and healthy, and I think it's really invidious to be doing that with something as basic as water.' It exacerbates what she calls 'health inequality', and she compares the effect to the often unintended exclusivity of the organic food movement, 'which the chattering classes are pushing forward, without realising that they're complicit in increasing this inequality'. A middle-class professional might feel it's neither here nor there to pay nearly twice a much for a couple of carrots with earth still clinging to them, or £1.49 for a bottle of water, but 'one pound is a hell of a lot on a low income. I used to work in disadvantaged areas where mothers would have to use any spare pound they might have to buy two packets of biscuits so the kids could get some calories. They're not going to use it on water. The choice wouldn't even come up.'

Of course, there are valid objections to water fountains. If they exist at all, they are often in toilets, which makes people squeamish about hygiene. In places such as railway stations, people might be worried about using fountains in poorly lit areas. So other options have begun to be explored. At present, cafes, restaurants and pubs are not obliged to serve free tap water on request, but many do so – albeit frequently with a measure of snootiness: tap water is cheap, and that makes you cheap. (New legislation will, however, make the provision of fresh water mandatory in Scotland from 2009.)

Free, or as near as possible to free vending machines are a possibility – the water filtration company Brita, for example, could be given council contracts; filtration and chilling would allay the fears of those who are still suspicious of tap water. Providing it in bottles or cups would create waste (another gathering argument against bottled waters: their impact on the environment, both in terms of long-distance shipping and the thousands of plastic bottles), but you could be given the option of using your own refillable receptacle. One company has launched vacuum-packed foil sachets for drinks; these could be used to dispense water. And you can market it, just like anything else. Make good, free drinking water cool. It may be an uphill battle, but it's a good aim.

# THE LONELINESS OF THE
# LONG-DISTANCE COMIC

## Nancy Banks-Smith

Well, that was downright moving. If David Walliams ever murders someone (possibly one of the fans who follow him around in frocks with funny voices), I will be happy to give him a glowing character reference in court. In *Little Britain's Big Swim* (BBC1) he swam the channel for Sport Relief, to keep an Ethiopian orphanage afloat.

His trainer, Greg Whyte, said, doubtfully, that he was pretty fit – for a comedian. He had never swum further than a mile in his life and he would have to swim 21. The first time he jumped into ice-cold water, I thought he was fooling around but he was hyperventilating. Not clowning but drowning.

When Captain Webb swam the channel in 1875, the Mayor of Dover said, 'I make bold as to say' – they knew how to make a speech, those men with big moustaches – 'that I do not believe that in the future history of the world any such feat will be performed by anybody else.' It took Webb more than 21 hours. Walliams did it in 10 hours 30 minutes.

He said, 'Channel swimmers never looked to me like natural athletes. They were in some ways misfits and loners. I suppose I identified with them. I was overweight at school and never really good at sport. Swimming was one thing I could do.' In fact, the way Jayne Torvill only looked beautiful on ice, Walliams looks wonderful in water.

Channel swimming threw incidental, accidental sidelights on being a comedian. He used exactly the same words for both. Amazing adventure … scary … terrible sense of foreboding. 'I'm used to always hiding behind characters. Anything other than being me would be nice. Now people are going to see me cold and tired and in pain. I want to be entertaining and jokey but I'll be really, really cold.'

After the stage, the sea is the loneliest place in the world. 'You really are alone with your thoughts. I try to think about pleasurable things and suppress all negative thoughts. There's something so scary about something coming from under the water and attacking you.' Your food is offered on the end of a pole. Your drink on the end of a rope. You are out of touch. 'I went through a kind of dream state. My thoughts were delirious, really. My brain felt like it had kind of melted. Weirdly, I even got a sort of anxiety, it was like a paranoia, that people in the boat were talking about me.' He dragged his hands hard down over his face as if to peel off the memory.

On a training swim to the Isle of Wight, Greg Whyte collapsed with hypothermia and was hauled, shuddering, into the boat. Walliams simply said 'Where do I go?' They pointed and he swam on alone, repeating to himself 'Be a man! Be a man!' How long since you heard that phrase, and how moved were you to hear it now?

Matt Lucas, who did the commentary, said, 'All joking apart, I haven't got what it takes and he has.'

Walliams set out at dawn to swim from Shakespeare Beach to Cap Gris Nez, which has no beach, only boulders. He had literally crawled from England to France and, when he got there, there was no strength left in his arms. He scrabbled at a boulder and slid. He tried to lever himself up with his legs and fell back. He looked dazed. On the boat, Greg Whyte was shouting: 'Get on the rocks! Get on the rocks!' If he didn't, the swim would be invalid. Then he found a low, sloping shelf and clambered out.

He had said something earlier that has a profound sound to it. 'Getting out is the bit I'm looking forward to. But you have to get in to get out.'

# A BLAST FOR THE PAST

## Alexander Chancellor

Crouching professorially over a lectern, Stephen Fry held forth last week on the subject of history. He was delivering a somewhat overblown dissertation to launch a campaign to 'raise awareness of the importance of history in our everyday lives and encourage involvement in heritage in England and Wales'. The campaign, with the oddly childish slogan 'History Matters – pass it on', is sponsored by the National Trust, English Heritage and every other heritage organisation of note, and aims, among other things, to get one million people to wear a badge saying that history matters to them. 'Some people sense in our world, even if they can't prove it, a new and bewildering contempt for the past,' Fry said. 'In the high street of life, as it were, no one seems to look above the shop-line. Today's plastic signage at street level is the focus; yesterday's pilasters, corbels and pediments above are neither noticed nor considered, save by what some would call cranks and conservationists.'

The audience, gathered outside the Orangery of Kensington Palace, included many grandees of the heritage industries, who were beaming with silent approbation when my mobile phone started ringing. 'Turn that fucking thing off,' said Fry, departing from his script. I hastily did as asked, and back to the text he went: 'And yet against this we measure the exponential growth in the public appetite for history. Has it ever been a better time to be a historian?'

Good point. The evening's master of ceremonies, David Starkey, has made successful television programmes on the Tudors, and others present have also made good money from their work. I was beginning to wonder why the campaign was necessary when my phone went off again.

'I said turn it off,' said a choleric Fry.

'I've been trying my best,' I replied feebly.

'Then put it on the ground and stamp on it,' he advised.

I know mobile phones are irritating, but we weren't at the opera and I wasn't sure my offence deserved such obloquy. But later, from the *National Trust* magazine, I learned that the mobile phone is a bugbear of the history promoters: 'We hope that by asking people to briefly step away from their emails, their mobile phones and their iPods, we can give them a moment to stand and stare and wonder; a pause from our fast-food culture, consumed on the run, and in its place a chance to slow down and savour our great and precious historical stew.' Fry also mentioned 'cheap celebrity culture' as one of those nasty, modern things, but his presence showed that you can't even launch an anti-celebrity movement today without a celebrity to do it.

And anyway, what's the point of the campaign when even its sponsors say history has never been so popular? The answer is found in the press release: it has been 'timed to coincide with important decisions about future levels of government investment in heritage'. It's just about money, in other words.

# 'YO, BLAIR,
# HOW ARE YOU DOING?'

## Jonathan Freedland

**Bush** Yo, Blair. How are you doing? [*Proof that the old saw – that politicians eventually morph into their caricatures – is true. Just as John Major came finally to resemble a pair of giant underpants, so here is George Bush sounding more like his* Dead Ringers *alter ego than any one would have credited. 'Yo Blair!' are the words of Jon Culshaw's Bush, rather than the real thing, surely? And is the use of the last name an example of presidential banter – such as 'Rummy' or 'Wolfie' – or does it contain a hint of disrespect, even frat-boy bullying?*]

**Blair** I'm just …

**Bush** You're leaving?

**Blair** No, no, no not yet. On this trade thingy … [inaudible] [*The trade 'thingy': that would be progress towards a global trade pact, on which turns the fate of millions struggling to escape poverty. But 'thingy' kind of captures it.*]

**Bush** Yeah, I told that to the man. [*Some dispute as to the identity of 'the man'. Insiders say a likely candidate is Pascal Lamy, director general of the World Trade Organisation – if only because he's someone whose name might well escape the president.*]

**Blair** Are you planning to say that here or not?

**Bush** If you want me to.

**Blair** Well, it's just that if the discussion arises …

**Bush** I just want some movement.

**Blair** Yeah.

**Bush** Yesterday we didn't see much movement.

**Blair** No, no, it may be that it's not, it may be that it's impossible.

**Bush** I am prepared to say it.

**Blair** But it's just I think what we need to be an opposition …

**Bush**  Who is introducing the trade?

**Blair**  Angela [*Angela Merkel, the German chancellor, at least gets the first name treatment.*]

**Bush**  Tell her to call 'em.

**Blair**  Yes.

**Bush**  Tell her to put him on, them on the spot. Thanks for [inaudible] it's awfully thoughtful of you. [*Apparently the prime minister gave the president a sweater. Clothes have been a bit of a theme with these two, ever since they first met at the infamous Colgate summit at Camp David, where Blair felt overdressed and ran off to change into jeans. And we know Blair takes his gifts to the president seriously: he took personal charge of the 2001 decision to lend Bush a Jacob Epstein bust of Winston Churchill. Normally suggesting the PM picked out a gift himself would be a sarcastic joke, but in this case, it's very plausible.*]

**Blair**  It's a pleasure.

**Bush**  I know you picked it out yourself.

**Blair**  Oh, absolutely, in fact [inaudible].

**Bush**  What about Kofi? [inaudible] His attitude to ceasefire and everything else … happens. [*Doubtless an expression of frustration with the UN secretary general, who has long been too dovish for Bush administration tastes. This suggests that Annan wanted the G8 to demand a ceasefire in the Middle East, a call Washington especially was reluctant to make, arguing that Israel has the right to defend itself.*]

**Blair**  Yeah, no I think the [inaudible] is really difficult. We can't stop this unless you get this international business agreed.

**Bush**  Yeah.

**Blair**  I don't know what you guys have talked about, but as I say I am perfectly happy to try and see what the lie of the land is, but you need that done quickly because otherwise it will spiral. [*The most embarrassing part of the exchange for Tony Blair. That he might want to visit the Middle East makes perfect sense, but why is he asking the president if he can go? He sounds less like the head of a sovereign government than a Bush official, waiting for the boss's green light – which he does not give. Another servant of the president, Condoleezza Rice, is going instead.*]

**Bush**  I think Condi is going to go pretty soon.

**Blair** But that's, that's, that's all that matters. But if you … you see it will take some time to get that together. [*Excruciating as Blair tries to affect a 'that's fine' tone, but stammeringly has another go. Condi will take ages, he says, whereas I'm ready to fly right away! Ever since the Good Friday Agreement, Blair has yearned to play the role of Middle East peacemaker. The craving is more urgent now, as he quests for a legacy.*]

**Bush** Yeah, yeah.

**Blair** But at least it gives people …

**Bush** It's a process, I agree. I told her your offer to …

**Blair** Well … it's only if I mean … you know. If she's got a … or if she needs the ground prepared as it were … Because obviously if she goes out, she's got to succeed, if it were, whereas I can go out and just talk. [*Verging on the David Brent, as Blair abases himself, suggesting he merely prepare the ground for the US secretary of state. He all but offers to carry her bags. He puts himself down further, implying that her visit would actually matter – whereas he can 'just talk'. A terrible admission of Britain's place in the scheme of things.*]

**Bush** You see, the … thing is what they need to do is to get Syria, to get Hizbullah to stop doing this shit and it's over. [*Despite his recent disavowal of Texan talk, the president shows he still has a cowboy's vocabulary. And confirms his view of the real source of the trouble: not Israel, not Hizbullah but Syria.*]

**Blair** Syria.

**Bush** Why?

**Blair** Because I think this is all part of the same thing.

**Bush** Yeah.

**Blair** What does he think? He thinks if Lebanon turns out fine, if we get a solution in Israel and Palestine, Iraq goes in the right way …

**Bush** Yeah, yeah, he is sweet. [*Who is the 'he', sweet as honey? British diplomats say it is Bashar al-Assad of Syria. The two men clearly distrust him, with Blair explaining that Assad is troubled by the prospect of success for US-led policies in the region and is therefore working to undermine them. One wonders if the PM has noticed that the 'ifs' he sets out – peace in Israel/Palestine, stability in Iraq – are pretty big ifs.*]

**Blair**  He is honey. And that's what the whole thing is about. It's the same with Iraq.

**Bush**  I felt like telling Kofi to call, to get on the phone to Assad and make something happen.

**Blair**  Yeah.

**Bush**  We are not blaming the Lebanese government.

**Blair**  Is this … ? [At this point Blair taps the microphone in front of him and the sound is cut.]

July 18 2006

# THE RIGHT TO SELF-DEFENCE IN THE MIDDLE EAST

## Ahmad Samih Khalidi

Much has been made in recent days – at the G8 summit and elsewhere – of Israel's right to retaliate against the capture of its soldiers, or attacks on its troops on its own sovereign territory. Some, such as those in the US administration, seem to believe that Israel has an unqualified licence to hit back at its enemies no matter what the cost. And even those willing to recognise that there may be a problem tend to couch it in terms of Israel's 'disproportionate use of force' rather than its basic right to take military action.

But what is at stake here is not proportionality or the issue of self-defence, but symmetry and equivalence. Israel is staking a claim to the exclusive use of force as an instrument of policy and punishment, and is seeking to deny any opposing state or non-state actor a similar right. It is also largely succeeding in portraying its own 'right to self-defence' as beyond question, while denying anyone else the same. And the international community is in effect endorsing Israel's stance on both counts.

From an Arab point of view this cannot be right. There is no reason in the world why Israel should be able to enter Arab sovereign soil to occupy, destroy, kidnap and eliminate its perceived foes – repeatedly, with impunity and without restraint – while the Arab side cannot do the same. And if the Arab states are unable or unwilling to do so then the job should fall to those who can.

It is important to bear in mind that in both the case of the Hamas raid that led to the invasion of Gaza and the Hizbullah attack that led to the assault on Lebanon it was Israel's regular armed forces, not its civilians, that were targeted. It is hard to see how this can be filed under the rubric of 'terrorism', rather than a straightforward tactical defeat for Israel's much-vaunted military machine, one that Israel seems loth to acknowledge.

Some of this has to do with the paradox of power: the stronger the Israeli army becomes, the more susceptible and vulnerable it becomes to even a minor setback. The loss of even one tank, the capture of one soldier or damage done to one warship has a negative-multiplier effect: Israel's 'deterrent' power is dented out of all proportion to the act itself. Israel's retaliation is thus partly a matter of restoring its deterrence, partly sheer vengeance, and partly an attempt to compel its adversaries to do its bidding.

But there is also something else at work: Israel's fear of acknowledging any form of equivalence between the two sides. And it is precisely this that seems to provide the moral and psychological underpinning for Israel's ongoing assault in both Gaza and Lebanon – the sense that it may have met its match in audacity, tactical ingenuity and 'clean' military action from an adversary who may even have learned a thing or two from Israel itself, and may be capable of learning even more in the future.

There has of course been nothing 'clean' about Israeli military action throughout the many decades of conflict in Palestine and Lebanon. Israel's wanton disregard for civilian life during the past few days is neither new nor out of character. For those complaining about violations of Israeli sovereignty by Hizbullah or Hamas, it may be useful to recall the tens of thousands of Israeli violations of Lebanese sovereignty since the late 60s, the massive air raids of the mid-70s and early 80s, the 1978 and 1982 invasions and occupation of the capital Beirut, the hundreds of thousands of refugees, the 28-year-old buffer zone and proxy force set up in southern Lebanon, the assassinations, car bombs, and massacres, and finally the continuing violations of Lebanese soil, airspace and territorial waters and the detention of Lebanese prisoners even after Israel's withdrawal in 2000.

It is unnecessary here to recount the full range of Israel's violations of Palestinian 'sovereignty', not least of which is its recent refusal to accept the sovereign electoral choice of the Palestinian people. Israel's extraterritorial, extrajudicial execution of Palestinian leaders and activists began in the early 70s and has not ceased since. But for those seeking further enlightenment about Hamas's recent action, the fact is that some 650,000 acts of imprisonment have taken place since the occupation began in 1967, and that 9,000 Palestinians are currently in Israel's jails, including some 50 old-timers incarcerated before and despite the 1993 Oslo accords, and many others whom Israel refuses to release on the grounds that they have 'blood on their hands', as if only one side in this conflict was culpable, or the value of one kind of human blood was superior to another.

If there ever was a case for establishing some form of mutually acknowledged parity regarding the ground rules of the conflict, Hamas and Hizbullah have a good one to make. And if there ever was a case for demonstrating that what is good on one side of the border should also be good on the other, Hamas and Hizbullah's logic has strong appeal to Arab and Muslim public opinion – regardless of what the supine Arab state system may say.

As George Bush and other western leaders splutter on about freedom, democracy, and Israel's right to defend itself, Tony Blair's repeated claim that events in the region should not be linked to terrible events elsewhere is looking increasingly fatuous.

The slowly expanding war in Afghanistan, the devastation of Iraq, the death and destruction in Gaza and the bombing of Beirut are all providing a slow but sure drip feed for those who believe that the west is incapable of taking a balanced moral stance, and is directly or indirectly complicit in a design meant to break Arab and Muslim will and subjugate it to untrammelled Israeli force.

Contrary to what Blair seems to believe, the use of force is unlikely to breed western-style liberalism and moderation. What is at issue here is not democracy but the right to resist Israeli arrogance and be treated on a par with it in every respect, including the use of force. If Israel has the right to 'defend itself' then so has everyone else.

Furthermore, there is nothing in the history of the region to suggest that Israel's destruction of mass popular movements such as Hamas or Hizbullah (even if this were possible) would drive their successors closer to western-style democracy, and every reason to believe the opposite. Israel's invasion of Lebanon in 1982 did away with the PLO and produced Hizbullah instead; the incarceration and elimination of Arafat only served to strengthen Hamas; and the wars in Afghanistan, the Gulf and Iraq gave birth to Bin Ladenist terrorism and extended its reach and appeal. And we should not be surprised if the summer of 2006 produces more of the same.

However Israel's latest adventure ends, it will not produce greater sympathy and understanding between west and east, or a downturn in extremism. Indeed the most likely outcome is that a new wave of virulent and possibly unconventional anti-western terrorism may well crash against this and other shores. We will all – Israelis, Arabs and westerners – suffer as a result.

# ON LEBANON

## David Grossman

Hizbullah's surprise blitz against the Galilee, Israel's northern region, proves – if anyone needed proof – how sensitive and explosive this region is, and how little it takes to bring it to the brink of war. Israel has launched a counter-attack, and it has every right to do so. There is no justification for the large-scale violence that Hizbullah unleashed this week, from Lebanese territory, on dozens of peaceful Israeli villages, towns and cities. No country in the world could remain silent and abandon its citizens when its neighbour strikes without any provocation.

For years, the government of Lebanon has avoided direct confrontation with Hizbullah. During this time, the fundamentalist Shia militia constructed a network of outposts and huge weapons depots, containing thousands of long-range missiles that can reach deep into Israel's territory. Israel, seeking not to heat up the border, also abstained from taking any real action against them. The result was an intolerable situation: within the territory of the sovereign state of Lebanon, which has no claims against Israel, an organisation the UN has classified as terrorist acts freely, and attacks Israel time and again.

Israel has attacked Lebanon because that country is officially responsible for Hizbullah. It is also the address from which missiles are being fired at Israeli cities. Hizbullah's leaders are members of the Lebanese cabinet, and participate in setting the country's policies. Even those who hope for an immediate end to violence and the opening of negotiations must acknowledge that Hizbullah deliberately created the crisis.

The scenarios for the future do not look good. Of course, Israel does not intend merely to respond to the Hizbullah attack. It is also acting to reshape the realities on its border with Lebanon, in accordance with UN resolution 1559, and to force the Lebanese government to move Hizbullah out of the country's south. Israel's goal is logical and just, but the aggressive conduct of the operation is dangerous. The Lebanese government is weak, and Lebanon could again slip into general collapse and civil war, which could well strengthen Hizbullah. Such a local conflict could easily develop into a regional one, with unpredictable consequences. In recent decades, Israel has gotten tangled up in military operations in Lebanon again and again. It never succeeded in achieving its goals. Attempts to shape the Arab world in accordance with Israel's needs have all failed.

Another goal declared by many of Israel's leaders is to utterly break Hizbullah's power and influence. This is doomed from the start. It recalls the shortsightedness of Israeli leaders in 1982, when they declared they would destroy the Palestine Liberation Organisation. Even though Israel has vastly superior forces, Hizbullah has very strong backing in Iran, Syria and the Arab world. Anyone who thinks Israel can achieve a knock-out victory is fooling themselves.

There is also a fundamental difference between the two fronts. Hizbullah is, openly, an Iranian agent in the Middle East, a bridgehead for its murderous plans against Israel. Iran is doubtlessly committed to the Palestinian cause, but its aspirations do not include an equitable peace between Israel and Palestine. Even if Israel and the Palestinians reach a peace agreement, Hizbullah will oppose compromises. It will continue to fight Israel, and will threaten whatever fragile stability such an agreement achieves.

Israel's relations with the Palestinians are utterly different. These two peoples must achieve peace if they wish to live. Their fates cannot be separated. Both have a clear interest in reaching a compromise in which each will give up some of its central demands. Both sides know that their conflict cannot be resolved by force. However, Hizbullah's deadly attack this week impels the great majority of Israelis to view the two fronts as one, both constituting threats to Israel's existence. While this instinct may not reflect the military balance, it has caused disproportionate harm to Lebanon. In the future, it could well lead to an indefinite postponement of a solution to the Israeli-Palestinian conflict.

What began as a justified Israeli response to aggression now looks like a trap with two doors, one for each side. Neither can defeat the other, but neither can concede. As the popular saying in these parts goes, each adversary is willing to lose an eye if that is the price to pay for gouging both of its enemy's eyes. Now is precisely the moment the international community must step in, mediate, formulate a compromise, and save both sides from self-destruction.

Many citizens of Israel, like those of prosperous, westernised Beirut, wanted to believe they were no longer really part of the Middle East conflict. Despairing of its bloody, fundamentalist, hopeless nature, they built themselves bubbles of comfort and escapism. The events of the past few days have shaken everyone awake. The war has reached their doorsteps, reminding them what materials make up life here. Diplomatic acumen will no longer suffice to turn those materials into a stable peace. It looks as if only an alchemist's lore could do that now.

August 31 2006

# TEN THINGS YOU CAN NO LONGER DO IF YOU'RE A BRITISH MUSLIM

## Urmee Khan

For the fastest-growing religion in the world, there have always been a lot of prohibitions connected with being Muslim. Many of the sacraments of secularism have been forbidden to us, which is a shame, perhaps, because so many of them – bacon, booze and bingo – are almost definitions of Britishness. Still, these privations have always been straightforward, and self-inflicted, and so they have been cheerfully borne by us Muslims.

But things are changing. Britain's top Muslim police officer put his finger on it when, following the travel restrictions put in place after the alleged Heathrow terror plot, Superintendent Ali Dizaei said, 'We are in danger of creating a new offence of travelling while Asian.' And a few days later the joke became real, when two Asian men on a flight bound for Manchester were removed from the plane after a passengers' revolt over their wearing big coats, talking in a foreign language which might have been Arabic and generally being shifty and not white. As one of the passengers said, 'Everyone agreed the men looked dodgy.'

I know, I know – there's a real threat of terror and everyone is frightened. But just as you didn't blame all Irish people for the IRA's bombing campaign, it doesn't seem fair to blame all us Muslims for al-Qaida.

Still, it is clear that what we need is a check-list of things to avoid if we want to be seen as 'ordinary, decent Muslims', if we want to be seen as above suspicion, as normal citizens.

This list will settle once and for all what Muslims in Britain can no longer do.

## 1. Don't wear a big coat

Terribly bad things, big coats. Palestinian suicide bombers during the intifada often wore unseasonal overcoats to hide their explosives. This has led to sartorial choices being forced on Muslims everywhere, and is a particular inconvenience in Britain, as in most English northern towns the sight of a grumpy-faced Muslim elder, fiercely wrapped up in a parka against the ravages of a perfectly mild day, is a very common sight.

In the aftermath of 7/7, the police asked the public to look out for people wearing unseasonal clothes. (The bombers were wearing jackets, and it was July, although not a particularly hot day – I myself remember wearing a jacket on July 7.) It would now take a Muslim from the lowest remedial class in the mosque to say to themselves any morning this summer that 'things are a bit parky today'.

The prohibition on big coats is so powerful that Scotland Yard's elite firearms unit let it be thought, after they had shot dead (the not-very-Muslim-looking) Jean Charles de Menezes, that he had been wearing a big coat. He hadn't, of course, so this otherwise cast-iron reason for shooting a chap in the head collapsed.

## 2. Don't go on holiday to Pakistan

What's the mantra that comes out whenever the police arrest someone for terrorist offences, the clinching final demonstration that, like the Mounties, they've got their man? 'Thought to have spent time in Pakistan.' That's how we know Siddique Khan and Shehzad Tanweer were the ringleaders in 7/7 – they had 'spent time in Pakistan'.

The problem is, spending time in Pakistan is what thousands of British Muslims do every year; it's the equivalent of white Britons trooping off to see old aunt Beryl in Bournemouth. It's a bit peculiar; going on holiday to see relatives in, say, Iran or Syria or North Korea won't raise the same eyebrows. It's Pakistan – where three-quarters of a million of British Asians have relatives – that signals you have been training in jihad.

So, Muslims – holidaying in Pakistan? Do yourselves a favour and don't bring your holiday snaps into the office.

### 3. Don't have a beard

The beard is top of the 'Watch out! Muslims about!' charts. We're not talking about designer stubble or a George Clooney five o'clock shadow – we mean scary Bin Laden bumper bum fluff. Think of those two Forest Gate lads. Yes, those two big bushy beards.

The beard is not an essential Islamic feature, yet any Muslim sporting one is instantly seen as a radical. And so, brothers (and a few sisters), get your razor out and shave it off!

### 4. Don't join groups or clubs

Somewhere there is a dusty office in Whitehall whose function it is to ban organisations (which are always labelled as being 'proscribed'). The room is probably full of mildewed, dusty files about Northern Ireland's paramilitary groups, and there is no doubt a faded map of Belfast peeling from the wall. But now the dust has been blown off, because there is a use for the office again.

A couple of months ago, two organisations – al-Ghurabaa and the Saved Sect – were banned in the UK. Now maybe that is right. These were the kinds of groups which, in my university days, used to hang around by themselves having beard-growing competitions, and never seemed to have any female friends. Their views on Jewish people, in particular, made my eyes water. But it cannot have escaped too many people's attention that while some merchants of hate get a good hard banning, others are free to wander the length and breadth of the country, like troubadours of bile. For example, the leader of one such crazed sect, the BNP, who says that, 'There is no such thing as a moderate Muslim.'

If you are a barking mad, dangerous extremist, in a group prepared to countenance violence to get their way, then you better make sure that you are white.

For Muslims, this is a no-no. So, to be a fully accredited ordinary, decent Muslim, you should join only the Scouts, the Brownies or – if force is your thing – the British army.

## 5. Don't wear the veil

The veil: up until the declaration of the 'war on terror', when guns, bombs and bottles of Lucozade took over, it was the hijab which, to many white westerners, was the symbol of being Muslim. It meant oppression – but with a vaguely sexual undertone. Whole BBC2 documentaries were made about it. But now, never mind that veils are a great way of repelling lechers and economising on lipstick, they symbolise either a) a militant female jihadist or b) a male bomber in disguise. (Mind you, John Simpson in a burkha wasn't exactly convincing.)

Most Muslims feel hard done by – nobody tells Catholic kids to take off their crucifixes, or Sikhs their turbans. In fact, Sikhs don't even have to wear a motorbike helmet because of the turban!

But it is becoming difficult to justify the clobber we don. When the BBC asked some Muslims about this, a woman called Salikah from London said that, as a Muslim woman, 'and visibly so because of my hijab', she had found people avoiding sitting next to her on the tube. 'I've thus resorted to standing to try and avoid any tense atmosphere, reading books such as Harry Potter, and wearing my Make Poverty History band,' she said.

So there you go – chuck out your salwar kameez and headscarves/ jilbabs/veils, and dress like them next door – as long as they are not also 'ethnics'.

## 6. Don't live in High Wycombe/Luton/Beeston/Walthamstow

Up until a couple of weeks ago, High Wycombe had a happily glum existence as one of Britain's many crap towns. But now, since several terror suspects were arrested there, it is vying for entry to the newly forming premier league of terrorist breeding grounds, along with Beeston, Luton and Walthamstow. Bad news for Muslims from those areas. I would advise packing up shop and going to live in, say, Lyme Regis, Wales or Cambridge. These days, it is perhaps best to live in an 'integrated' way, as far away as possible from your family and friends.

## 7. Don't be apathetic

A funny one this – many Muslims make the mistake of thinking that what mainstream Britain wants from us is apathy, a withdrawal from presumptuous political comment, a retreat to the days of corner-shopkeeping and waggling our heads as we talk. But no, this is denial. My 13-year-old brother is more interested in the World Wrestling Federation than global jihad. But in a few years' time, his non-Muslim fellow citizens are going to start expecting some more cogent opinions from him on subjects other than muscular men in underpants. There seems to be a growing expectation that any vaguely coherent Muslim, certainly if they enter professional or public life, needs to take sides, make their position clear, constantly trim their views to incorporate the necessary ritual condemnation of extremists. However, it is a delicate balancing act – don't be too unapathetic, but don't, at the same time, be a community leader (see below).

## 8. Don't be a 'community leader'

The phrase 'community leader' when used in Britain today is almost never applied to anyone who isn't a Muslim. Frequently it has 'self-appointed' added to it. Almost anything can qualify; any form of elected office, of course, but even owning a business or shop on some fleetingly significant street. Being cast as a Muslim community leader is a thankless task. No other community is so replete with a similar cast of leaders, so be prepared for the calumny that will pile upon your head from those who say you are taking an insufficiently tough stance against extremism.

## 9. Don't be a successful sportsman/woman

Or, in fact, show any sporting prowess at all. It isn't worth it. A Muslim sports star nowadays carries a burden of representation that black athletes have long since sloughed off. To evade it, there is really only one course of action – wrap yourself in the union flag the way black stars did in the 1980s. Amir Khan now must follow where Daley Thompson trailblazed.

That said, you might still be called a 'terrorist', the label applied to a South African Muslim cricketer of Asian origin, Hashim Amla, by the former Australian cricketer and (subsequently sacked) commentator,

Dean Jones. Or 'the son of a terrorist whore', as most believe Marco Materazzi labelled Zinedine Zidane in the World Cup final. (And you also might be labelled a 'traitor' by Pakistani fans, as happened to England players Sajid Mahmood and Monty Panesar. And Monty ain't even one of us!) You also run the grave risk of falling into the old Orientalist stereotype of the haughty, touchy, slightly ridiculous Muslim martinet; think of how Prince Naseem used to be described, or the reaction to the Pakistani cricket team's behaviour last week.

**10. Don't draw cartoons**
Hold on, I've got that wrong – it was we who were trying to ban this after those crazy Danes drew the Prophet (may peace be upon him) in a series of offensive 'comedy' depictions. But we can all get carried away.